RUN*FAST*

How to Beat Your Best Time
EVERY TIME

By **Hal Higdon,** senior writer, ***RUNNER'S*** *WORLD.* magazine,
and author of ***Marathon: The Ultimate Training Guide***

RODALE

Cover and Interior Designer: Joanna Williams
Cover Photographer: John P. Hamel/Rodale Images

Library of Congress Cataloging-in-Publication Data

Higdon, Hal.
    Run fast : how to beat your best time every time / by Hal Higdon.
        p.   cm.
    Includes index.
    ISBN 1–57954–269–7   paperback
    1. Running—Training.   I. Title.
    GV1061.5.H5395   2000
    796.42—dc21   00–032322

Distributed to the book trade by St. Martin's Press

    6 8 10 9 7   paperback

Visit us on the Web at www.runnersworldbooks.com, or call us toll-free at (800) 848-4735.

WE **INSPIRE** AND **ENABLE** PEOPLE TO IMPROVE
THEIR LIVES AND THE WORLD AROUND THEM

To Carey Pinkowski
A fast runner and a great race director

CONTENTS

Introduction . . . . *vii*

Chapter 1
Flying without Wings
The Thrill of Running Fast *1*

Chapter 2
First Base
"Legging Up" Gets You in Shape *13*

Chapter 3
Slow Down to Speed Up
Speed Training without Speedwork *25*

Chapter 4
Speed Endurance
Where Time Meets Intensity *38*

Chapter 5
Juggling Workouts
Make the Most of Training Time *48*

Chapter 6
Good Form
Smooth Out Your Stride *55*

Chapter 7
Speedwork
Fine-Tune Your Training *73*

Chapter 8
The Magic Workout
Interval Training Can Improve Your Speed *89*

Chapter 9

Speed Play
Fartlek and Tempo Training 117

Chapter 10

Pure Speed
Improve Your Kick 135

Chapter 11

Dynamic Flexibility
Speed in Motion 149

Chapter 12

Hit the Hills
Climb Your Way to the Top 165

Chapter 13

Strength Does It
More Muscle Means More Speed 182

Chapter 14

The Polishing Touch
Be Your Own Best Coach 199

Chapter 15

Detraining and Retraining
The Best Way to Get Back in Shape 210

Chapter 16

Ready to Race
Test Your Ability to Run Fast 219

Epilogue 234

Index 239

INTRODUCTION

The runner paused at my booth at the expo of a major marathon. He observed the various titles spread out on the table before him, including the first edition of this book, *Run Fast*. He tapped its cover and frowned. "I don't want to run fast," he said and chose instead a copy of *Marathon: The Ultimate Training Guide*.

Not a bad choice, I thought, for an individual whose primary focus as a runner was participating in marathons. But his attitude puzzled me. What runner wouldn't want to run fast? What golfer wouldn't want to smash the ball straight down the fairway? What tennis player wouldn't want to hit the corners with every serve? What skier wouldn't want to carve graceful turns down the side of the mountain?

Yet I understood the runner's concern. He equated running fast with pain. Running fast can both get you out of breath and cause your muscles to ache after workouts. The runner probably worried that by changing his training regimen he might be courting injury. He just wanted to get out and run on the roads and not have to listen to some expert tell him that by doing something different, he could improve all his times from 5-K to the marathon.

Yet *Run Fast* is not merely about seeking Personal Records at various race distances. Sure, we'd all like to return home from the local road race with a trophy in hand—but that's not the only reason we run. We like to *feel good* running. We like to *look good* running. We like to feel of the wind in our hair. And yes, we'd all like to be able to run just a little faster—even if only to cut our 5-K best from 30:01 to 29:59.

It is a physiological fact that if you can teach yourself to run faster at shorter distances such as the 5-K, you will be able to improve your performances at longer distances as well. All of your times will improve. "Speed is basic to performance at all levels," insists David L. Costill, Ph.D., former director of the human performance laboratory at Ball State University in Muncie, Indiana. Check the performance charts if you don't believe Dr. Costill. Run a mile in 7:30 and—theoretically at least—you should be able to do about 25:00 for a 5-K, 52:00 for a 10-K, 1:56 for the half-marathon, and 4:00 for the full marathon.

But nudge 15 seconds off that mile time and—again, theoretically—your times at longer distances should improve to about 24:30, 51:00, 1:54, and 3:55. Equally important, you'll feel better running. Your stride will feel smoother. You'll be able to converse while jogging, rather than gasping for breath with every step. Get in really good shape, and you'll recover more rapidly, which will allow you to run more often, or run longer distances, or have enough energy left over after your workout to want to go out dancing in the evening. All sorts of good things will happen if you learn how to run fast. Of course, to do so, you'll need to teach yourself how to train for speed—which is what this book is all about.

While numerous books have shown people how to start jogging and how to finish their first marathon, less attention has been paid to running short races faster. Yet while the marathon has captured the attention of the populace at the beginning of the Millennium, the 5-K remains America's most popular race distance—and it's becoming more popular. According to the USATAF Road Running Information Center, 2.5 million runners completed 5-K races in 1999, an increase of 10 percent from the year before. Most runners run a 5-K, or the near equally popular 10-K, as their first competitive experience. Others skip straight to the marathon but eventually return to 5-K and 10-K races because running road races is fun, and you can't run marathons every weekend.

Unfortunately, few of the millions participating in the current running boom learned to run fast while younger. Most skipped high school track and cross-country, where they might have learned the necessary skills for successful running. They didn't run in college either, except recreationally. They never were coached as part of an athletic team. As a result, they missed the training opportunities at that level. They never learned how to warm up properly. They never learned about interval training, fartlek, and bounding drills. "They never learned how to train for speed," explains Robert Vaughan, Ph.D., a coach from Dallas.

While researching the first edition of this book, I spoke with numerous world-class runners and their coaches. Talented and well-trained, these fast athletes often felt that the answers to my questions about improving speed were almost too simple. More than one told me, "To run fast, you simply run fast." That included Lynn Jennings, three-time world cross-country champion. Jennings said, "The trick to running fast is to make sure you run fast in training. Just covering the mileage won't do the job."

Keith Brantly, who ran the marathon for the United States in the 1996 Olympic Games, agreed, adding, "You have to drill your body to run fast."

Jennings and Brantly instinctively knew the type of training required to reach peak performance. From years spent as highly competitive runners, they also understood that achieving top speed in a specific race requires more than a few fast workouts. It requires a base of endurance before beginning those workouts. It requires planning and organization and a knowledge of other disciplines, from diet to flexibility to racing tactics. It also requires a lot of trial and error, realizing that what works for others in training may not necessarily work for you—and vice versa. It requires body knowledge and body sensitivity, and even with all that in place, you may need the assistance of an experienced coach.

During a long running career, I have worked with numerous

coaches and have learned something new from each. I also have had the opportunity to visit the laboratories of eminent exercise physiologists and physicians. They tested me on treadmills to increase their own knowledge, but I also usually went home a wiser runner.

As senior writer for *Runner's World* magazine, I have shared this information with millions of readers who run. In that position, I have had the opportunity to meet and interview many more of the world's most knowledgeable coaches. Although their techniques often differed, these coaches shared a basic ability to motivate athletes. They also knew how to teach athletes—some of them gifted, some of them less gifted—to run fast.

Finally, I found myself working as a coach of other athletes: both gifted youngsters on high school teams and eager oldsters just learning how to run. Some of the youngsters I coached went on to win state championships. Some of the oldsters I coached went on to finish their first 5-K races or marathons. And a lot of runners of all ages learned that it can be fun to run fast.

During the summer of 1999, nearly 1,300 runners enrolled in a class I taught to prepare runners for The LaSalle Bank Chicago Marathon. An additional 7,000 runners signed up for my Virtual Marathon Training on the Internet, where I provide daily training directions by e-mail. Since I rarely spend time coaching other runners without increasing my own knowledge, I felt it was time to revise and update *Run Fast*, originally published in 1992.

This book, then, is a compilation of all I have learned about running fast over the last 8 years and the years before that. I hope that it will help make you a better and faster runner.

FLYING WITHOUT WINGS

THE THRILL OF RUNNING FAST

The feel of the wind in your hair. That's the best way I can describe running fast. Doing it provides almost a sensual pleasure. Simply stated, running fast feels good. It doesn't happen in every workout, or in every race, but on those special occasions when you're rested and eager and ready to run and you've found a perfect course featuring breathtaking scenery or you have a pleasant running partner, nothing could be better. Our urge to run fast is what pushes a lot of us out the door and down the road or onto a winding forest path each day. We like running, and we especially like running fast.

"When you're running fast, it's pure joy," says Julie Isphording, a marathon runner on the 1984 U.S. Olympic Team. "It's the exhilarating moment—the moment when you are breezing by the world. It's hot-blooded ecstasy, soaring intensity, when you can't feel the pavement, you can't hear your heart pounding and you're flying without wings."

Can anybody be taught to run fast? I think they can.

Fast, of course, is a relative term. Fast for one runner is slow for another—and vice versa. Recently, I competed in the Vulcan Run, actually a weekend festival of races (5-K, 10-K, half-marathon, marathon) in Birmingham, Alabama. It was my second trip to Birmingham for Vulcan. In 1984, I had competed in the 10-K, running it in about 35 minutes. On my second trip 15 years later in 1999, I competed in the 5-K, running slower than 25 minutes. Speaking at the postrace dinner, I joked to the audience, "As I age, my times for the 5-K have begun to sound like my former times for the 10-K."

But it didn't really matter. I felt fast on both occasions. You should have seen me coming down the final straightaway of the 5-K: I was flying! Toward the end of his racing career, Jack Foster, the New Zealand Olympian, once commented, "I feel like I'm running as fast as always—as long as I don't look at my watch." You might not be able to break 30 minutes for a 5-K, or 60 minutes for a 10-K, but you can still feel fast doing so.

Running fast requires mainly a change of attitude and a willingness to experiment with different workouts and training methods.

Running fast doesn't take special talent. You don't need expensive equipment. You don't need to hire a coach or train on a track—although good coaching certainly can help, and tracks are where a lot of fast runners do hang out. Some skills are required, but the average runner can learn those skills. You don't need to participate in 5-K and 10-K races every weekend, although many runners enjoy a full racing schedule. Running fast requires mainly a change of attitude and a willingness to experiment with different workouts and training methods.

If you're a beginner, running fast means merely getting started. If you've never run before, except when you were a child (when running was perceived as fun and not as hard work), simply to jog for a few hundred meters is to move faster than if you were to walk that same distance. Improvement comes rapidly—if not always easily—when you begin from a base of zero fitness.

YOUR FIRST STEPS TO A FASTER PACE ■

Consider, for a moment, beginners, who have not yet even run their first 5-K, much less begun to worry about running the 3.1-mile distance faster. If you are an experienced runner who bought this book to help you set a PR (Personal Record) or qualify for the Boston Marathon, you may want to skip over to chapter 2.

The best advice anyone can offer a beginner is: Just do it! Begin easily. Take a few fast steps forward. Walk and jog without worrying whether there is anybody looking over your shoulder. Don't be shy. Don't be embarrassed. Stride forth with purpose. Anybody looking at you—specifically nonrunners—probably does so in envy. Not everybody has the courage to begin.

In the words of Priscilla Welch, "If you want to become the best runner you can be, start now. Don't spend the rest of your life wondering if you can do it." Of course, Welch also knows it's never too late to start. A former heavy smoker, she did not even begin competitive running until she was in her midthirties—but she went on to make the British Olympic team and win the New York City Marathon.

Beginners occupy a unique—and fortunate—position in the running world because every move is upward. "One of the joys of being a beginning runner is that you continue to get better," says Mary Reed, a coach with the Atlanta Track Club. "Everything is improvement until you reach that first plateau. It's an innocent time of joy in any runner's life that a lot of us would like to go back to."

How do you begin? The answer to that question is both simple and complicated. Let's start by talking about motivation.

One winter night some years ago, I was changing in the locker room of the local racket club near where I live in Northwest Indiana when a tennis enthusiast inquired about the group of people that surrounded me. "What are you doing?" he asked.

I explained about the beginning running class I was then teaching with my wife, Rose. At that time, we met with the group once a week to run together around the racket club's indoor track.

The tennis player seemed surprised: "I didn't know you could teach running."

He was right, of course. You don't need to teach running—or shouldn't need to. Children learn to run almost as soon as they learn to walk. Visit any elementary school playground, and you'll see kids running all over the place. An athlete who goes out for any sport in high school—football, basketball, tennis—runs as part of the conditioning program for that sport, or should! It is only as adults that people forget to run and sometimes have to "relearn" the motion.

Running is basically a simple movement. To quote 1976 Olympic marathoner and *Runner's World* magazine senior writer Don Kardong: "First, you put your right foot forward. Then, you put your left foot forward. Then, you do it again." It's that simple.

When Rose and I taught people to run, we tried to get them to start slowly. Some beginners (particularly if they're overweight) need to walk first, beginning with a half-hour, 3 or 4 days a week. In starting, we suggested that they jog a short distance until they got slightly out of breath, walk to recover, then jog some more. Jog, walk. Jog, walk. After a while, they would be able to run a mile without stopping. (Interestingly, the jog-walk-jog-walk approach used by beginners mimics interval training, a very sophisticated method for improving racing performance. I'll cover interval training in detail in chapter 8.)

GOAL SETTING

Motivation is important for all runners, but particularly so for beginners. They may have not yet had a chance to recognize the positive values of running, which are not always easy to explain or measure. Before you take your first steps, establish a goal. Make the goal challenging but realistic. Do not give up until you reach that goal.

Many people start exercising to lose weight. Some people exercise as a means to quit smoking. For others, the goal may simply be to relieve stress or to find some private and peaceful time for themselves.

Establishing mileage goals works for many runners. Completing a mile nonstop for the first time can provide you with your first glimpse of Runner's High. Running that mile progressively faster or increasing the distance you can cover to 2, 3, or more miles can keep you going. Each new step you take creates another Personal Record.

PREACHING MODERATION ■

We preached moderation, following the motto coined by New Zealand coach Arthur Lydiard: "Train, don't strain." We also talked about efficient running form, diet, equipment, safety, and avoiding injuries. Every now and then we showed a film featuring a running guru, such as Ken Cooper, M.D., or the late George Sheehan, M.D.

But mostly, we did not teach running; rather, we peddled motivation. Every coach of a beginning running class does the same. A lot of us who have been running more than a few years forget it, but it does take courage to don a pair of running shoes and step out on a sidewalk for the first time, in front of friends and neighbors. Quite honestly, a lot of beginning runners never get moving out of fear of looking foolish. They lack self-confidence. They fear failure.

One advantage of a class situation, of course, is the group

support you get from others of similar ability. This certainly is true with the marathon class I teach in Chicago, but it's also true at every level from novice to expert. One reason why the Kenyans have been able to dominate the world distance running ranks recently is that they train together and push each other every day in practice. Top runners gather in cities like Eugene, Oregon or Boulder, Colorado, for mutual support. Group dynamics can be very important in achieving success. If you have the opportunity to join a class or hire a coach or train with other runners, do so. You'll greatly increase your chances to run better—and faster!

Group dynamics can be very important in achieving success. If you have the opportunity to join a class or hire a coach or train with other runners, do so.

LOOKING GOOD ■

The most important thing you can tell a rookie runner is not how to hold their arms or how far to jog without stopping, but simply, "You're looking good. You're doing great. Keep it up." Give them basic motivation. Natural running instincts, developed in child-hood, simply take over.

Meet Bette Murray. She worked in the computer center at Purdue University North Central in Westville, Indiana. Her motivation was simple: She wanted to lose a few pounds.

Murray started slowly in our class at the racket club. We had her walk and encouraged her to do a little more each week. Finally one evening, she set out after her goal: to run 1 mile (16 laps around the club's indoor track) without stopping.

When she completed her 16th lap, she was more exultant than tired. "I never believed I could do it," she said.

Of course, Rose and I knew she could do it. She didn't need us to teach her to run; we simply supplied a little motivation. As far as I know, Murray never did compete in the Boston Marathon, and I haven't seen her in any 5-K races recently, but she did experience a victory. She reached her goal of running 1 mile without stopping. To some people, that may sound like a small achievement, but as Murray's motivators, we were very proud.

Finding a good class is an important first step. You're more likely to find running classes offered in the spring, a time when warm weather beckons people outdoors. To find classes in your area, check with local running or fitness clubs or hospital "wellness programs." Or, try surfing the Internet. Community colleges, such as Southwestern Michigan College in Dowagiac, often offer classes in fitness, walking, jogging, and even marathon running. Running clubs usually welcome beginning joggers. Some, such as the Atlanta Track Club or New York Road Runners Club, offer personalized coaching.

To locate a running club in your area, contact the Road Runners Club of America, 1150 South Washington Street, Suite 250, Alexandria, VA 22314-4493. I frequently use the RRCA's Web site (www.rrca.org) to locate out-of-town running clubs when I'm traveling. This is one way to plug into the network of runners; you'll be surprised how eager other runners or running clubs are to assist novice runners who are seeking advice and help.

YOUR FIRST TIME AT THE STARTING LINE ■

Sooner or later, most runners want to test their newfound fitness in a race, typically a 5-K or a 10-K. Although too many runners in recent years seem to choose the marathon for their first racing experience, most wisely select a shorter distance as an interim goal. Not much serious training is required to finish a 5-K: perhaps three or four workouts a week over a period of several weeks. (See the schedule on page 12.) Logging an average of a dozen miles a week will do the trick. That does not mean you will finish the race comfortably or near the front, but you will finish.

Should you at least be able to run the full distance in a workout to prove that you can do it on race day? You can, but it's not absolutely mandatory. Most marathoners, for example, run no farther than 20 miles in a climactic "long run" session before attempting the entire distance of a 26-mile race.

If you can cover 2 or more miles in practice several times over a period of weeks, without excessive straining, the spirit of the moment should carry you across the finish line of a 5-K—as long as you start slowly and keep a steady pace. (Reaching a 10-K finish line requires slightly more training mileage.)

Not much serious training is required to finish a 5-K: perhaps three or four workouts a week over a period of several months.

Once you've finished your first race, however, you will most likely find that a new goal beckons. You'll realize that it is no longer enough for you to merely cover the distance; you will want to cover it progressively faster. You will enter the world of performance, complete with training logs, lightweight racing shoes, and inside expertise to shave seconds from your PR.

SETTING PRS ■

The term *PR* is part of the running jargon; it means Personal Record. (Some runners use PB, or Personal Best.) Few of us will ever set a world or national record, but anybody can establish a PR. Any time you've recorded a time over any distance (even odd distances in training), it becomes your PR. Every time you run that course or distance, you will have an opportunity to improve upon that PR. Going after PRs can be fun and, perhaps more important, it can be motivational.

There is a downside to constantly chasing PRs, however. As you become more involved in improving your performances, keep in mind that setting new PRs may not always be easy—or advisable. To improve, runners gradually increase their training mileage, the quality of their training sessions, or both. Eventually, however, they risk losing that initial feeling of joy described by coach Mary Reed and find that their performances have inexplicably leveled off. This performance plateau can sometimes confront novice runners with this perplexing, diabolical question: Are they training too little, or too much?

Jack Daniels, Ph.D., an exercise physiologist and coach at the State University of New York at Cortland, writes, "Almost anyone can stay happy and injury-free simply by jogging a couple of miles a day. Fine. But these same runners would be even happier if they could run faster. That's simply human nature. We want to get better, and that brings us face to face with the quintessential training question: How can you train hard enough to improve, but not so hard that you get burned out and/or injured?"

Few of us will ever set a world or national record, but anybody can establish a PR.

But first things first. To establish your PR, of course, you'll need to run some distance—any distance (though I strongly suggest you keep the 26.2-mile marathon for somewhere down the road in your running career). To begin, follow the 8-week schedule on page 12. If you've already run a 5-K and you're eager to run a 10-K or work on increasing your speed, move on to chapter 2 to learn how to begin this process.

Training for Your First 5-K

How much do you need to train to be able to run your first 5-K race? Most individuals who possess a reasonably high level of fitness (because they bicycle or swim or participate in other sports that involve cardiovascular development) could probably go out and run 3.1 miles on very little training. They might be sore for a few days after the race, but they still could finish.

But if you've made the decision to run a 5-K race, you might as well do it right. The training schedule that follows will help get you to your first finish line. Before you embark on the schedule, it is assumed that you have no major health problems, are in reasonably good shape, and have done at least some jogging or walking. If running 1.5 miles in the first week seems too difficult, you may want to schedule more than 8 weeks to reach your goal and begin by walking, rather than running.

The terms used in the training schedule are somewhat obvious, but clear-cut definitions never hurt.

- **Rest:** Rest days are as important as training days. They give your muscles time to recover so you can run again. Actually, your muscles will build in strength as you rest. Without recovery days, you will not improve.

- **Run:** Put one foot in front of the other and run. It sounds pretty simple, and it is. Don't worry about how fast you run or whether or not you have "perfect" running form; just cover the distance—or approximately the distance suggested. Ideally, you should be able to run at a pace that allows you to converse comfortably while you do so.

- **Walk/Run:** This is a combination of running and walking, suggested for those in-between days when you want to do some running, but only "some." There is nothing in the rules that suggests you have to run continuously, either in training or in the 5-K race itself. Use your own judgement. Another option for in-between days is to cross-train: Bike, swim, hike, or simply walk.

- **Walk:** Walking is an excellent exercise that a lot of runners overlook in their training. In the training schedule, I suggest that you go for an hour-long walk on the day after your longest run. Don't worry about how fast you walk, or

SORE MUSCLES

No matter how fit you may be from other physical activities, when you begin to run, you're probably going to experience sore muscles. Even after running becomes easy, you're still going to experience sore muscles from time to time. People get sore muscles for three reasons.

1. They are not used to exercising.

2. They are used to a *different* exercise.

3. They greatly increase the typical duration (or effort) of their regular exercise routine.

Exercise physiologists say that soreness starts as a result of tiny tears in the muscle fibers, similar to a paper cut on your finger. (It's uncomfortable, but you can still use the finger.) What happens next is that the body's defense mechanism kicks in, white blood cells come to the rescue, and fluid moves into spaces it normally doesn't occupy, resulting in swelling. Swelling and soreness often peak 48 hours after exercise, which is one reason why your muscles can sometimes hurt more the second day.

To relieve the pain of sore muscles, first use ice to reduce swelling. Once your pain has peaked, heat helps to speed recovery by improving your circulation. Massage and pain-relieving rubs may help. But if you want to become a faster runner, you may need to accept some soreness as a natural part of the conditioning process.

After your muscles recover, they actually should be stronger. Tearing and repairing your muscles is what gets you in shape and allows you eventually to run farther and faster. One way to avoid sore muscles is not to do too much too soon. That's why coaches recommend that people new to running begin slowly and that even experienced runners schedule regular periods of rest.

how much distance you cover. Not all training should be difficult. If a 60-minute walk seems too much at first, begin with about 30 minutes and add 5 minutes a week until you reach your time goal. A hike in a natural setting can add a little adventure to your walking routine.

Week	Mon	Tue	Wed	Thu	Fri	Sat	Sun	Total Miles
1	Rest or run/walk	1.5 m run	Rest or run/walk	1.5 m run	Rest	1.5 m run	60 min walk	4.5
2	Rest or run/walk	1.75 m run	Rest or run/walk	1.5 m run	Rest	1.75 m run	60 min walk	5.0
3	Rest or run/walk	2.0 m run	Rest or run/walk	1.5 m run	Rest	2.0 m run	60 min walk	5.5
4	Rest or run/walk	2.25 m run	Rest or run/walk	1.5 m run	Rest	2.25 m run	60 min walk	6.0
5	Rest or run/walk	2.5 m run	Rest or run/walk	1.5 m run	Rest	2.5 m run	60 min walk	6.5
6	Rest or run/walk	2.75 m run	Rest or run/walk	1.5 m run	Rest	2.75 m run	60 min walk	7.0
7	Rest or run/walk	3.0 m run	Rest or run/walk	1.5 m run	Rest	3.0 m run	60 min walk	7.5
8	Rest or run/walk	3.0 m run	Rest or run/walk	Rest or run/walk	Rest	5-K race	60 min walk	6.1

The schedule above is only a guide. Feel free to make minor modifications to suit the weather and your work and family schedule. The progression suggests adding a quarter-mile to most runs each week. That's one lap on most outdoor tracks. If you train on the roads or on trails, it's more difficult to measure precisely how far you run. So don't worry about it: Simply run for an amount of time that's comparable to what it usually takes you to cover a quarter-mile.

Once you finish a 5-K, you will have set your first PR. Pick a new goal, whether to run that distance faster or to run a longer distance. Keep reading and I'll tell you how. ■

FIRST BASE

"LEGGING UP" GETS YOU IN SHAPE

On a crisp winter morning, I rose early while staying at a hotel near Arlington Park (a racetrack northwest of Chicago) and went for a slow run on the bike paths of nearby Busse Woods. As I encountered other joggers, walkers, and cyclists, I greeted them with a nod or brief hello.

Two of the joggers apparently recognized me. I heard one say to the other after I passed, "What's he doing out here?"

I was not there to bet on the horses, since the track was closed for the season. Actually, while on the way home from a track meet in Madison, Wisconsin, I stopped with my wife, Rose, at the hotel to attend a wedding reception. As to why I was in that particular forest preserve early on a Sunday morning, I was doing some base training to get in shape for speedwork planned later that spring. I might have replied to the pair, "I'm legging myself up."

That's an expression used by horse people. Ed Benham, a retired jockey from Ocean City, Maryland, who has sct nearly 100

American track and road records for runners age 70 and older, taught it to me.

LESSONS FROM THE HORSE TRACK ■

Horses move pretty quickly, so what's good enough for a horse should be good for a runner. While legging it up, I was moving at a pace so slow as to bore even most beginners. During a 90-minute run near the racetrack that morning, I covered 9 or 10 miles. That's barely a 10-minute-mile pace. Run that slow in most 10-K races, and you'll finish toward the back of the field. But that's part of Benham's method, even though he ran considerably faster when he raced.

As pedestrian as they may seem, those slow miles near the racetrack would result in fast finishes later during the year. My performance earlier in Madison certainly indicated that I needed a good shot of speed. In the 1500-meter race, the top two runners left me after one lap. I paced the rest of the field for five more laps. Then three runners swept past me on the last circuit.

After that defeat, the logical training response would seem to be to run sprints to improve my finishing kick—perhaps some lung-searing 400-meter repeats on the track. The experts all tell us: You can't run fast unless you train fast.

This is true if your fast training is done at the right time of the year. But another adage says that you can't run fast unless you first train slow. Here's where base training comes in. You first need a base of long distance training. You need to get in shape before you're ready to play. That's basic to all sports. In baseball terms, you need to reach first base before you can cross home plate. Melvin H. Williams, Ph.D., an exercise physiologist at Old Dominion University in Virginia and a top-ranked masters runner, believes that base training is vital to success in running at any distance.

"Over a long period of time, even small numbers of miles add up to large numbers," says Dr. Williams. "I was never a distance runner in high school, but I always ran to get in shape for other sports. I continued running in the military, and after that was simply trying to stay in shape. All that background running helped to lay a groundwork of base training that I took advantage of immediately when I got serious about being a runner."

> *Over a long period of time, even small numbers of miles add up to large numbers.*

Thus, those slow miles in the woods near Arlington Park were designed to prepare me to run fast.

BASE TRAINING ■

Ed Benham learned that on the job. He rode his first race as a jockey in Culver City, California, at age 14. Two years later, he scored his first victory. Benham rode competitively until 1940, then worked as an outrider and equipment handler until he retired in 1976.

Soon afterward, Benham started to run with his two sons and achieved instant success as an age-group competitor. "I trained myself just like I trained the horses," says Benham.

That meant starting slow. Or, as Benham describes the base training he used to give horses, "You leg them up." For 6 to 8 weeks, the horses would gallop very slowly. Finally, Benham would throw in a little speed, "breezing them," as they say at the track. He would run the horses, first $\frac{1}{8}$ mile, then $\frac{1}{4}$ mile, until they worked up to $\frac{5}{8}$ mile fast. (In metric terms, that would be runs of 200, 400, and 1000 meters.) If the horses seemed tired, he would back off on the hard training 1 or 2 days, walking them around the shed for an hour each day until they recovered their pep.

"One way you could tell if a racehorse was overtrained," says Benham, "was that the horse wouldn't finish his feed." Loss of appetite is a symptom of overtraining among runners, too, although sometimes we are less likely to react with rest, unless we have a coach or trainer advising us.

Other warning signs for overtrained runners are restlessness at night, a slightly elevated pulse rate just before rising, or dead legs and a general feeling of fatigue. Race times suffer, too. You're more likely to catch colds because of lowered resistance. A certain amount of muscle soreness and stiffness is a natural part of the training process, but if symptoms of fatigue persist for more than 2 or 3 days, don't take an aspirin or see a doctor as you might for that cold. The best advice is simply to cut your mileage until, like Benham's horses, you recover your pep.

When Benham turned to running at the age of 71, his approach to his new sport was similar to the way he had approached his horse racing. "Nobody told me how to run," he says, "so I legged myself up first. Once I got into shape, then I stretched out." Benham means he cut his training distance and increased the speed of his runs, thus stretching his stride.

RUN LONG TO RUN FAST ■

For any running machine—human or horse—success depends on the development of a strong aerobic base. Endurance is the foundation of your running performance. That's true even for sprinters running the 100 and 200 meters.

The fastest sprinters (Carl Lewis and Michael Johnson come to mind) are not always those fastest out of the blocks, but rather

SIMPLIFY YOUR TRAINING

"Fortunately, running is a sport that fits easily into most people's schedules. You don't need to reserve a court or find a playing field. You don't need a partner—although sometimes it's nice to have companionship. You just head out the door and do it.

"Despite running being my profession, I've simplified my training to a couple of options. I go out to my mailbox and turn left or right. One way's a short run; one way's a long run. Depending on how much time is available, I can run fast or I can run slow—relatively speaking, that is.

"A lot of runners get upset because an issue of *Runner's World* or some book had a program saying you do your long run this day and your speedwork that day. You don't always need to follow a precise schedule. Let your schedule follow you."

—Joan Benoit Samuelson

those who slow down the least in the later stages of the race. "Endurance training must come first," insists Bill Dellinger, former track coach at the University of Oregon and a bronze medal winner in the 1964 Olympic Games. "Speed is merely a supplement to strength."

If you are a beginning runner, that means gradually increasing the distance of your daily runs from 1 to 2 to 3 miles or more and, at the same time, including a weekend long run of a somewhat longer distance, such as 4 to 6 miles. Even with such a simple program, great gains can be made in fitness, strength, and even speed. You can develop endurance by taking long runs—and for a beginner, even 3 or 4 miles can be a long run.

Benji Durden, a 1980 Olympic marathoner and now a coach in Boulder, Colorado, says, "One thing I strongly believe in is the value of a long run. A lot of people, when trying to run fast, overlook the need for strength. There's great value in the weekly long run. If you're pointing for a short race, you still need to run long in training. Just because you're not running more than 2 hours in a race, that doesn't mean that runs that long have no value in your training program."

Russell H. Pate, Ph.D., director of the human performance laboratory at the University of South Carolina in Columbia and a past president of the American College of Sports Medicine, talks about the benefits of *cumulative caloric through-put*, a term he claims to have borrowed from another runner and researcher, Peter Wood.

For any running machine—human or horse—success depends on the development of a strong aerobic base.

"That refers to your overall caloric expenditure, your cumulative activity," says Dr. Pate, who twice placed in the top 10 of the Boston Marathon. "You need to burn lots of calories to succeed in running, even at modest intensities."

Dr. Pate admits that there's a certain risk to that kind of training. "The long run, particularly, can be overdone, if too often or too long. Once a week worked well with me. There are both physiological and psychological benefits to the long run that we can't always measure in the laboratory. Only in the long run do you encounter the muscle glycogen depletion that occurs in competition. There are some adaptions with that form of training that are difficult to get any other way."

He concedes that the above theory may be controversial. "Some physiologists might challenge me on that. But when you get into a glycogen-depleted state, you have to make greater use of fat as an energy source. It's probably advantageous to experience what that means in training. Having been there before on a regular basis helps.

"It also helps from a psychological point of view. You have

to tune your mind to focus intently on your running for a long period, whether that period is 30 minutes or 3 hours. That's why long runs are critical to success in any training program, even for distances shorter than the 5-K."

HOW LONG IS LONG? ■

How far should you run? How long is long? Those aren't easy questions to answer, not merely for beginners but also for experienced runners. Let's talk about ways you can improve as a runner.

Exercise physiologist Dr. Jack Daniels states, "To improve your running capabilities, you need to impose a stress that is not an overstress." Think about that for a minute. It's a very important point.

That means runners have to be very cautious when it comes to increasing workload. "You want to create a *positive* reaction to stress, not a negative one," instructs Dr. Daniels.

Selecting the correct dose of exercise stress is no easy task, either for a runner or for a coach like Dr. Daniels. If you run 20 miles a week and do it for 1 month, what do you do next? Do you shift to 25? To 30? Should you set your sights on 40 weekly miles? Guess wrong and you might get injured—or experience training burnout, which will similarly detract from your performances.

According to Dr. Daniels, "When you go from zero running to 20 miles a week, you'll achieve *enormous* gains in fitness and your ability to perform. Doubling your mileage from 20 miles to 40 will result in nowhere near that much improvement. It's a case of diminishing returns. The more and more you do, the tougher it is to improve—and at some point, the curve tips downward. So be cautious in increasing workload."

The same applies to intensity. If you run the same number of miles but at a faster pace, you're also increasing your stress load. Whether mileage or intensity, Dr. Daniels's rule is to not increase stress more often than every third or fourth week. "Allow yourself time to adjust to a certain amount of stress before imposing another," he suggests.

One way to determine your mileage progression is to decide how many miles you want to be running at peak performance. (When I design training programs, such as those you see in this book, invariably, this is where I begin.) If you want to run 40 miles and you're currently running 20, you can achieve that mileage by adding 5 miles to your training program every fourth week. You can go from 20 miles to 25 to 30 to 35 to an ultimate 40 weekly miles and theoretically do it in 16 weeks (or 4 months). If you have 6 to 8 months, you can pick a gentler progression and decrease your risk of injury.

"Determining levels of stress," says Dr. Daniels, "is one of the most difficult tasks for any coach or athlete."

Running long and slow is a good way to develop your endurance base, but in terms of developing speed, a danger exists if runners train only with long runs. They eventually develop the gait and the rhythm of the long-distance runner. They become efficient at running slowly for a long period of time. Their strides may change, and they lose their speed. They can no longer run fast at shorter distances in an efficient way.

"The major disadvantage of concentrating on volume in training is that long, slow distance training is considerably slower than racing pace," states former Ball State researcher Dr. David Costill. "Such training fails to develop the neurological patterns of muscle fiber recruitment that will be needed during races that require a faster pace. Since the selective use of muscle fibers differs according to running speed, runners who train only at speeds slower than race pace will not train all of the muscle fibers that they need for competition."

Determining levels of stress is one of the most difficult tasks for any coach or athlete.

The best method for developing speed, therefore, is to begin with a slow aerobic base, then move to the fast anaerobic training.

THE HEART OF THE MATTER ■

To run fast, you must have a cardiovascular system that is capable of delivering oxygen efficiently. Within certain limits, the more oxygen your muscles receive, the faster you can run. Scientists don't entirely understand the reasons why, but an efficient oxygen delivery system—aerobic base—is best developed by training within 70 to 85 percent of your maximum heart rate (MHR).

When a runner moves beyond 85 percent of his MHR, he crosses his anaerobic threshold, or lactate threshold, with different physiological effects. By training anaerobically, you can develop your muscular system's ability to readily release energy from your muscles. But you must possess a solid aerobic base first. If you don't, you won't be able to deliver oxygen to your muscles and your performances will diminish.

Robert H. Vaughan, Ph.D., who coached world-class distance runner Francie Larrieu Smith, described this in his doctoral dissertation at the University of North Texas in Denton. Dr. Vaughan noticed that some of the runners he coached were more capable than others of maintaining their competitive ability over a longer period of time. One was Larrieu Smith, who set personal records at the 1988 Olympic Trials in July,

EVEN PACE

Russian coach A. Yakimov explains how running slow can help you run fast—as long as you do it at even pace: "At first, it was thought that long, continuous running helped perfect only the aerobic processes, but specialists have since come to the conclusion that it also helps develop the anaerobic potentials of the runner." Yakimov suggests that coaches and runners be very careful in selecting both the speed and duration of the run. Yakimov wrote in *Track Technique*, "The problem is that the athlete must be able to distribute his effort in order to run the whole way at an even pace. If the pace drops off at the end, the problem has not been solved."

In other words, a workout that starts fast and finishes slow may fail to train the muscles properly, either in developing base or in developing speed. Learn to monitor your pace carefully.

then ran still faster 2 months later at the Olympic Games in Seoul, Korea, where she placed fifth in the 10,000 meters.

Looking back on Larrieu Smith's training, Dr. Vaughan realized that one key to her consistency was that she had maintained her aerobic base by running regular 20-mile workouts, even while preparing for a race one-third that distance. Larrieu Smith was training for seemingly selfish reasons, though. Not only was she primed for the Olympics, she also was looking 5 weeks beyond the Games to running in the Columbus Marathon. Theoretically, training for this marathon could have had a negative effect on Larrieu Smith's Olympic performance; in actuality, it was one of the reasons she ran so well in Seoul.

Larrieu Smith's long runs maintained her aerobic base and, in effect, kept her oxygen delivery system open. With this sound base remaining in place, she was better able to benefit from the anaerobic (speed) training she also was doing. Other runners coached by Vaughan did primarily anaerobic training and found that without as sound an aerobic base, they could not maintain their peak conditioning that long into the season.

Building a Base: Training for Your First 10-K

Assuming that you followed the training schedule in chapter 1 and competed in your first 5-K, the following schedule will take you to the next level and help you build the aerobic base that will allow you to train anaerobically further down the road. It nudges you gently upward in distance. "The secret to success," suggests Larry Mengelkoch, Ph.D., an exercise scientist at the University of Florida, "is to be consistent in your

Week	Mon	Tue	Wed	Thu	Fri	Sat	Sun	Total Miles
1	Rest or run/walk	3.0 m run	Rest or run/walk	2.0 m run	Rest	3.0 m run	60 min walk	8
2	Rest or run/walk	3.0 m run	Rest or run/walk	2.0 m run	Rest	3.5 m run	60 min walk	8.5
3	Rest or run/walk	3.0 m run	Rest or run/walk	2.0 m run	Rest	4.0 m run	60 min walk	9.0
4	Rest or run/walk	3.0 m run	Rest or run/walk	2.0 m run	Rest	4.5 m run	60 min walk	9.5
5	Rest or run/walk	3.0 m run	Rest or run/walk	2.0 m run	Rest	5.0 m run	60 min walk	10
6	Rest or run/walk	3.0 m run	Rest or run/walk	2.0 m run	Rest	5.5 m run	60 min walk	10.5
7	Rest or run/walk	3.0 m run	Rest or run/walk	2.0 m run	Rest	6.0 m run	60 min walk	11.0
8	Rest or run/walk	3.0 m run	Rest or run/walk	2.0 m run	Rest	**10-K race**	60 min walk	11.2

training and not attempt sudden jumps. With moderate intensity, you'll see gradual improvements and can avoid injury."

To help motivate you, I've included a 10-K race at the end of the tunnel. But if there's no convenient race at that distance near you, feel free to pick a race at any shorter distance, even a 5-K. You may surprise yourself by setting a PR.

Don't worry about adding speed training yet. That will come after you've built your endurance base.

Once you finish your first 10-K, you will have set another PR at this new distance. More important, you will have learned how even small increases in mileage can help you improve as a runner and teach you how to run fast. ■

SLOW DOWN TO SPEED UP

SPEED TRAINING WITHOUT SPEEDWORK

While training for the 1960 Olympic Games, Peter Snell ran one Sunday with veteran Murray Halberg on an extremely hilly 22-mile loop in Owairaka on the outskirts of Auckland, New Zealand. At that time, Snell was an up-and-coming 800-meter runner; Halberg was a veteran miler, moving up to the 5000 meters. Considering their specialty distances, the Owairaka loop (still renowned among distance buffs) seemed to offer an excessive amount of miles. The pace, much slower than his racing pace, both fatigued and frustrated Snell.

"I'm going to stop at 15 miles," he finally told Halberg.

Halberg warned the younger runner not to quit. "If you stop now, you'll completely waste the value of this workout. You have to run 15 miles before reaping the benefits that come in the last 7."

Snell wasn't entirely convinced, but he persevered through that workout and other long, slow training runs prescribed by his coach, Arthur Lydiard. At the 1960 Olympics that summer in Rome, the unheralded Kiwi astonished everybody by winning the 800 meters in a record 1:46.3. Halberg, his training partner, won the Olympic 5000 meters. Four years later, Snell won both the 800 and 1500 meters at the 1964 Olympic Games in Tokyo. In between, he also set world records for the mile of 3:54.4 and the 800 of 1:44.3 that surprised him even more than it did track fans.

"It was a total shock because I had done almost no fast training leading up to that race," Snell now recalls. "I spent most of the winter running slow workouts. I even ran a marathon in about 2:30 as part of my practice! After the marathon, I went to the track, added some speed training, and boom: world record. I couldn't believe at the time that you could learn to run fast by running slow."

Later, Peter Snell, Ph.D.—currently a research scientist in the cardiology department at the University of Texas Southwestern Medical Center at Dallas—came to understand the scientific principles that permitted him to use slow running to train his predominantly fast-twitch muscles. After Snell retired from competition, he moved to the United States to study for a degree in exercise physiology at Washington State University under Phil Gollnick, Ph.D.

In 1974, Dr. Gollnick collaborated on a study with Bengt Saltin, Ph.D., one of Sweden's top exercise physiologists. Dr. Gollnick and Dr. Saltin studied a group of cyclists in their laboratories. They took muscle biopsies of the cyclists as they exercised and discovered that after 60 or 90 minutes, most of the glycogen stored in the cyclists' slow-twitch muscles had become depleted.

Slow-twitch muscles are used most often in aerobic en-

A QUICK SCIENCE LESSON

Through the use of muscle biopsies (slicing out a minuscule piece of muscle and examining it under a microscope), exercise scientists have been able to divide muscles into two distinct types: fast-twitch and slow-twitch. Fast-twitch muscles fire quickly but also tire quickly; slow-twitch muscles react more slowly but do not fatigue as easily. Not too surprisingly, most sprinters have a preponderance of fast-twitch muscles, while distance runners most often have more slow-twitch muscles.

It's one of the reasons why Michael Johnson, who ran a world record 19.32 while winning the Olympic gold medal for 200 meters in 1996, will never be able to match Khalid Khannouchi's 2:05:42 world record in the marathon. And also why Khannouchi will never dust Johnson in the sprints. Even ordinary joggers are programmed to have more success at certain distances than others. Some people are born to be better 5-K runners; others, to be marathoners. It's all in the genes, although training can effect some changes. (One subcategory of fast-twitch muscles can be trained more for endurance than another subcategory.)

How well fast-twitch and slow-twitch muscles perform depends partly on how much fuel is available during exercise. Both muscle types burn fuel to function. Glycogen is the most efficient form of fuel for energy. Glycogen is a substance similar to sugar that is most easily stored in the muscles when you consume carbohydrate. Fats and proteins also can be converted into energy, though less efficiently. When glycogen becomes depleted, diminished performance results. Glycogen depletion is one reason why marathoners "hit the wall" 20 miles into their 26-mile races.

durance activities; fast-twitch muscles are used more for anaerobic speed activities. (See "A Quick Science Lesson.") With glycogen depleted from the slow-twitch muscles, the cyclists' bodies began to recruit the fast-twitch muscles for their supplies of additional glycogen. As a result, Dr. Gollnick and Dr. Saltin discovered, the body "trained" these fast-twitch muscles.

"When I reviewed the results of the Gollnick and Saltin study," says Dr. Snell, "I finally realized what Murray meant when he said the 'benefits' of our 22-mile run at Owairaka didn't begin until we had gone 15 miles. Murray was no exercise scientist—and neither was our coach Arthur Lydiard—but both realized instinctively that by pushing into that netherworld of glycogen depletion, you could actually improve your speed as well as your endurance."

> *As your body begins to recruit your fast-twitch muscles for additional glycogen, you speed up, giving those muscles an extra training boost.*

BANISHING SPEEDWORK ■

Although the Gollnick and Saltin study was completed many decades ago, competitive athletes from high school cross-country runners to world-class track stars have used various forms of long, slow running to prepare for their competitive seasons. But the adult runners who might most benefit from long, slow running have not always understood how jogging along at a gentle pace might make them fast and allow them to set PRs at popular distances such as the 5-K or 10-K.

Certainly, articles in *Runner's World* magazine and various books (including this one) have popularized the idea that if you want to maximize your ability at shorter distances, you need to do speedwork: interval training on the track, hill repeats, fartlek in the woods, and demanding tempo runs near race pace. (If you want to run fast, you have to run fast.) Those training methods still work, but they don't work equally for all runners. Not everybody is capable of pounding out a series of fast quarters or hill repeats without getting injured. Many individuals—including increasing numbers of women coming into the sport—are unfortunately intimidated by the thought of sharing a track with elite athletes. The bulk of readers of this book probably will feel relieved at Peter Snell's message that slow running can help improve your speed. Maybe most important, slow running carries with it less risk of injury than certain forms of speedwork.

But just any slow running won't work, suggests Dr. Snell, who reported his theories at a meeting of the American College of Sports Medicine. It must be slow running carried on for a period of 60 to 90 minutes, at which point glycogen becomes depleted from the slow-twitch muscles. It is this slow-twitch depletion that allows the fast-twitch muscles to undergo a similar depletion. It is at this point that the fast-twitch muscles are trained. This process can be enhanced, suggests Dr. Snell, if the runner then speeds up his pace.

During a visit to New Zealand several years ago, I was driven over the famed Owairaka course by John Davies, who placed third in the 1964 Olympic 1500 meters behind Snell. I was able to see firsthand how athletes trained under the direction of Arthur Lydiard. Over the first third of the 22-mile distance, they faced a series of climbs culminating in one final, steep ascent to loop through a forest area overlooking the city of Auckland.

This middle third of the run was relatively flat. The final third involved more downhill running. This encouraged Lydiard's runners to increase their pace toward the end of their workouts. It was at this point during his workout with Murray Halberg that a younger Peter Snell had considered stopping.

When Snell, Halberg, Davies, and Lydiard's other runners trained on the Owairaka course in the 1960s, it was mostly farmland. Today, farmland has become urban sprawl, an endless stretch of gas stations, housing developments, and shopping centers leading up to the forest. Fewer runners train on the Owairaka course today, and, whether coincidentally or not, New Zealand no longer wins medals at the Olympic Games. But the training principles that resulted in Snell's and Halberg's successes remain today and can be applied by runners at all levels.

The secret is to start slow during your long runs, but finish fast.

3/1 Training

The contour of the Owairaka course prompted Snell and his training companions to pick up the pace toward the end. They ran the Owairaka course every Sunday, although usually they held back every other Sunday to prevent overtraining. Even if you can't find a course that provides a downhill push at the end, you can adjust your training into a similar slow/fast pattern. The result might be called 3/1 training, an approach favored by John Davies, who now serves as a coach. Runners coached by Davies include former world record holders Dick Quax and Anne Audain.

Not just any slow running will work. It must be slow running carried on for a period of 60 to 90 minutes.

In 3/1 training, you run at a comfortable pace for the first three-fourths of the workout. In the final one-fourth, you gradually accelerate to a pace 30 to 90 seconds faster per mile than the pace you had been running. In the typical 20-mile run that is the climactic long run of many runners training for a marathon, this would mean running the first 15 miles at a slow pace, then running faster in the final 5 miles. If running an 8-mile workout, you would pick up the pace for the final 2 miles.

Of course, you don't have to be a marathoner to benefit from 3/1 training. As Dr. Snell explains—and as the Gollnick and Saltin research demonstrated—you need run only 60 to 90 minutes to deplete the glycogen from your slow-twitch muscles. If you run at a 10-minute pace per mile, you would enter this zone after 6 miles of your 8-mile run. As your body begins to tap your fast-twitch muscles for additional glycogen, you speed up, giving those muscles an extra training boost.

In the 8-mile workout mentioned above, someone running at 10-minute pace would run the first 60 minutes at that slow pace; the final 20 minutes would be done somewhat faster.

How much faster? It depends on the individual runner and what he defines as slow or fast. A runner accustomed to running his longer workouts at 8-minute-mile pace might begin by running 8:30 or 9-minute miles, pushing to 7:30 or even 7-minute pace toward the end of the run. For those who use heart monitors to guide them in their training, the first three-fourths of the run might be executed at an easy pace (65 to 75 percent of maximum heart rate) before moving to a medium pace (75 to 80 percent of maximum).

Will adapting 3/1 training allow you to banish speedwork from your bag of workout tricks? If you want to attain peak performance, probably not. But 3/1 training certainly provides a useful addition to the 5-K runner or marathoner's arsenal. The training technique is not revolutionary; Lydiard's runners began using it decades ago. Somewhat revolutionary is the idea that this type of training can be adapted to fit the needs of the majority of runners who do not have their sights on an Olympic gold medal. Regardless of your motives in adapting 3/1 training, it can help you to your next PR at the popular 5-K and 10-K race distances.

The training schedule on pages 36 and 37 is a modification of the program used by Davies for his championship runners. Designed to accommodate the time constraints of runners with regular jobs and family commitments, it involves less time than is necessary for racing at a world-class level. Davies prescribes training loads in minutes, rather than miles. "That way, it can be

(continued on page 34)

JUNK MILES

They are disparagingly called junk miles—those slow, extra miles done on our easy days or in second workouts, sometimes to inflate training mileage: to be able to say we ran 25 miles last week rather than merely 15, or 50 rather than 45. I certainly plead guilty. During my peak years, I ran twice daily, often dragging myself through extra workouts so I could hit 100 miles a week, an important psychological barrier—or so I thought.

But did those junk miles do me any good? Would increasing your weekly mileage from 20 to 30 to 40 or more make you a better runner or simply increase your risk of injury? Are junk miles like junk food: burning empty calories with little training effect? A high school coach I know considers slow miles wasted effort. "If you're going to run, run hard!" he grumbles. He promotes the idea of running less mileage at a faster pace.

That point of view is not without merit. Nevertheless, junk miles may have an overlooked value. One study at the University of Wisconsin–La Crosse by Carl Foster, Ph.D., showed that athletes' performance improved when they incorporated recovery days featuring so-called junk miles. "You need *true* recovery days in order to allow the real training to work," says Dr. Foster.

Gerrit Briun, Ph.D., of the Netherlands, defines monotony (everything at the same hard pace) as causing overtraining even more than high mileage.

Another study, conducted at the University of Georgia by Michael J. Breus and Patrick O'Connor, Ph.D., demonstrated that exercising even at 40 percent of maximal capacity significantly lowered anxiety levels, and thus could help prevent staleness. "These results are good news for those who want to get benefits from exercise, but who don't enjoy working out at a high intensity," summarizes Breus.

It's also good news for those of us who enjoy running slow and don't want to feel guilty about not "going all-out" every time we lace up our training shoes. Even so-called junk miles benefit runners in many ways.

- Strength. Running farther increases strength, which also increases speed. "It's the principle of multiple repetitions of a light weight," suggests coach Roy Benson of Atlanta. "Every step you run does count."
- Calorie burn. Junk miles burn calories as efficiently as fast miles; it just takes longer to burn them. Regardless of pace, each mile you run burns approximately 100 calories.
- Economy. Extra miles can make you a more efficient runner. "A low, shuffling stride is faster than a high, bounding stride," says Benson. Run longer miles and you'll improve running economy.
- Relaxation. For someone who enjoys running, taking a day off is not an easy training option. "Junk miles on recovery days help prevent runners from becoming depressed and stale," says Dr. O'Connor.

How do you fit junk miles into your training? On days between hard workouts, make sure your pace is slow enough to promote recovery. The same goes on weekend long runs. Not every workout has to be conducted flat-out fast. Still another approach is to substitute easy running for some of your cross-training.

The downside to junk miles, however, is that running long and slow can tighten as well as strengthen your muscles. "You need to do more stretching to stay loose," warns Benson. Thus, while adding junk miles, be sure to stretch after each workout. Also, adding miles to your training should be done on a gradual basis. One rule is to never increase your mileage by more than 10 percent a week—and even that percentage may be too much when your mileage starts soaring past 30 or 40 miles a week. While increasing mileage, occasionally schedule a "stepback" week featuring lowered mileage before pushing upward again.

Don't overlook the value of good junk. Don't be shy about including some very slow miles in training, particularly on days between your hard sessions. Cross-training is not always the best option. Your performances can improve if you know when and how to use junk miles.

used by runners of different abilities," explains the New Zealand coach. (If you think in miles instead of minutes, simply divide the number of minutes prescribed by your usual training pace to find out about how many miles you should run. Thus, a 60-minute run for a runner used to doing 10-minute pace becomes a 6-mile workout.)

One secret in running longer distances is to slow down. Cut your training pace and don't be afraid to take a short walk break.

This 3/1 program is divided into two phases: an endurance-building phase and a second phase involving competition. The object of the first, endurance-building phase is to build aerobic power through long, easy running. "The volume builds gradually but steadily during this phase," says Davies. Runners start with approximately 4 hours of running in the first week, including a single long run of 75 minutes. After an 8-week buildup, they have increased their weekly total by several hours, with two weekly long runs of 90 minutes.

If you are a novice runner who has progressed by using the 5-K and 10-K training schedules in the first two chapters, you should be able to slide relatively easily into this new training regimen. If running 75 minutes in the first week seems too difficult, repeat the last few weeks of the 10-K training program for as many weeks as you need to adapt to the distance. One secret in running longer distances is to slow down. Cut your training pace and don't be afraid to take some short walk breaks. You're being judged in this program by the number of minutes you run, not how far you run in those minutes.

If running 6 days a week also seems too difficult, substitute a day of rest for the 30-minute jog suggested for Fridays. The weekly total of hours and minutes run in the final column of the schedule assumes that you have done just that.

Level	% of Max	Description	Definition
Jog	50–65	fairly light	slow pace, jogging
Easy	65–75	somewhat hard	conversational (not a jog)
Medium	75–80	hard	out of the comfort zone

Most runs are done at an easy pace, or 65 to 75 percent of maximum heart rate as described in the pace chart. "Easy" for a world-class athlete might be 6:00 mile pace, allowing that athlete to cover 10 miles in 60 minutes. Someone with less speed might cover half that distance but still would benefit at his own level. Also prescribed are recovery workouts at a jog pace and 3/1 workouts every other weekend, where the runner runs easily for the first three-quarters of the run, then picks up the pace in the last quarter, finishing at a medium pace.

"The important goal of the first phase," instructs Davies, "is to achieve two runs each week which last for at least 90 minutes each. Wonderful changes occur to your physiology when you run for this length of time on a regular basis."

Phase 1: Endurance Building

The climax of this first phase is a competitive race, mainly to test your level of fitness after 8 weeks of (relatively) slow running. (If a race at some other distance than 5-K is more convenient, feel free to run it.) But don't expect a miracle or a PR—that will come later. If you want to spend more time building endurance, repeat weeks 6 and 7 before the climactic test race in week 8. The 3/1 workouts every other weekend are described as easy/medium.

Week	Mon	Tues	Wed	Thurs	Fri	Sat	Sun	Total Time
1	rest	30 min jog	60 min easy	30 min easy	30 min jog or rest	30 min easy	75 min easy	3:45
2	rest	30 min jog	60 min easy	30 min easy	30 min jog or rest	40 min jog	75 min easy/med	3:55
3	rest	30 min jog	70 min easy	30 min easy	30 min jog or rest	40 min easy	80 min easy	4:10
4	rest	30 min jog	70 min easy	30 min easy	30 min jog or rest	50 min jog	80 min easy/med	4:20
5	rest	30 min jog	80 min easy	30 min easy	30 min jog or rest	50 min easy	90 min easy	4:40
6	rest	30 min jog	80 min easy	30 min easy	30 min jog or rest	60 min jog	90 min easy/med	4:50
7	rest	30 min jog	90 min easy	30 min easy	30 min jog or rest	60 min easy	90 min easy	5:00
8	rest	30 min jog	90 min easy	30 min easy	30 min jog	rest	**5-K race**	3:30

Phase 2: Competition

Following the endurance buildup, you move into a second phase that continues to focus on slow running, but also includes competition every second week. The 8-K and 10-K "races" in weeks 10 and 12 should be run in the spirit of the 3/1 long runs. Start toward the back of the pack, forcing yourself to run at least the first mile slower than if you were serious about the day's competition. Then pick up the pace and finish strong. This will give you an opportunity to stretch your legs, plus it's more enjoyable passing people in the last mile than being passed.

Notice that during 4 of the 8 weeks, your maximum weekly time commitment is only 5 hours. This is not an excessive amount of time, even for a fitness jogger who works at a 9-to-5 job. During weeks when you race, your time commitment is even less. (Of course, you will probably spend more time at the race than you would during a workout, because you'll want to hang around afterward and talk to everybody about how well you ran.)

By weeks 14 and 16, the benefits of the training buildup should begin to take effect. At the end of each of these weeks is a race, one in which you do *not* want to start in the back row. It's PR time. Go for the gold! The race distances chosen are arbitrary. If your racing goal involves different distances, modify the schedules accordingly.

Week	Mon	Tues	Wed	Thurs	Fri	Sat	Sun	Total Time
9	rest	30 min jog	90 min easy	45 min easy	30 min jog or rest	45 min jog	90 min easy/med	5:00
10	rest	30 min jog	60 min easy	45 min easy	30 min jog or rest	30 min jog	**8-K (3/1)**	3:35
11	rest	30 min jog	90 min easy	45 min easy	30 min jog or rest	45 min jog	90 min easy/med	5:00
12	rest	30 min jog	60 min easy	45 min easy	30 min jog or rest	30 min jog	**10-K (3/1)**	3:45
13	rest	30 min jog	90 min easy	45 min easy	30 min jog or rest	45 min easy	90 min easy/med	5:00
14	rest	30 min jog	60 min easy	30 min jog	30 min jog or rest	rest	**5-K race**	2:30
15	rest	30 min jog	90 min easy	30 min easy	30 min jog or rest	45 min easy	90 min easy	5:00
16	rest	30 min jog	60 min easy	30 min jog	30 min jog	rest	**10-K race**	3:00

SPEED ENDURANCE

WHERE TIME MEETS INTENSITY

Dr. Russell Pate of the University of South Carolina believes that even well-trained runners can improve speed by simply improving endurance. He links the two concepts in a single term: *speed endurance*.

Dr. Pate—who once ran the marathon in a world-class time of 2 hours, 15 minutes—defines endurance as the ability to continue activity of a designated intensity for a prolonged period. You go far. But speed endurance couples the ability to go far with the ability to go fast. In other words, you attain the ability to go farther faster. Dr. Pate believes that three major physiological factors contribute to speed endurance.

Oxygen uptake. Referring to the maximum volume of oxygen your body can transport and absorb, scientists often use the term max VO_2 to describe aerobic power potential—the ability to deliver oxygen to the muscles, particularly for endurance activity. But be careful. Don't confuse this scientists' max with the coaches' max, which more often describes maximum heart rate. (See "The Two Maxes" on page 40.)

Lactate threshold. Some individuals start to accumulate lactic acid sooner than others. "An untrained person may accumulate lactic acid at as low as 30 to 40 percent of their max VO_2," says Dr. Pate. Their lactate thresholds are very low. "More highly trained endurance athletes, on the other hand, will be able to work at 80 percent or more without accumulating lactic acid." They have developed a high lactate threshold, so they can perform longer and harder at sub-max levels. Dr. Pate notes that max VO_2 sets a cap on the entire system. "I don't think we've ever found an individual who can work for more than a few minutes at 100 percent of max VO_2," he says, "because you start accumulating lactic acid too rapidly."

Efficiency. Efficiency relates to biomechanics and economy of motion. The smoother you are, the less oxygen you consume at a particular running speed. "The lower the rate of oxygen consumption, the lower the amount of metabolic and cardiorespiratory stress, and the farther you can run," says Dr. Pate. Efficiency, scientists agree, is most difficult to modify by training.

"To acquire speed endurance, you need to put these three factors together," Dr. Pate explains. "The optimum would be to have a high max VO_2, have a high lactate threshold, and be very economical." A program that develops these three factors produces high-powered performances. Regardless of your level of ability, you can improve by following such a program.

ACQUIRING SPEED ENDURANCE ■

Some of your endurance capacity is natural. If you possess the ability to endure, it is probably because you have a higher percentage of slow-twitch than fast-twitch muscles. Thus, genes determine our endurance capacity. But to improve your base endurance, you need to train. "Anybody, regardless of their muscle composition, can improve endurance with training," says former Ball State researcher Dr. David Costill.

To develop speed endurance, you need to use specific types of training. How do you achieve that end? Let's begin by expanding our discussion on developing your base endurance that began in chapter 2. To do so, I need to use some difficult scientific terms, but bear with me for a moment.

Improving endurance requires muscle adaptations, claims

THE TWO MAXES

The term *max VO₂* is often used by exercise physiologists as a convenient benchmark to measure human performance, but runners frequently confuse it with another "max" more often used by coaches: maximum heart rate, or MHR.

Your max VO_2 relates to the maximum volume of oxygen transported to your muscles. Usually, scientists obtain the measurement by monitoring athletes while they run on a treadmill or ride an exercise bike, breathing into a device that measures gas volume. This permits researchers to arrive at a figure that defines the amount of oxygen an athlete can consume per kilogram of body weight per minute (ml/kg/min).

That's the researchers' max, best forgotten unless you have easy access to a human performance laboratory. More handy is the coaches' max: MHR for maximum heart rate.

Coaches find MHR the best measure of ability, since they are dedicated to training athletes rather than testing them. MHR is just what it says. It's the maximum number of times your heart beats under extreme stress, usually measured per minute.

One hundred percent of max VO_2 is the same as 100 percent maximum heart rate, but after that, the two maxes diverge. For instance, to achieve 50 percent of max VO_2, you actually exercise at 75 percent of your MHR.

It's also possible to achieve levels above 100 percent of max VO_2, at least for short periods of time. In dealing with MHR, 100 percent is the max. With the exception of this chapter, you'll encounter the term MHR more frequently than max VO_2 in this book because I believe MHR is easier to measure and put to use.

William Fink, who worked closely with Dr. Costill at the human performance laboratory at Ball State. The key, says Fink, is producing more mitochondria, a subcellular organelle that makes adenosine triphosphate (ATP), the energy that fuels your muscles. "When someone exercises aerobically," Fink explains, "we see increased activity in a number of specific enzymes involved in the utilization of ATP. The muscle also develops more capillaries, which enhance the delivery of blood and oxygen to the muscle."

According to Stan James, M.D., an orthopedic surgeon and cross-country skier from Eugene, Oregon, "There's a certain amount of endurance associated with increased strength, which also comes with endurance training."

Dr. Pate adds, "The muscle develops more connective tissue; a larger cross section. All of this improves endurance."

The key to endurance training, according to Dr. Pate, is to gradually increase your exercise stress. He explains: "In order to induce an adaptation, you have to force the system to do something it is not currently adapted to. The trick is to apply a stress sufficient to adapt the system without the undesirable side effects and injuries that come with doing too much. This all needs to be individualized. People vary in how much exercise they can tolerate."

Nevertheless, scientists can now state with some precision how much training is necessary for the average runner to improve endurance, specifically speed endurance. Howard A. Wenger and Gordon J. Bell of the School of Education of the University of Victoria in British Columbia have identified three factors necessary to achieve maximal gains in aerobic power, the essential quality of speed endurance. They are intensity, frequency, and duration.

Intensity. According to Wenger and Bell, "The magnitude of change in max VO_2 increases as exercise intensity increases from 50 to 100 percent max VO_2, and then begins to fall as the intensity exceeds max VO_2."

That statement certainly requires some explanation because of possible confusion again between the scientists' max and the coaches' max. To begin to get improvement in your max VO_2, you must exercise at an intensity equal to at least 50 percent of your max VO_2. This means you need to train at 75 percent of your maximum heart rate (MHR), a pace that we might call your minimum aerobic pace. (Ironically, the better condition you are in, the harder you have to train to improve your max VO_2.)

The trick is to apply a stress sufficient to adapt the system without the undesirable side effects and injuries that come with doing too much.

Translation: To improve your endurance, train at 75 percent of your MHR or higher.

Frequency. Wenger and Bell go on to say, "Improvements in max VO_2 are greater in both absolute and relative terms up to six sessions per week (for low fitness). In the high-fitness category, however, no improvements are elicited with only two sessions per week, and maximal gains accrue at a frequency of four."

Translation: To improve endurance, train with some intensity (at minimum, near race pace) four times a week, approximately every other day.

Duration. Wenger and Bell note some improvements in training sessions of 15 to 30 minutes. They identify the most improvements when exercise exceeds 35 minutes. They write, "This improvement could reflect the greater involvement of fast-twitch motor units as slow-twitch units begin to fatigue."

Beyond 45 minutes, however, improvements decline, most likely because it becomes difficult to maintain intensity (as described previously) for that long a time or to train that hard with the right frequency.

Translation: To improve endurance, the hard portion of your average workout should last 35 to 45 minutes.

To summarize the results of the Wenger and Bell survey:

The combination of intensity and frequency that elicits the greatest absolute and relative change is 75 to 90 percent of your MHR four times per week, with exercise duration of 35 to 45 minutes. The scientists add, however, "It is important to note that lower intensities still produce effective changes and reduce the risks of injury in nonathletic groups."

SMART TRAINING ■

One of the appeals of an endurance sport such as running, of course, is that you can overcome a lack of natural ability—considered by many the most essential ingredient for athletic success—with dedication and training. Does that statement motivate you? It should. Acquiring speed endurance requires some natural talent, but with the mental focus to train hard—and to train smart—anyone can develop a faster, stronger pace.

Dr. Pate, drawing on both his research as an exercise physiologist and his own experiences as a world-class marathoner, believes that smart training is the key to improving speed endurance. What is smart training? One key factor, he claims, is regular pace changes. Here are four different paces that you can use to bring variety to your workouts.

Pace 1: High Intensity

"For decades," says Dr. Pate, "exercise physiologists have studied changes in max VO_2, and have learned that you can modify it. I think it's debatable whether or not we know the best way to modify max VO_2, but clearly, high-intensity activity is a key. Exercising at intensities that go beyond the individual's current max VO_2 is important."

What type of training would this be? A typical Pace 1 workout would be three 1-mile repeats, with 5 minutes or more of walking or jogging in between. (A "repeat" is any distance run at a set pace, followed by fairly complete rest and more runs at that same distance.) Dr. Pate suggests a speed close to your most recent 5-K race. A runner capable of a 25-minute 5-K, for instance, would run his mile repeats at about an 8-minute-mile pace. (For more on repeats, see chapter 7.)

The combination of intensity and frequency that elicits the greatest absolute and relative change is 75 to 90 percent of MHR four times per week, with exercise durations of 35 to 45 minutes.

In designing training schedules, I often use the term *race pace*—which sometimes confuses beginning runners. They often post questions to my bulletin boards on the Internet: "What do you mean by race pace?" The answer is fairly simple. Race pace is the pace you plan to run in the race for which you're training. If you're training to run the 5-K in 25:00, race pace would be 8:00, as stated above. If you're training for a 10-K, half-marathon, or marathon, then race pace for you would be slower, depending on the race distance. For a faster runner (someone capable of doing a 5-K in 20:00, for example), race pace would be faster.

One side benefit of working out at race pace is that it gets you to recruit fast-twitch muscle fibers, according to Dr. Pate. "If those fibers have not been used in training, they may not be recruited easily when you get into a competitive situation."

Pace 2: Medium Intensity

Also important to training are lactate threshold runs. (The lactate threshold in a trained runner would be 80 to 90 percent of his max VO_2. It's the point where lactic acid—produced when the body is working at high effort—begins to accumulate in your bloodstream, which will force you to slow down.)

Dr. Pate prescribes running longer but somewhat slower in Pace 2 workouts: 20 to 60 minutes at 70 to 90 percent of your

MEASURING YOUR MAX

Various training programs use maximum heart rate (MHR) as an aid to dictating workouts. Do you know yours?

The average person probably has an MHR somewhere around 200 beats a minute. But don't get too hung up on numbers, since people vary greatly depending on age and level of training. Also, various formulas used to predict MHR don't always work for everyone.

One formula is to take the number 220 and subtract your age. But *Aerobics* author Kenneth H. Cooper, M.D., suggests 200 minus half your age as more accurate for very fit people. That doesn't work for everybody. At age 35, my predicted MHR should have been 185 using the first formula, 165 using the second. Actually, my MHR as measured in Dr. Costill's human performance laboratory was 160, suggesting the second formula as reasonably accurate. But for several decades as my age increased, my MHR declined very little.

On the other end of the scale, while coaching a high school cross-country team, I once placed a heart monitor on ninth-grader Megan Leahy during an interval workout. Leahy's pulse jumped to 240 while running 400-meter reps on the track. I was ready to call 911, but that actually was normal for her. She was a very fit athlete who later placed second in the state championships while leading her school to the team title.

You can measure your pulse rate with some accuracy using a watch and, holding the vein in your wrist, counting pulse beats per minute. Or, you can purchase a pulse monitor to do the job for you. This handy device uses a chest strap with a monitor that broadcasts a signal to a wristwatch, giving you continuous readouts while you run. If you check your numbers at the end of a hard interval workout on the track or in the last few hundred meters of a 5-K or 10-K race, you'll probably come pretty close to determining your MHR.

For complete accuracy, you need to be tested on a treadmill at a human performance laboratory. The standard stress test given by cardiologists during physical exams doesn't always produce the right number because cardiologists often are conservative and stop the treadmill before their patients reach maximum stress levels.

MHR. "Not as fast as an interval workout, but faster than the pace used on a long run," he instructs. In other words, set a pace slower than your 5-K time. The runner capable of an 8-minute-mile pace, for example, would do lactate threshold runs at about an 8:30 pace.

One of the appeals of an endurance sport such as running is that you can overcome a lack of natural ability with dedication and training.

When Dr. Pate was training for the Boston Marathon (he had top 10 finishes there in 1975 and 1977), he would add a lactate threshold run to his Saturday routine as a prelude to his Sunday long runs.

He picked that workout intuitively. Later, as an exercise physiologist, he understood its scientific base. "Training studies have looked specifically at how to increase endurance performance," he says, "and some evidence suggests prolonged activity at intensities close to your current lactate threshold is helpful to increase that threshold."

Pace 3: Low Intensity

This is the longer run taken at a slower pace—a typical Sunday morning workout for most serious runners. Many runners who are training for a marathon, for instance, choose 20 miles as the distance for their longest runs. They run aerobically, at a steady pace near 70 percent of their MHR. "Longer runs are valuable," says Dr. Pate, "even if you're not training for a marathon."

The pace used in low-intensity runs should be slow enough so that you can converse with your training partners. Some runners have dubbed this the talk test. (If you cannot talk with your partner, then you are running too fast.) In designing training programs for marathoners, I usually recommend doing the long runs 45 to 90 seconds slower than race pace. A runner capable of an 8-minute-mile pace in a 5-K would run at an 8:45 to 9:30-mile pace (or slower) on long runs if training for a 5-K, slower if training for a marathon.

Pace 4: Rest

Equally important is rest, which might consist of slow running at short distances or even a complete day off. "Some people do quite a lot of running on their recovery days," according to Dr. Pate, "but for others, any activity should be minimal. If they do too much on rest days, they either are going to get injured or they become so tired they need to back off on their hard days, which defeats the purpose of the entire training plan."

Dr. Pate considers variety the key to any training program. He also subscribes to periodization, or peaking. "I continue to be attracted to the concept of building on intensity as one works toward achieving a major goal in some particular competition," he says. "There is risk associated with high-intensity exercise. Experience indicates that such workouts are more demanding and stressful. Carrying on high-frequency training for prolonged periods is risky in terms of overtraining and even riskier in terms of injury."

So to improve your speed endurance, surround your key sessions with sound recovery activities—like short, easy runs; swimming; or walking. Build your program on priorities. The highest priority is attached to the key hard sessions, so take the rest days necessary to prevent breakdown and injury.

To vary the mix, I often prescribe cross-training on easy days, particularly for novice runners. Biking, swimming, or even walking can allow you to log some aerobic training while still resting the muscles specific to running. Don't make the mistake, however, of biking, swimming, or walking too hard or too much, or you'll defeat the purpose of the rest day. ■

CHAPTER 5

JUGGLING WORKOUTS

MAKE THE MOST OF TRAINING TIME

A runner from Salt Lake City once asked me if he could do his long runs on Mondays, instead of weekends as I advise in my training schedules. Yes, I responded. Schedules should not be followed mindlessly. Later, I used this example in lectures to illustrate the fact that workouts can be juggled for convenience. My audiences would chuckle at this runner so nervous about making a seemingly meaningless change.

But in many respects, the Salt Lake City runner gets the last laugh. It does matter whether you do that long run on a Saturday, Sunday, or Monday. Which day you do your long run affects every other type of workout you do the rest of the week. Do your long run too close to a speed session, and your speedwork will suffer. Even worse, you could wind up injured.

How then do you balance long runs with speedwork? How do you mix easy runs, cross-training, and total rest? Those are

REST IS BEST

When juggling workouts, scheduling rest is as important as scheduling stress. The late Bill Bowerman, the great University of Oregon mentor and 1972 Olympic team coach, popularized the hard/easy approach to training. That worked well with his college athletes, but many fitness runners bent on performance often run too hard, then don't rest enough. "When 'hard' becomes 'too hard,' you're in trouble," warns exercise physiologist Dr. Jack Daniels.

Dr. Daniels suggests that if you're on a hard/easy pattern, you may need to convert some of those hard days into "not so hard." Also, one easy day between hard runs may not be enough—particularly as you get older. One or two tough workouts a week may be all many runners can tolerate.

Knowing how and when to schedule rest is particularly essential during the racing season. Dr. Daniels recommends that runners rest one day for approximately every 3,000 meters in a race. The following chart suggests the amount of rest required after racing at common distances. ("Rest" can mean either easy running or no running at all depending upon the runner's state of fitness.)

Race	Rest	Race	Rest
800-meter	1 day	15-K	5 days
1500-meter	1 day	half-marathon	7 days
5-K	2 days	25–30-K	8–10 days
8-K	3 days	marathon	14 days
10-K	3 days	50-K	16 days
12-K	4 days	50 miles	28 days

some of the most difficult decisions made by coaches and runners. Get the formula right, and you set Personal Records. Get it wrong, and you become injured—or do less than your best.

Unfortunately, the scientific community offers little guidance. Dr. Russell Pate of the University of South Carolina admits: "It's difficult to find funding for training-related issues, but it's also very difficult research to do. You're trying to control the behavior patterns of athletes who are not very inclined to be controlled."

Nevertheless, scientists have begun to at least identify the questions that runners need to ask in designing their own workout schedules or applying the schedules of others, such as those in this book. David Martin, Ph.D., chairman of sports science for USA Track & Field, asks the following questions of the athletes he advises.

- **Recovery.** How much rest do you need after your last workout? Muscle soreness, carbohydrate and fluid depletion, fatigue, and age all dictate how soon you can do another hard run.

- **Rest.** How much rest do you need before your next workout? You can't run well while suffering from the symptoms above. Resting before a hard workout allows you to train even harder and build more muscle.

- **Fitness.** What shape are you in? Your current fitness level dictates not only how hard you can train but also how quickly you recover. Very fit athletes can squeeze more hard runs into their workout weeks.

- **Schedule.** What is your overall plan? Pre-set schedules are not meant to be followed precisely, but deviate too much and you may fail to achieve your goals.

- **Distraction.** What's in your way? No matter how well-designed your training plan, distractions (the flu, a snowstorm, an important business engagement) may force you to make adjustments. (Interestingly, at least for elite athletes, Dr. Martin classifies a boyfriend or a girlfriend as a distraction.)

Fail to ask these questions, suggests Dr. Martin, and you'll never achieve success. Yet answer incorrectly, and you're also doomed to failure. Most critical when it comes to juggling workouts is how to mix hard days with easy days so that you recover to run hard again. According to Edward F. Coyle, Ph.D., of the University of Texas at Austin, "Recovery is related to how long it takes you to refuel your muscles with glycogen. This becomes especially important if the intensity of exercise is high."

> *Get the formula right, and you set Personal Records. Get it wrong, and you become injured—or do less than your best.*

So which hard training sessions do you select and how much do you rest between them. Dr. Pate offers the following advice.

1. Think recovery first. Athletes do better when given adequate periods of recovery between extremely demanding exercise sessions. Know how much rest you need to retain quality in your schedule.

2. Decide what's important. Whether long runs for marathoners or speedwork for 5-K runners, plug that "kingpin" workout into your schedule first.

3. Build around the kingpin. One or 2 other days a week, include other hard workouts to also build speed endurance. Marathoners might add long repeats at race pace (5 × 1 mile); 5-K runners might include a medium-long run such as a 10-miler on the weekend.

4. Fill in the gaps. On the remaining days, add some low-stress running to contribute to your overall base mileage. Don't get hung up on numbers, but train consistently.

5. Monitor body signals. No coach can look inside your body. You need to recognize symptoms of overtraining and make adjustments.

The patterns are the same," advises Dr. Pate. "Only the specific training activities differ." Learn to juggle your workouts properly, and you are on your way to success in your next race.

PLOT YOUR PROGRAM ■

But how do you blend theory and reality? What can you learn from eminent scientists quoted in this book to help you run faster? Can the same training methods that permit American record holder Bob Kennedy to run 5,000 meters faster than 13 minutes and challenge for an Olympic gold medal work for someone whose goal at that 5-K distance is a performance twice that length of time? Yes, because regardless of your ability or performance potential, you can improve if

Most critical when it comes to juggling workouts is how to mix hard days with easy days so that you recover to run hard again.

you train correctly. If you learn how to blend hard work and easy work, fast running and slow running, all combined with adequate rest, you will run faster.

Keeping in mind the principles covered in this and the previous chapter, here is one way of structuring a program to develop speed endurance. The distances vary depending upon the race you are training for. Someone training for a 5-K would run shorter distances than someone training for a marathon, but would also train at a faster relative pace. (Paces 1, 2, 3, and 4 relate to the various intensities described in Smart Training on page 27.)

SUNDAY: Long run

> **Distance:** 10 to 20 miles
>
> **Intensity:** Low
>
> **Pace 3:** 45 to 90 seconds slower than race pace
>
> **Purpose:** To strengthen aerobic base

SOMETHING DIFFERENT

Runners often get trapped in the same training patterns. They find a pattern that works for them (whether speedwork or distance) and often follow it to the exclusion of other patterns. This is not entirely bad—particularly if you achieve success—but sometimes resistance to change can stifle your improvement.

One way to improve, claims Jack Daniels, Ph.D., is to do something different: "This may mean focusing on different distances, which will force you to change training patterns. If you're primarily a 5-K or 10-K runner, you may benefit from a season where you train for a marathon. If running two or three marathons a year is your life focus, you may be able to achieve a breakthrough performance after a season working on your short-distance times. Switching from the roads to cross-country to the track can offer similar benefits. When you return to your true running specialty, you can do so with a new array of training tools."

One warning: When you shift training patterns, think like a beginner. Just because you can run 20-milers every Sunday doesn't mean you can survive 10 × 400 meters at a fast pace on the track without discomfort. You'll suffer undue fatigue and sore muscles if you try to do too much too soon of any training regimen. Back off when you begin, running at a reduced effort until you adapt to your new routine.

MONDAY: Recovery

Distance: 0 to 6 miles

Intensity: Low

Pace 3: 45 to 90 seconds slower than race pace

Purpose: To recuperate from Sunday's long run

TUESDAY: Speedwork

Distance: 3 to 6 miles

Intensity: High

Pace 1: Race pace (depending on race trained for)

Purpose: To increase max VO_2 and efficiency

WEDNESDAY: Recovery
> **Distance:** 3 to 6 miles
> **Intensity:** Low
> **Pace 3:** 45 to 90 seconds slower than race pace
> **Purpose:** To recuperate from yesterday's speedwork

THURSDAY: Lactate Threshold Run
> **Distance:** 5 to 10 miles
> **Intensity:** Medium
> **Pace 2:** 15 to 30 seconds slower than race pace
> **Purpose:** To increase lactate threshold

FRIDAY: Rest
> **Distance:** 0 miles
> **Intensity:** None
> **Pace 4:** No running except for advanced runners
> **Purpose:** To store energy for a weekend of hard work

SATURDAY: Swing Day
> **Distance:** 5 to 10 miles
> **Intensity:** Medium to high
> **Pace 1 or 2:** Race pace or slightly slower
> **Purpose:** Competition or other fast training

Developing a training program is as much an art as a science. As we continue, we'll begin to discuss some of the increments that can be included in a training program such as this to make you a better runner. ■

GOOD FORM

SMOOTH OUT YOUR STRIDE

While writing an article on American long-distance star Bob Kennedy for *Runner's World* magazine several years ago, I traveled to Indiana University in Bloomington and watched the two-time Olympian training on Old Kinser Pike, a country road south of the campus. I was struck by his economy of motion.

While his legs and arms churned rapidly, Kennedy's torso did not move. From hips to head, he looked like a statue being towed along a rail. His body gleamed with moisture (the only symptom of the stress of running near 5-minute-mile pace on a warm day), but his face was a mask. His eyes stared straight ahead. No smile. He seemed totally focused on the act of running as fast as he could.

Kennedy was running that day with Andy Herr, a training partner with 29:30 10-K credentials, who nevertheless had to struggle to stay close. Kennedy and Herr had run the opening miles of an 8-mile workout over a series of imposing hills at a variety of paces. They were followed in a car by Sam Bell, the Indiana coach, who stopped the car each mile to call split times. As Kennedy cruised by 4 miles, Bell shouted to him, "You're 20:21! This next mile is supposed to be hard."

"Hard" has different meanings to different people. Kennedy had been running lockstep to that point with Herr, but in shifting to hard he moved effortlessly away.

Bell called out the next split: "4:19!"

For most runners, who might be hard-pressed to run even a half-mile in the time of 4:19, it's difficult to imagine the combination of talent and training that would result in a mile split—in practice nonetheless—that fast. Yet talent and training are only part of the picture. Much of Kennedy's ability to run fast comes from his efficient running form. But is Kennedy's smooth stride a result of natural ability, or a result of practice-makes-perfect?

It's probably a combination of both.

PRACTICE MAKES PERFECT ■

A videotape of Kennedy winning the U.S. national high school cross-country championship his senior year, claims coach Bell, shows him smooth but hunched and using wasted up-and-down motion. While Kennedy was a student at Indiana University and being coached by Bell, those minor form faults disappeared. "My form definitely became more refined during my years at Indiana University," concedes Kennedy.

Good form is a skill that's sometimes overlooked when experts discuss what makes a top distance runner. We know that we need strong legs, a strong heart, and a strong mind in order to run fast, and it also helps to have only about 10 percent body fat. But one important factor that determines whether you finish near the front or rear of your local 5-K race is an efficient running style, or effective biomechanics. In other words: good form.

We can change our form, but only to a certain point. An experienced coach can tell a runner how to incline his head, how to hold his arms, and how to land on—and push off with—his feet. In essence, how to look like a refined runner. "We spend a lot of time on body awareness," states coach Bell. But coaching can only refine what Mother Nature gave you. Some of us are born with an efficient form, and some of us have to learn to live with what we have. We come from the womb preprogrammed for success or failure as runners, the biomechanical relationship of arms to legs to trunk already determined.

Good form is a skill that's sometimes overlooked when experts discuss what makes a top distance runner.

Nevertheless, even inefficient runners can improve. Former Ball State researcher Dr. David Costill remembers the time when three girls from one family, the Cartwrights, began running local road races. "When they started," recalls Dr. Costill, "they finished behind me, but as they got older, they gradually moved past." At age 13, Lora Cartwright, the oldest, set an age-group record of 2:55:00 in the marathon. She won several state championships and later competed for Purdue University.

Dr. Costill continues, "The most noticeable thing from year to year was that they began as bouncers, because that's the way kids run. The older they got and the more they ran, the smoother they got. Exercise physiologist Dr. Jack Daniels did some research in which he followed elementary and junior high school kids at 6-month intervals, measuring their oxygen uptake while they ran at a set speed. What he learned was that as they got older, their max VO$_2$ didn't change. What happened was that they became more efficient. As a result, their times got faster. These improvements seem to be natural in young, developing kids, so the big question is: How do you help older runners improve their form?"

Dr. Costill believes that motor patterns developed early in life become "frozen." While subtle adjustments can be made in those motor patterns to improve performance, major changes will not occur. This is particularly true in Dr. Costill's primary sport of swimming. "You learn a smooth stroke early," he believes, "or you never learn." He also cites speech patterns, because they, too, become locked in place early. I have four cousins, for example, who emigrated from Italy to the United States at various ages, from 6 to 26. Their accents are related to the ages at which they arrived. Nearly 4 decades later, the youngest sounds typically American; the oldest sounds like he just got off the boat. Speech therapy and study can help people improve their speech patterns, but some accents never fade.

Similarly, running stride patterns may also resist improvement. An economical form is not achieved easily. Some experts even insist that it happens naturally, that it should not be taught. Emil Zatopek had terrible upper-body form, yet he was arguably the greatest distance runner of all time, winning the 5000, 10,000, and marathon "triple" in the 1952 Olympic Games. Alberto Salazar ran with the grace of a mailbag thrown from a truck, yet he set a world marathon record. "People run as they do because they have to," one college coach told me. "They don't have any choice. A lot of time is spent coaching things you don't have to, and this is one of them."

Yet coach Bell took exception to that statement when I repeated it to him. "What he's saying is that you can't coach," countered Bell. "I happen to disagree with that."

TEACHING FORM

What allows Bob Kennedy to run so effortlessly? Coach Sam Bell described Kennedy's form, a form he demanded of all his runners when he coached at Indiana University. "Bob runs tall. He wastes little energy. His head is parallel to the ground as he stares off into the distance. His back is straight, and his arms churn easily forward and back. As his arms come forward, they bend slightly as the relaxed hands (thumb resting on index finger) come to chest level.

"As the arms return backward, they straighten somewhat as the hand reaches back to the hip. Torso and head remain perpendicular to the ground. The whole body is relaxed."

How did Bell's runners achieve such form?

Coach Bell emphasized acceleration sprints, body coordination drills, and relaxation sprints.

Acceleration sprints are simple: Runners dash easily out 50 meters, progressing to near speed, then jog back to begin again. They concentrate on relaxation.

Coordination drills include a series of exercises. In one called High Knees, each runner runs in an exaggerated style, raising knees to waist height on each step. They also Skip for Distance, gliding forward while swinging arms to shoulder height. Heel-to-glute drills emphasize quick, high backward kicks, the runner's heel hitting his butt with each stride. Several sidestepping routines, including one called The Carioca, complete the routine.

Bell next has his runners run a series of relaxation sprints "loose as a goose." Arm and leg movement is exaggerated as runners lope along as fast as possible, as though running on air or skimming across water, with each movement relaxed and light.

Eventually, the runner is shaped into an efficient and economical machine. Kennedy says, "Coach Bell told me that when finishing a race, you don't think, 'faster, faster, faster,' you think, 'form, form, form!' You relax, keep your form, and all of a sudden, speed comes."

Regardless of which point of view is correct, questions arise: Can your natural style or form be changed? How can you learn to run economically?

POSITIVE GAINS ■

You can make your style somewhat more economical, even if you started running as an adult. Joanne Kittel is a perfect example. When she joined a beginning running class I taught, Kittel was not the world's least economical runner, but she was close.

At one time, Kittel weighed 196 pounds. Over a period of years, before joining my class, she lost 80 of those pounds. So she at least looked like a runner—that is, when she was standing still. In motion, she was what Zorba the Greek might have called "the full catastrophe." She ran bent over, almost stumbling, gasping for breath. I was afraid to correct her running form for fear that any distraction would send her tumbling to the ground.

Kittel, however, persevered. She became every coach's dream—a runner with the desire to improve. Gradually, she built her running base. She went from slogging through 1 or 2 miles to covering 3 or 4 miles without tripping over a crack in the pavement. At classes and clinics, she paid attention when much swifter runners talked about speedwork. Soon, Kittel was doing strides on the same golf course where I trained in the mornings. Later, she did some interval training by making $\frac{1}{4}$-mile marks on a flat stretch of road that paralleled some railroad tracks. I taught her a few of these tricks, but mostly she learned by listening to others.

One morning, I was working in my office overlooking Lake Shore Drive, a superhighway for joggers, walkers, inline skaters, and cyclists, particularly on Saturdays. I glanced out the window and saw this fast female striding smoothly past my house. It was Joanne Kittel! I remembered the stumbling woman who had seemed so uncoordinated when I first saw her in my class, and I was amazed. Eventually, Kittel would run 3:45:00 for the marathon, nowhere near the Olympic standard but a solid performance that many runners would be proud to achieve. Her accomplishments taught me that running economy can be a learnable trait, not merely a gift of genetics. Coach Bell was right.

LESS IS MORE ■

But exactly what is an economical runner? Owen Anderson, Ph.D., discussed the subject of economy in an article in his *Running Research News*. "An economical runner is one who burns modest amounts of oxygen at a given pace; an uneconomical runner requires large amounts of oxygen (and energy) for the same running speed." In other words, when you're running at the same speed as your competitors, the pace feels easier to you than it does to them. Or when you're running with the same effort as your competitors, you're running faster than they are.

Dr. Anderson believes, as I do, that running economy is a neglected aspect of training. He indicated that while exercise physiologists seemingly have solved the secrets of boosting max VO_2 to create faster runners, little is known about which training methods best improve equally critical running economy, the skill that often separates good runners from bad.

> *While exercise physiologists seemingly have solved the secrets of boosting max VO_2 to create faster runners, little is known about which training methods best improve equally critical running economy.*

Martyn Shorten, a professor from Loughborough University in Great Britain, admits that trying to turn inefficient runners into smooth striders was not easy. He did suggest two possibilities.

Flexibility. First, lack of flexibility restricts range of movement and may limit economy. Thus, runners interested in improving their forms should first improve their flexibility. This is why so many coaches stress stretching drills, a subject covered in chapter 11.

Smoothness. Second, Shorten added that jerky movements incur an energy cost without contributing to efficient propulsion. "In coach's terms," he summarized, "an efficient running action will appear to be smooth, relaxed, and rangy—but you don't need a computer to tell you that." Converting jerky movements into smooth movements is no easy task, but it's one that sometimes can be accomplished with the use of speed drills, also covered in chapter 11.

One of the smoothest runners I competed against was Curt Stone. Stone attended Pennsylvania State University and later competed for the New York Athletic Club. He was America's premier distance runner when I first became involved in track-and-field. He placed sixth in the 1948 Olympic 5000 meters. I was still in high school then, but 4 years later, I ran against him at the 1952 Olympic Trials in California, where he won the 10,000 and set an American record. Later, I watched as he also won the 5000 meters and set another American record.

Of all the dozen or so runners on the Los Angeles Coliseum track that day, Curt Stone easily was the smoothest. He moved along the surface with minimum effort, his inevitable triumph seemingly preordained by his ability, whether practiced or God-given, to run with economy of style. Of course, Stone didn't win every race—no runner does. In fact, at the Olympics in Helsinki, he lost decisively to Zatopek—the man who moved like a maniac. Even then, I continued to admire Stone for his economy of motion.

But my story does not end there. A half-dozen years later, at a meet in which I ran well, a track aficionado approached me and asked, "Do you know who you look like when you run?" I replied, "Who?" To my surprise, he said, "Curt Stone!"

> *Jerky movements incur an energy cost without contributing to efficient propulsion.*

Did I run like Stone because after that day in the Coliseum, I modeled my running after his? Or did I merely think he ran better because I already realized, at least subconsciously, that I ran like him?

SHORT STRIDES, FAST FINISH ■

I recalled another runner from my past: Jim Beatty, one of the world's best milers and 5000-meter runners in the early 1960s and later a TV commentator. Beatty is now a member of the USATAF Hall of Fame, but in 1956, the two of us were unheralded members of an American track team that spent 3 weeks training and competing in Finland. During a workout one afternoon at Suomi Urheilupisto, a sports camp near the town of Vierumaki, Finnish coach Armas Valste watched Beatty run an interval workout. Beatty was relatively short and stocky, but he had a long, flowing stride that allowed him to swallow long stretches of ground in large gulps. Valste observed him and commented tersely, "He overstrides!"

At the time, Beatty was still attending the University of North Carolina and had a mile best of about 4:07. He graduated and retired from the sport. Then, while watching the U.S.-Soviet track meet on television a few years later, he wondered how good he could become if he fully dedicated himself to excellence. He moved to Los Angeles to train under Mihaly Igloi, the former Hungarian Olympic coach who had defected to the United States in 1956. Igloi placed Beatty on a twice-daily, 100-mile-a-week program that consisted almost entirely of interval work on the track.

I next saw Beatty in 1959 during the telecast of an indoor mile race, and my first reaction was that he had cut his stride length in half. In actuality, Beatty probably had sliced only inches from it, but it appeared to be a short, quick-tempo, efficient running style, well-suited to his height. He employed this short stride for maybe 10 of the 11 laps that made up the mile race. Then, almost as though he had shifted gears, he began a powerful, long-striding sprint that swept him past his opponents. He won that day in 3:59, a considerable improvement over his college time—and in an era when sub-4-minute miles still remained a rarity.

Beatty had shown me that you can improve your running form to make it more efficient. Whether this improvement had come from a conscious manipulation of style by his coach or from an unconscious reaction by Beatty's body for protection during an exhausting training regimen, I don't know. His shift mirrored my own experience in seeing my stride length shorten as I went from 25 miles a week in college to 100 miles a week several years later.

FIVE ELEMENTS OF EFFICIENT FORM ■

So what is good running form? And how do you recognize it? The late Fred Wilt, a contemporary of Curt Stone, made an interesting analysis of running form in his book *The Complete*

Canadian Runner, produced for the Canadian Track and Field Association. Some of coach Wilt's views are included in this list of elements of form and how efficient runners use them. How do you stack up?

Footstrike. Most better runners land on their midfoot, that is, at a point just behind the ball of the foot. They then drop down on their heel, and their body glides above a foot that is planted firmly on the ground before they push off with the toes. Some land more forward on the ball of the foot (toe runners); others land more flat-footed (heel strikers). Different runners have different plants, dictated by how the parts of their bodies fit together, otherwise known as biomechanics.

If you possess an imperfect footplant (which can cause injury), you may need to see a podiatrist for orthotic inserts, although most runners can control such problems by carefully selecting shoes. The worst you can do to your footstrike is to try to adjust your landing to accommodate what you think other runners do.

Stride length. There is no definition of a perfect stride length; the best stride lengths depend on each runner's natural form. In general, however, a short, quick-tempo stride may be more economical in a 5-K or 10-K race. A long stride causes the runner to lose momentum and waste energy by pushing too far ahead of his center of gravity—thus, the term overstriding. But understriding can be just as great a mistake.

Carriage. Your trunk should be more or less perpendicular to the ground and your hips should be forward. American Olympian Garry Bjorklund once told me, "Novice runners have a tendency to sit down, to put their weight behind them. They need to bring their center of gravity forward and get their weight over their metatarsals (the part of your foot between the ankle and the toes)."

Arm carry. Your arms should move in rhythm with your legs. They should swing forward more than sideways, with your elbows in and your hands cupped (rather than clenched). The late Bill Bowerman, who was track coach for the University of Oregon, liked to have his runners carry their arms high across the chest. Villanova University's Jim "Jumbo" Elliott wanted his runners to carry their arms low, "thumbs in their pockets." If these two renowned coaches can differ as to what is proper form, then there may be no proper form.

Head position. The head serves as keystone for the rest of the body. Back in some Paleolithic era, a coach once told me to fix my gaze 10 yards up the track and use my eyes to anchor my head in a relaxed position. That is probably as good advice as any. If you allow your eyes and gaze to wander all over the road, you probably will wander with them.

HIDDEN FORM FLAWS ■

I wonder how much even the most experienced coach can learn about a runner's form merely by observing with the naked eye. Once during a visit to the Nike Sport Research Laboratory, I observed Joan Benoit Samuelson running on the treadmill. From the side, her legs seemed a blur as she used 200 steps a minute to run at a 6-minute pace. I could tell little by observing her from different angles. She seemed to move very smoothly, another Curt Stone.

Yet the laboratory director, E. C. Frederick, Ph.D., pointed out that Samuelson favored her right leg, the result of a fracture while skiing years before. He knew this because they had analyzed her style by camera and computer. That was 3 years before Samuelson strode into history with her victory in the first Olympic marathon for women, at Los Angeles in

1984. But it also was 3 years before a severe knee injury, perhaps caused by the imbalance detected by Dr. Frederick, forced her to have surgery that almost caused her to miss the Olympics.

Dr. Frederick told me that when they test various individuals, they sometimes discover that runners who appear to have the worst form are judged most efficient in the laboratory. By now it is common knowledge, for example, that four-time Boston and New York City Marathon champion Bill Rodgers, for all his other virtues, has a strange right arm swing that compensates for a slight foot imbalance. And Frank Shorter swings his left arm outward. You wouldn't want to pass him on that side for fear of getting struck. Dr. Frederick said that Tony Sandoval, winner of the 1980 Olympic Trials marathon, functioned like two separate runners in the area of footstrike: flat-footed on the left, a classic mid-footstrike on the right.

Woe to the coach who would have attempted to modify their forms. In the closing stages of a race, they move with relentless energy and efficiency.

During another project, the scientists at the Nike Sport Research Laboratory tested footstrikes by having a group of top runners adjust their forms during different runs on the treadmill—one time landing on the balls of their feet, another time midfoot, another time more flat-footed, and even on their heels. They expected to discover that the midfoot landing was most efficient, since film and force plate analysis suggests that the world's fastest runners run that way.

During the tests, most of the runners found landing on their heels to be least comfortable. One subject described heel running during the test as a truly horrible experience, akin to Chinese water torture. Yet when the results were computed, heel running proved the most efficient, even for that one reluctant subject.

10 TIPS ON RUNNING FORM

Fred Wilt was a distance runner on the 1948 and 1952 U.S. Olympic teams and became famous for his legendary indoor mile encounters at that time with Wisconsin's Don Gehrmann. After retiring from the FBI, Wilt coached the women's running teams at Purdue University. He edited the publication *Track Technique* and advised various runners, including 1964 Olympian Buddy Edelen, who once held the world marathon record of 2:14:28. (Wilt also coached me when I achieved my PR at the Boston Marathon that same year.) The following is excerpted from a book he produced for the Canadian Track and Field Association, *The Complete Canadian Runner*.

1. Running form is a completely individual issue. Each athlete differs from every other at least to a minute extent in height, weight, bone structure, length and size of muscles, point of muscle origin and insertion, strength, flexibility, posture, and personality, in addition to numerous other features. Therefore, no two runners should ever use identical form, even though they all adhere to basic mechanical principles.

2. It is a form error of the highest magnitude to run without permitting the heel to touch and rest on the ground with each stride, without reservation, in a ball-heel grounding action. This is true at all running speeds, especially sprinting.

3. It is physically possible to land heel-first in running, but this is quite incorrect and almost never seen, since it jars the body excessively and can be done only at very slow running speeds. Landing heel-first

"Sometimes the more you learn, the more you realize how little you know," Dr. Frederick admits. He cautioned runners against using this one experiment to justify a major shift in their running style. "There may be other reasons, beyond what we can measure easily in a laboratory, why a runner should stick with a particular style," he warns.

and "toe running" (refusing to permit the heels to ground) are both incorrect.

4. Ideally, the position of the feet in running is one in which the inner borders fall approximately along a straight line. Athletes should run in a straight line, but not necessarily on such a line. When one foot is placed directly in front of the other, lateral (sideways) balance is impaired.

5. Runners in races longer than sprint distances wherein economy of energy is the paramount consideration should use a natural stride: not exaggerated, not long, not short, but of a length in keeping with maximum economy of effort for the running speed required.

6. Both understriding and overstriding are faults. Each runner has his own optimum stride length at any given speed, depending upon leg length, muscular strength, and joint flexibility.

7. At uniform top speed with zero acceleration, if the athlete was running in a vacuum with no wind resistance, there would be no body lean at all.

8. The hands should be carried in a relaxed, cupped position at all running speeds. They should never be rigidly clenched in a fist while running, since this produces tension, which causes unnecessary fatigue.

9. The head should be aligned naturally with the trunk, and the eyes should be focused a few meters ahead while running.

10. Usually, the best solution to apparent form problems is many repetitions of running short distances, such as 100 meters, at a fast, though not exhausting, pace.

CREATING FORM AWARENESS ■

Let me offer not necessarily a magic formula but rather some suggestions as to how you might at least be aware of your running form, if not improve it. In his article in *Running Research News*, Dr. Anderson quoted several techniques used by Dr. Daniels to improve running form: interval training, downhill running, uphill running, and bounding drills. I've devoted a chapter to each of these techniques. But for now, let's briefly discuss how to use these drills to enhance your form.

Interval training has been proven as a way of improving running ability. It can strengthen you aerobically and anaerobically. It can strengthen your legs. It can strengthen your confidence. I've always felt that one of the greatest values of interval training is that it strengthened my ability to concentrate. It permitted me to maintain good form. During interval sessions at the beginning of the season, I would often find my mind drifting and my form lagging in the backstretch. As weeks went on and I became more comfortable with the training routine, I found I could concentrate and maintain an efficient form for the full lap. Maintaining peak efficiency over a longer period of time inevitably helped me to run faster. My times would improve not merely in workouts but also in races.

> *One of the greatest values of interval training is that it strengthens your ability to concentrate.*

Dr. Daniels apparently agrees, suggesting to Dr. Anderson that runners should combine short bouts of 400 meters, carried out at a rapid (but not maximum) velocity, with maximum rest: a work-to-rest ratio of 1 to 4 or greater. That is, for each quarter-mile you run in 75 seconds, you should rest 5 minutes or more. "The idea is to be completely rested and refreshed for every 400-meter run," Dr. Anderson says, "so that you can maintain good running form throughout."

Dr. Daniels also recommends downhill running to become accustomed to running faster by increasing your leg turnover without increasing your effort. He suggests running very gradual downhills—no more than 2 percent grade—preferably on golf fairways. Uphill running, on the other hand, is good for improving the power of your butt muscles, getting them more involved in the motion of running and forcing you to use more effort. "The idea is not to sprint, but to move steadily," Dr. Daniels says.

Bounding drills, championed by coach Bell, similarly improve strength, flexibility, and running form.

Apart from what the experts say, I'm convinced that runners need to develop what Bell calls body awareness and what I call a feel for form. You need to become aware of how your body moves as you run. One way of achieving that is to attend a running camp where you can be videotaped, so that you can see what you look like running. Or, if you own a video camera, you can have someone else videotape you. One advantage of the current generation of video cameras is that you can employ stop action to check your form at different stride points. The latest models even allow you to download these single-frame pictures onto a computer and print them.

To improve your running economy, try these form drills.

Run barefoot in the park. On a summer day, go to the beach or golf course and find a smooth stretch of sand or fairway. Remove your shoes. Jog or run at a comfortable pace for a distance of 50 to 100 meters. Can you feel the point where your foot contacts the ground? Do you land midfoot or more toward your toe or heel? Can you run more comfortably by adjusting your footstrike? Probably not, but at least you will be aware of your landing. Running gently on the grass is one way to develop body awareness. Running on wet sand and studying your footprints is another way.

Run fast at the track. Visit a 400-meter track. Begin running at the 300-meter starting line, at the head of the back straightaway. Slowly accelerate throughout that straightaway until you are running near race pace through the turn. As you come into the home straightaway, continue your acceleration to top speed at the line. What happens to your form during this acceleration run? At what point and pace do you become a more efficient or less efficient, runner? Focus on what happens to your knee lift, your stride length, your posture, your arm carry, and your head angle. At what point does fatigue cause your running form to deteriorate? Trot out the video camera again if it helps you to answer these questions.

Run straight on the road. Pick a lightly trafficked road where you can follow a straight line: a painted stripe, a crack in the pavement, or the separation between pavement and shoulder. Run at a steady race pace for 1 mile or more. Focus your attention on that line and think of yourself as a machine moving along it, like a train on a rail. Be a Buddha, like Bob Kennedy. Can you run straight along the line without wavering back and forth? Is your head straight; are your eyes level? Are your arms moving smoothly back and forth, in rhythm with your legs? Are your legs moving straight forward and kicking straight back?

Run focused in a race. As you're running your next 5-K, try to concentrate completely on your movements. Can you ignore the scenery, the sights and sounds of the race around you? Can you run without talking? Are you only peripherally aware of other runners around you? Can you maintain the form you practiced on the grass, on the track, on the road? You may need to do so if you want to maximize your ability to run fast. ■

SPEEDWORK

FINE-TUNE YOUR TRAINING

"There's only one way to get faster," Francie Larrieu Smith once told me. "You have to teach your legs what it feels like to run fast." She recommends some sort of speedwork, whether repeats, intervals, fartlek, or whatever. She concedes that runners can improve their times by slowly conditioning themselves—the same pace, day after day—but eventually, improvement ceases. Runners hit a plateau. That's when speedwork can help.

But a lot of runners are like the individual I mentioned in the introduction to this book. He claimed he didn't want to run fast, possibly because he felt threatened by the type of training he might be forced to do to achieve that end. A trio of older runners once told me that they had a conversation one day and decided they didn't want to try any more training tricks. They felt that by sticking to their usual regimen, they would be less likely to get injured. And they might be right. I also remember one of the runners on my cross-country team once saying that she didn't have the speed for running speedwork. I eventually convinced her otherwise, and she finished her high school career as captain of the team.

MAKING SPEEDWORK FUN ■

A lot of runners want to run fast, but they are unconvinced that they have either the ability or the determination to follow the advice of experts such as Larrieu Smith.

Once, at a meeting of our local running club, Joanne Kittel told me how much she despised speedwork. "Does it ever become fun?" she asked.

I had no ready answer. I find speedwork fun, maybe even exhilarating on occasion. Sure, I enjoy long runs on a path through the woods or along backcountry roads—but there also are times when I want to get out on an ugly asphalt track and simply pound away. Is this being masochistic? Possibly so.

Even elite runners who average more than 100 miles a week in their training concede that quality is more important than quantity. They know that you can't abandon speedwork in favor of so-called junk miles. Junk miles have their place in any runner's training plan, but not to the abandonment of other forms of training.

During the club meeting, Kittel told me about the sort of speedwork she did. For one workout, she had marked a nearby road in 440-yard increments. Running over this marked road, she would alternate going fast and slow. It reminded me of some of the workouts of Czech running star Emil Zatopek, who would use telephone poles as guideposts for his sprints, sometimes also seeing how many poles he could reach while holding his breath. Such speedwork could hardly be classified as fun.

A second workout Kittel used was to go to a nearby golf course and do sprints of 130 yards, jogging and walking in between. I doubt if she knew much about Zatopek's training, but I recognized the source of inspiration for that second workout. It was my own method. I often described it at my clinics. Why did we both use 130 yards? Because that was the distance from one tree to another on a particularly flat fairway where I trained. Kittel even might have been using the same trees.

I enjoy that particular golf course workout, because I rarely push it. I go fast but seldom do so many repetitions that I finish tired. Typically, I do a set of four to eight sprints, jogging between, then I walk to full recovery. When I was in top shape, I would do a second set of eight. I usually finished the workout feeling more refreshed than when I started. Why sets of eight? Why not? Good training is often as much an art as a science.

Does such a workout sound difficult or excessively painful to you? With those sprints done only slightly faster than race pace, and following a thorough warmup, would they be likely to cause more injury than a long run on the road? Done in the cool early morning at sunrise in the bucolic setting of a golf course, would the workout lack beauty? I don't think so. And I believe that if you incorporate only this one workout into your training program for at least a few months during the summer, you will see an improvement in your performances.

Like many fast runners, I came to road running with a track background. I competed in the mile and half-mile while at Carleton College in Northfield, Minnesota, and won conference titles in those events. To me, speedwork seems natural, but it could hardly seem so to Kittel, who, as I described in chapter 6, came to one of my running classes as your classic beginning jogger. Like most runners who are more involved with personal achievement than with Olympic aspirations, she began by running slow and progressed to running long. Speedwork, therefore, was unnatural to her. It was a beast to be conquered.

So it was not fun for Kittel. What was fun, however, was her 44:23 10-K finish several weeks before our conversation. It was her first 10-K run faster than 45 minutes. And to what did she attribute the improvement?

Speedwork!

Kittel would continue to mix fast running with her long training, whether she liked it or not. Speedwork may not have been the only reason—or even the major reason—for her success. Over a period of years, she had built a base of miles that led to her improvement. But speedwork certainly contributed to her breaking 45 minutes for the 10-K. It can help you become a better runner too.

If you incorporate only this one workout into your training program, you will see an improvement in your performances.

ACCEPT THE CHALLENGE ■

Before you begin to add speedwork to your training, you should consider whether you are ready to accept this challenge. Coach Bob Glover of the New York Road Runners Club recommends that runners not use speed training until they train for 1 year, complete one race, run at least 16 miles per week, and race faster than their training pace at distances between 3 and 6 miles.

"Be careful about how quickly you add speed training to your schedule," warns Bob Williams, a coach from Portland, Oregon. "Don't jump too rapidly from the base phase of your training program to two or three speed sessions a week. Many so-called overtraining injuries are simply the result of too much intensity too soon."

I'll add another warning. You should be willing to push into the discomfort zone. I dislike using the word "pain," which has a negative connotation. I also find it difficult to understand why marathoners, who willingly suffer the agonies accompanying the last 6 miles of their race, are unwilling to accept what they consider to be painful sensations associated with speedwork. If you want to be a fast runner, you must be willing to accept a certain amount of discomfort. That doesn't mean speedwork is all discomfort. Integrated rest intervals act as a counterbalance. Just as quickly as you enter the discomfort zone, you leave it again by walking or jogging.

Many so-called overtraining injuries are simply the result of too much intensity too soon.

WHY SPEED TRAINING WORKS ■

There are physiological reasons why speedwork is necessary if you want to maximize your potential at any distance, from the mile to the marathon. The primary reason, according to Ball State physiologist William Fink, is that you need to train your system to recruit the muscle fibers necessary to be able to run fast. "I must admit, a lot of the evidence is still out," suggests Fink, "but obtaining a sense of relaxation at race pace apparently comes as a result of training your muscle fibers to function at that accelerated pace."

But certain metabolic adaptations also occur, Fink explains, that relate to the pH levels of the muscles. When you run at an anaerobic level—that is, at a pace so fast you cannot absorb oxygen fast enough to eliminate your body's developing waste products— your muscles accumulate lactic acid. Your pH level declines. Eventually, so much lactic acid accumulates in your muscles that they lose their ability to contract. This is why a middle-distance runner who sprints a 400-meter race usually crosses the finish line stiff-legged, in a state of near collapse. His muscles (at least temporarily) no longer function properly because of excessive lactic acid. Although the phenomenon occurs over a much longer period of time, the same happens to someone running an all-out 5-K or 10-K.

ADD SPEEDWORK CAREFULLY

Bob Williams, a coach from Portland, Oregon, warns against adding speed training too quickly to your training schedule. "Begin with 1 day of speedwork a week," advises Williams. "Allow at least 6 weeks to *gradually* adapt your body to this change of pace."

As an example, Williams suggests that a miler might begin with 4×400 meters and bit-by-bit build up to 8×400 meters. "Don't let the total mileage get too high," says Williams.

A 5-K or 10-K runner might use a slightly different approach, using 800-meter repeats instead of 400 meters. Marathoners might do 1-mile or even 2-mile repeats. Williams suggests that a 10-K runner not do more than half the race distance at speed (thus 5-K, or a dozen 400s on the track as maximum). A miler might do equal race distance at speed, but a marathoner would do considerably less.

"There's no perfect rule that suggests how fast you can progress, or how much speedwork you can tolerate in any one session or during a week," says Williams. "If you begin conservatively, there's less chance you will get hurt. Be particularly careful about mixing volume and intensity, a sure formula for disaster."

Training, and particularly speed training, can modify this effect. According to Fink, "One of the adaptations is the development of a 'buffering' capacity on the part of the body. A runner who is well-trained, through use of the proper amounts of speedwork, can limit the degree to which his muscles become acidic. He can run faster for a longer time before accumulation of lactic acid brings him to a halt."

Also part of the training process is the psychological ability to continue to perform under high stress: in effect, to push on through the pain barrier. But a lot of what many runners, including beginners, assume to be psychological adaptations may actually be metabolic ones—particularly pushing back the anaerobic threshold.

In the words of the late physiologist Al Claremont, Ph.D.,

"Too many people write themselves off as having bad bodies, when they possess more potential than they realize. They simply are unwilling to do the hard work, including speed training, necessary to convert their supposed bad body into a good one."

The anaerobic threshold for someone with "poor" ability might be 60 percent of maximum; that is, they might begin to accumulate lactic acid in their muscles while running at half their maximum heart rate (MHR). For an "average" runner, it could be 70 percent, and a "good" runner may still be able to function aerobically at 85 percent of maximum. Speed-trained runners push into the world beyond. This level of conditioning permits runners like marathon world-record holder Khalid Khannouchi to run seemingly endless miles below a 5-minute pace without apparent distress, because lactic acid has not yet started to accumulate. But even a less gifted runner can push his anaerobic threshold to the right of the scale: from 50 percent toward 85 percent. And the way to do this, as Joanne Kittel discovered, is by doing speedwork.

A runner who is well-trained, through use of the proper amounts of speedwork, can run faster for a longer time.

FAST TWITCH VERSUS SLOW TWITCH ■

Not all of us are born physiologically equal, and it is true that some possess more natural speed than others. Former Ball State researcher Dr. David Costill popularized the theory of fast-twitch versus slow-twitch muscles. Everybody is blessed with both. Most of us have equal numbers of each, but some have more of one than the other. Along with biomechanical differences, this is one reason why some people succeed as sprinters and others as distance runners.

Fast-twitch muscles fire quickly, of course, but they also quickly exhaust their supply of fuel in the form of glycogen.

Fast-twitch muscles are geared for short bursts of energy. Slow-twitch muscles contract more slowly, but they maintain that contraction for a longer period of time. They excel for activities that require continuous effort.

Along with these two basic types, scientists recognize a third type of muscle that fits somewhere in the middle: a fast-twitch muscle that can be trained for endurance, or a slow-twitch muscle that can be trained for speed. In an article in *Esquire* magazine on the subject, Kevin Shyne wrote, "Although it's long been believed that the ratio of fast- to slow-twitch fibers is genetically determined, a number of coaches and sports scientists have recently challenged that view. They hold that speed is much more learnable than previously believed and that anyone can substantially improve his ability to run fast through proper training."

Bob Glover says, "Many runners, especially beginning racers, underestimate their abilities as athletes. Through speed training, they often discover that they are tougher than they had realized."

Apart from physiological considerations, I look upon speedwork as a fine-tuning device, a means by which you become able to extract the maximum amount of energy from an already well-conditioned machine, the human body. Speedwork is a training method that may allow you, after many months or even years of long, steady running, to continue to progress after you seem to have reached a performance plateau.

At the top competitive levels, speed also is important for tactical reasons. Former University of Oregon coach Bill Dellinger says, "The distance runner who has the potential to sprint at the end of a race has a distinct advantage. He can relax and allow the other runners to do all the pacing, relying on his ability to accelerate at the finish. It's known as a kick.

"The problem," he adds, "is that distance runners spend hundreds of hours and thousands of miles training, yet neglect that one weapon—acceleration, or the ability to sprint—that all would love to have."

SPEEDWORK'S MANY FACES AND PACES ■

What is speedwork? Speedwork consists of any training done at race pace or faster. This definition allows for variation in abilities. But by what "race" do you define race pace? During the course of a year, I may compete at distances from 800 meters to a marathon, and while my range is greater than that of many competitive runners, it is not unheard of.

Olympic champion Frank Shorter relates race pace to his average speed in a 2-mile run. During the period when he ranked as one of the world's top 10,000-meter runners, Shorter would consider speedwork as running done faster than 65 seconds for a 400. A number of respected coaches, from Jack Daniels to Bob Glover to Owen Anderson, tie speedwork to the 10-K because it's a popular race distance and most runners can easily relate to it. Since my most recent 5-K times have been in the 25-minute range (8-minute-mile pace), my speedwork begins around 2 minutes for a 400.

Choose your pace carefully. A common beginner's mistake is to run speedwork flat out—faster than race pace. While a certain amount of flat-out training can contribute to your fitness level, too much of it can increase your risk of injuries.

There are various forms of speedwork. Some of them are quite difficult, some of them quite easy, some of them quite similar, some of them quite different. Different coaches have favored certain forms over others, based partly on their own intuitive perception of what works best for their runners. And a form of speedwork that works best for one runner may not necessarily work best for another.

Some forms of speedwork are best for improving strength; others, for improving endurance. Some help you with your form; others, with your concentration. Another important consideration is the confidence that comes from training hard in a measured environment. How you conduct your speed sessions may depend on your specific situation and surroundings. Your training plans will be dictated by whether you live near a track, a golf course, or a wooded area with trails, for example. Weather conditions may be a factor, as will be the length and importance of the race for which you're training.

Some forms of speedwork are best for building strength, others, for boosting endurance, improving form, or sharpening concentration.

In this chapter, I'll cover one type of speedwork, called repeats. In the chapters ahead, I'll also describe intervals, sprints, strides, surges, fartlek, and hill training—and how to successfully implement and use them in your training schedule.

REPEATS ■

A repeat workout is one in which you run very fast, usually over a very short distance, and take a relatively long period of time to recover before repeating that distance again.

A typical repeat workout for me might be 3 × 300 meters. I run 300 meters flat out and walk until fully recovered (usually about 5 minutes). I repeat the 300 two more times.

Running repeats was the first type of training I encountered when I went out for track as a youngster. It was a simple, basic method for working on your speed, one employed by sprinters as well as distance runners.

Repeat running, as taught by many track coaches, was a fairly unsophisticated form of training. It was easy for a coach to pull out a stopwatch and tell his runners to sprint a fast lap. After timing the runners, he could tell them to "walk it off" while he gave his attention to the high jumpers or shot-putters. Looking up 5 minutes later, he would see his runners standing around and send them sprinting around the track again.

At a luncheon in New York, Glenn Cunningham, America's greatest miler in the 1930s, described to me the training methods that had brought him close to 4 minutes for that distance. Cunningham ran little else but repeats, claiming he rarely ran more than a dozen miles a week. A typical Cunningham workout was to sprint 220 yards as fast as he could. After resting, he would sprint another 220, then go home. All of the milers from that era trained similarly.

I graduated from college in 1953 and, during graduate school, trained with Ted Haydon at the University of Chicago. Haydon patterned his training after that of Billy Hayes, the successful Indiana University coach whose runners included Don Lash and Fred Wilt. After an overdistance run of 3 miles on Mondays, we would do three or four 440-meter runs on Tuesdays, a couple of 880s on Wednesdays, five or six 220s on Thursdays, rest on Fridays, and race 2 miles on Saturdays, taking Sundays off. Although it was not identified as such, our training consisted mostly of repeats, because we paid little attention to what we did between fast runs. We recovered by jogging, walking, or sometimes, sitting down.

In 1956, I traveled to Berlin to participate as a member of a U.S. team in the Conseil Internationale du Sport Militaire (CISM) Championships, a track-and-field meet for athletes serving in the armed forces of various nations. On our team was Tom Courtney, a Fordham University graduate who would win the 800 meters at the Olympic Games later that year, running 1:47.7. He also had won the National AAU 400 title that same year.

I would like to tell you that I trained with Courtney, but as someone with considerably less speed, I mostly watched as he ran through a series of 300-meter repeats. Courtney explained that he would begin the track season running 8 × 300; then as he got fitter and faster, he would actually cut the number, but run each repeat faster. At peak training, he would run 3 × 300 at full speed.

It seemed like a reasonable way to train, so eventually I copied Courtney's workout, modifying it to my own needs as a distance runner. I developed a pattern for repeat running, which I described as "three of something." Three became my magic number. I rarely did more, because too many repetitions converted a speed workout into an endurance workout. My body quickly told me that to do more than three, I would need to slow down. The purpose of the workout was to run near maximum speed. There was nothing scientific about my approach; it simply felt right.

Typical workouts that I used, and still use, were: 3 × 200, 3 × 300, and 3 × 400, or for variation, a 200, a 300, and a 400. I seldom go beyond one lap on a track anymore in a single repeat, although years ago, one of my favorite workouts was to crowd 3 flat-out miles within the space of an hour. Were I to do that workout today, it would probably be over a measured road course. At peak training, I include one repeat workout in my schedule each week—but never exactly the same workout. For psychological reasons, I do not want to be able to look at this week's workout and realize that I ran $1/10$ second slower than last week.

Dr. Owen Anderson recommends that each rest period be about five times as long as it takes you to run each fast repeat. This 1 to 5 ratio sounds about right to me. Usually, I would rest by walking the same distance that I had just run. After finishing a 300, I would turn and walk back to where I had started. If I felt

I needed more recovery time after I got back to the starting line, I would take it. While coaching high school runners, I sometimes found that they liked to jog and walk back to the start, anxious to go again. I'd hold them to a 5-minute break to be certain they were well-rested. I would watch them and talk to them, and if they looked like they needed more time, I would give them more time. I stressed to them, and I stress to you, that repeats should not be a punishing workout. You should finish a repeat workout refreshed and feeling positive about running hard with good form.

CONTROL INTENSITY FOR BEST RESULTS ■

One word of caution (I mentioned it before, but I think it's important enough to repeat): Runners new to speedwork (particularly masters runners) should not begin by running repeats flat out. Build your speedwork the way you build your distance. Start easily and gradually increase the pace for the full length of the repeat. Over a period of weeks and months, improve your total time by gradually accelerating toward the end of each repeat. Try to maintain enough control so you can finish each repeat at a speed faster than you start.

In training runners in Dallas, Dr. Robert Vaughan has them run 400s with the second 200 faster than the first. If you finish your repeats struggling and with your form deteriorating, you're running too far, too fast, or too many. Pick a distance, speed, and number that you can run while maintaining good speed form.

That's one reason why I like 300 meters as a distance for repeats. It's longer than the sprint distances of 100 and 200 meters, so you don't (or shouldn't) run it full speed. And it's shorter than 400 meters, so you stop before lactic acid slows your pace and tightens your legs.

On most tracks, the start for the 300 meters is after the first turn, at the beginning of the back straightaway. That's also the start for the 1500 meters. I recommend that my runners begin relatively slowly in the first 100 meters down the back straightaway, build through the second 100 meters coming around the turn, and then kick the final 100 meters down the home straightaway. I ask them to visualize running the last 300 meters of their races. Repeats thus become an exercise to fine-tune a finishing kick. When the runners reach that point in a race, they can relate their kick to the repeats they run in practice.

At Indiana University, track coach Sam Bell used a similar philosophy, but he fine-tuned his runners using 150-meter sprints. Bell coached a series of fine milers on his teams, and felt that the last turn and final straightaway of a 1500 is where the race is won or lost. But regardless of the distance you choose for repeats, they should be done with control.

In an article translated from Russian and published in *Track Technique* magazine, former Russian coach A. Yakimov advises, "Repetition training is not a sprint nor a run at full strength. The athlete runs at a set and controlled pace, which depends on what distance and pace he is preparing himself for. This type of training is a method for developing speed and speed endurance, and can be considered as a method used to develop tempo and a sense of pace. Repetition training brings out a reaction from the body similar to that of a race. So this method finds its main use in the competitive season."

USE REST INTERVALS WISELY ■

"Some runners rest sitting down," Yakimov continues. "At this, they have noticed that the heart rate drops to normal faster than when jogging. However, the recovery of the heart rate is not the only important issue. It's possible that it's better to jog than to sit, especially after an intense run. Slow running offers the muscles a massaging effect, which helps clear waste products and increase the supply to the muscles of oxygen and sugar. In repetition work, the rest should consist of jogging followed by walking, and then sitting or lying down."

When doing repeat miles on the track while at the University of Chicago, I'd walk or jog over to the gymnasium and lie down on the wrestling mats during my 20-minute recovery period. This had the advantage of getting me out of the heat and the sun, since I usually did this workout in midsummer. Today, while running repeat 400s, I sometimes will continue around the track, walking 100 meters, jogging 200 meters down the back straight away and around the turn, then walking 100 meters down the home straightaway before running hard again.

Why? Because it feels right. Every runner needs to determine the best form of rest for his or her particular needs.

Yakimov notes that lengthening the rest intervals (within certain limits) and going faster on the runs increases the workout's effect on your speed. Conversely, shortening the rest periods and slowing the runs decreases the effect on your speed and increases the influence on your endurance.

The chart on page 88, which shows the rest intervals recommended by Yakimov, can help you determine how long to rest during various forms of speed training. You also can use the table for interval training (see chapter 8).

Had Yakimov included my favorite distance, 300 meters, in his table, his rest period would probably have come close to matching the 5-minute rest I suggest. When I ran 3 × 1 mile, my rest periods were close to the 20 minutes the Russian coach recommends for runners doing 2000-meter repeats, which are a quarter-mile longer. What many coaches determine scientifically, runners learn intuitively. Actually, the best coaches simply watch the workouts done by intuitive runners, learn from them, and systemize their training for the benefit of other runners.

Distance of Fast Run (in meters)	Length of Rest (in minutes)		
	Easy Pace	Hard Pace	Flat-Out Pace
100	Up to 0:30	Up to 1:30	Up to 3:00
200	1:00	2:00	4:00
400	1:30	3:00	7:00
800	2:30	5:00	9:00
1,000	3:00	6:00	12:00
1,200	4:00	7:00	15:00
2,000	5:00	8:00	20:00

SHARPEN YOUR RUNNING ECONOMY ■

Repeats also promote running economy. Writing in *Runner's World* magazine, Dr. Anderson describes research by a team of exercise scientists from Arizona State University that followed miler Steve Scott's training over a period of 9 months in 1980 and 1981.

Scott improved his running economy by 5 percent, but, Dr. Anderson suggests, only after he added fast 200- to 600-meter runs to his training program. After improving his economy, Scott set two American records: 3:31.96 for the 1500 meters and 3:49.68 for the mile.

"The key to improving economy is to run fast while you're feeling strong and relaxed, not when you're tired and struggling and your running style is unnatural and fatigued," Dr. Anderson advises. ■

THE MAGIC WORKOUT

INTERVAL TRAINING
CAN IMPROVE YOUR SPEED

Each Wednesday throughout the year, just before 5:30 P.M., members of the Jacksonville Track Club begin gathering in the parking lot of The Bolles School. In any given week, as many as two dozen may show, more in the weeks leading up to that Florida city's major road race, the Gate River Run in March. The group leader is Bob Carr, who started running in 1969 while in the Navy, to get in shape before being shipped to Vietnam. Carr persisted and has run each of the 23 River Runs, most recently winning his age group (70-74) in the year 2000 race.

The group starts by jogging along San Jose Boulevard to and from Epping Forest, a fashionable club nearby. The distance is about 2 miles, a good warmup. Then, the runners move into the Bolles athletic complex, which even late in the afternoon is usually crowded with students involved in different activities: football, soccer, swimming, tennis, baseball, cheerleading. The runners, however, have come to use the track for interval training.

After several minutes of stretching, Carr gathers the group and announces the evening's workout: a half-dozen or more 400s, 800s, or some combination of those and longer distances, the fast repetitions punctuated by recovery 400s, which are jogged and walked. The group varies in ability from runners used to winning their age categories in local road races to those who come to the Wednesday workouts mainly for the camaraderie and an opportunity to stretch their legs and feel the wind in their hair.

"We've been meeting for 18 years," says Carr. "It breaks the usual routine of running the roads at the same old pace."

Not only in Jacksonville, but in many areas, from Eugene to Boulder to Albuquerque to Chicago, runners look to the track—and interval training done on the track—as a major means of improving performance. Certainly, the value of interval training has been recognized for more than half a century, dating back to the late 1930s when the German coach Waldermar Gerschler asked his top athlete Rudolf Harbig to train by running alternate fast and slow laps. In 1939, Harbig ran a world record 1:46.6 for 800 meters, a mark that remained on the books for nearly 2 decades, long after he was killed in action during World War II.

Tom Ecker, an expert on coaching techniques from Iowa, once described interval training as "the most effective single training system ever devised."

Former Ball State researcher Dr. David Costill claims that a runner shifting to interval training often can improve speed after only a single session.

The University of Oregon's Bill Dellinger states, "Interval training—if it's done properly—develops speed in a runner more quickly than any other form of training."

The magic workout? If I had to name one single type of training capable of converting a plodder into a runner, this would be it. Interval training, carefully structured into a well-designed workout regimen, may not necessarily turn you into an Olympian, but it can make you a better runner.

An article by Brian Mitchell in *Athletics Weekly* magazine presented the case for interval training. "In this type of (training), the runner gets the best of two worlds because he keeps moving throughout and is able regularly to raise the pace above what would be done in a steady run, and thereby also extend the range of body movement, with all that implies for muscles and nerves. The session is under as much control as you want. It is systematic and definite, and it is tailored for each individual, so long as he does not allow himself to be overrun by a group of fellow athletes and forced to go their pace rather than his own."

interval training if it's done properly— develops speed in a runner more quickly than any other form of training.

Mitchell adds, "Interval training can also be intelligently progressive, month by month, season by season, accessible and adjustable."

If proof were needed of the effectiveness of interval training, James Stray-Gundersen, M.D., provided it during a study he did in collaboration with Dr. Peter Snell at the University of Texas in Dallas. The researchers asked 10 experienced runners, whose 10-K times averaged between 34 and 42 minutes, to train for 6 weeks at 50 miles a week, building a base. They then divided the runners: One group did lactate threshold training, the other group did interval work: 400s in 75 to 85 seconds, 200s in 33 to 38 seconds.

At the end of 10 weeks of training, the researchers tested both groups by having them race at 800- and 10,000-meter distances. Analysis showed that the interval-trained group improved their 800 times by 11.2 seconds and their 10,000 times by more than 2 minutes. The control group demonstrated lesser improvements: 6.6 seconds in the 800 and just over 1 minute in the

10,000. Improvements in max VO$_2$ showed a similar division: 12 percent in the interval group, 4 percent in the control group.

Dr. Stray-Gundersen and Dr. Snell worked with well-conditioned runners. But at the University of Miami, Arlette C. Perry, Ph.D., tested 66 college-age women in an aerobic dance class, training two groups 3 days a week for 35 minutes a day at 75 to 85 percent of their maximum heart rate (MHR). The control group did aerobics for 35 minutes nonstop. The interval group alternated 3 to 5 minutes of aerobics with brisk walking, which stretched the workout past 35 minutes.

After 12 weeks, the control group had improved cardiovascular endurance by 8 percent; the interval group had improved by 18 percent. Other studies at the University of Massachusetts and Arizona State University showed similar benefits for interval training.

But is this a training method that can benefit every runner? What about someone whose only goal, admirably, is to nibble a few seconds off her 5-K time, not win an Olympic medal? Let's discuss this magic training method in greater detail.

WHAT IS INTERVAL TRAINING? ■

"Contrary to popular belief," says coach Dellinger, "interval training isn't superfast, all-out running as much as it is controlled running." Control, of course, is important in any intelligent training program. The subtle difference between running repeats (as covered in chapter 7) and doing interval training—other than the fact that you usually include more repetitions in the latter— is that you control the rest interval between the fast runs as well as the speed and distance you are running.

That's an important point. The key word is *between*. Many runners mistakenly refer to intervals as the fast part of the speedwork. ("I ran my intervals in 70 seconds a lap.") Not so. Check a dictionary. Interval is defined as an intervening period of time, a period of temporary cessation, or a pause.

Remember that. The interval is the rest that happens between. The fast run is more properly referred to as the repetition (although this term could be confused with repeats). Many coaches call the fast segments reps.

But what's more important than what you call them is how you do them.

MEET WALDERMAR GERSCHLER ■

The individual credited with the development of interval training as an important means of improving speed and endurance is the German coach Waldermar Gerschler, who trained Rudolf Harbig to his 800 world record. Gerschler was not the first coach to ask his athletes to alternate fast and slow running. Earlier, the Finnish coach Pehhala had developed a system of "terrace training," which consisted of repeated speed runs with slower running between.

Czechoslovakia's Emil Zatopek also employed this pattern in his training, running as much as 60×400 meters, although slower than race pace. After Zatopek's three victories at the 1952 Olympics, coaches and athletes began to examine his training methods. They realized the biggest advantage of fast/slow training: Runners could work at race paces for race distances and with race intensities by utilizing recovery segments midworkout.

Gerschler's contribution was to systemize interval training, which he did in collaboration with Hans Reindell, M.D., a cardiologist. Reportedly, Gerschler and Dr. Reindell studied more than 3,000 individuals. According to an article by Paul A. Smith in *Athletics Journal*, the German coach and physician together pinpointed when the greatest stimulus for heart development occurs—during the first 10 seconds of the recovery interval. "The run provides the stress, while the interval allows for the development response," Smith explained. "Because Gerschler and Dr. Reindell realized during their research that the rest period was the key to development, they named this exercise interval training." And it became a successful formula for improving speed and endurance that could be applied to almost any workout at any level.

Before going any further, I should note that there was little or no masters competition when Gerschler and Dr. Reindell did their research. So we can assume they worked with young athletes, whose MHRs would have been around 200. If so, heart rates around 170 to 180 beats a minute for the fast run (cited in the study) would have been the equivalent of 85 to 90 percent of their MHRs. Heart rates of 130 to 140 beats a minute during the recovery would have been the equivalent of 65 to 70 percent of their MHRs.

In describing interval training, Gerschler and Dr. Reindell identified the following variables.

1. Distance. How far you run during each repetition. Gerschler and Dr. Reindell determined that the time for each run should not exceed 90 seconds. (This suggested a distance no longer than 600 meters, although 400 meters became the distance most favored by runners for interval workouts.) The intensity should be sufficient to produce a heart rate of 170 to 180 beats per minute, which they measured during the first 10 seconds of the recovery period.

2. Interval. How long you rest during each interval. They also deduced that the interval should not exceed 90 seconds. They noted that it took only 30 seconds into the interval for the pulse to drop to approximately 130 beats per minute. If the pulse failed to fall below 140, they slowed the pace or shortened the distance. If the pulse remained elevated, they stopped the workout.

3. Repetitions. How many times you run the distance. (Or, in coaching jargon, how many reps.)

4. Pace. How fast you run the specified distance.

5. Rest. What you do during the interval.

Let me offer you an example based on my own training. While researching the first edition of this book, I visited the National Institute for Fitness and Sport in Indianapolis to interview exercise physiologist Dean Brittenham. It was December, and I arrived early to use the institute's indoor track: 200 meters, approximately eight laps to the mile. The institute is located a short distance from the Indiana University and Purdue University in Indianapolis outdoor track, which was used for the 1984 and 1988 Olympic Trials.

For various reasons, I decided that morning to run 300-meter repetitions, a lap and a half on the track. Thus, that became my distance, the first variable. The distance usually remains constant during any single workout, but may vary from one workout to the next. "The important thing," says Ecker, "is that the distance is shorter than the athlete's race distance, usually in multiples of 100."

At the institute, fast runners are asked to use the outside lanes, leaving the inside lanes for walkers and joggers. I chose lane 5, which meant that after finishing each 300, I would need to continue around the track approximately another 140 meters to get back to the starting line. This became my interval, the second variable.

Not knowing how I would feel, since this was my first run on the institute's track, I simply ran until I felt I had a good workout. I stopped after 11 repetitions, the third variable. "The exact number of runs is not important," says Ecker. "The important thing is that they have been run to their absolute limit." Ecker considers this the biggest guessing game the coach (or athlete) has to play. "If too low, [the number of reps] reduces the effective-

AN INTERVAL WORKOUT

Below is an example of a classic interval workout: 11 × 300 meters, averaging 61.1 seconds per rep, resting by jogging 140 meters between in approximately the same time. Notice that in the 11th and final rep, I reached my maximum heart rate of 150. But between reps, the interval of rest allowed my heart rate to drop to near 110.

Number	Rep Time (in seconds)	Pulse Rate (beats per min)	Interval Time (in seconds)	Pulse Rate (beats per min)
1	62.1	136	63.5	103
2	61.0	138	63.4	108
3	61.4	141	65.9	105
4	61.5	140	65.4	106
5	61.2	142	65.1	109
6	58.7	147	65.9	109
7	64.0	140	60.1	109
8	63.3	141	62.3	111
9	61.3	145	65.4	111
10	61.6	144	66.7	110
11	56.2	150	72.6	111

ness of the workout," he says. "If too high, the runner crashes."

My time for each 300 was around 61 or 62 seconds—although borrowing a tip from coach Dellinger, I ran two of my reps (the 6th and the 11th) faster, 58 and 56 seconds. The pace I ran was the fourth variable. "The speed of each repeat run," suggests Ecker, "is determined by the runner's projected race pace."

Between reps, I jogged at a moderate speed, covering the 140-meter interval distance in 60 to 65 seconds. (That converts to approximately 12-minute miles, 5 mph).

The rest between bouts of running fast was the fifth and final variable. "For interval training to be a truly effective system for conditioning the runner's cardiorespiratory system," says Ecker, "the heart rate must be alternately increased during the runs and decreased to a level of semirecovery between runs."

This resulted in a rather neat workout package: 1 minute of hard running followed by 1 minute of easy running, repeated 11 times. My heart rate on the fast runs rose to above 90 percent of my MHR; during the intervals, it dropped to 70 percent of my MHR. (Keep in mind that my maximum heart rate is 150 or slightly higher.)

Gerschler would have been proud of me, had he been present to witness the workout. As a German scientist, he also would have been fascinated with the digital watch I wore (capable of storing 30 times) that allowed me to precisely record the times for my reps and intervals. The fact that I was wearing a second watch that recorded my pulse every 5 seconds would have convinced Gerschler that, indeed, he had been born in the wrong era.

In shortened form, the workout could be described as: 11 × 300 (61.1 seconds average), 140 rest between (65.1 seconds average). That sounds scientific, but actually, I just showed up at the track and did what my body told me was a reasonable workout for my level of training and my feelings of energy on that particular morning. I might add that I finished the workout comfortably, feeling that I put in some hard work that felt good, whether or not it would help me in my next race.

That single well-measured workout would provide a database for future workouts. One week later, I was in New York City on business and worked out one morning on the cinder path (approximately 2,000 meters around) that circles the reservoir in Central Park. I set my watch to beep every 60 seconds to remind me to alternate running fast and slow. I ran 11 fast sprints in this manner, jogging between. My measured heart rates were slightly lower than in Indianapolis, possibly because chilly weather prevented me from going full tilt. Otherwise, this New York workout was a carbon copy of the first. While interval training most often is done on the track, it need not be.

WHY DO INTERVAL TRAINING? ■

Interval running, even at relatively slow speeds, is more demanding than ordinary running. It is a high-stress workout. It also can be more time consuming. You may need to travel to a track, or somewhere flat and marked, to do it. So why train that hard when jogging in the park is more fun and less stressful?

The main reason for interval training, of course, is improvement. Although some may consider interval training painful, it actually can be a rather benign way to train at race pace. Certainly, running 400 meters at your best pace for 10,000 meters, then slowing down to rest before taking on another 400, is easier than running 25 laps at your best possible pace. Practically all research done on distance runners suggests that they improve when they add intensity to their programs.

The other side of that coin, of course, is a study of walkers and joggers executed by the late Michael L. Pollock, Ph.D., who was director of the University of Florida's Center for Exercise Science, that showed that intensity is exactly what scares beginners away. It also subjects them to higher injury risk, said Dr. Pollock, and I'll buy that. As a result, when you mention intensity or interval training to the people who run for T-shirts in 5-K races, their attention sometimes drops. They don't want to go fast or do speedwork; they just want to get in their daily 5 miles and burn a few calories to feel good and look good.

If that is your approach, don't change. Yet beyond a desire to improve race times, those who embrace intensity comprehend that there is a mystical aspect to interval training. "Pushing the edge of the envelope" (to steal a term from the test pilots)—testing your own personal speed barriers—can be exhilarating. Interval training done in the company of like-minded fellow runners results in a shared experience, even if you're too stressed during or afterward to talk. Running with the group at The Bolles School, simply stated, was fun! It was obvious to me after one workout with coach Bob Carr's training group that the runners liked each other's company. They enjoyed seeing each other for these weekly sessions. And the fact that they were participating in an intense training session didn't prevent many from chatting during the interval recovery jogs between the fast reps. Being able to see improvement from week to week—both in yourself and in others—also offers a form of motivation. And interval training can improve your concentration and refine your technique and form. After running with the group at Bolles, I vowed that anytime I was in town, I would try to find time to join them.

The main reason for interval training is improvement.

MORE ART THAN SCIENCE ■

How fast should you run your interval training? That's a tricky question, despite all the expert advice and the charts published in running magazines that seem to offer exact answers. An experienced coach like Bob Carr, observing you in training over a period of 6 months or more, might be able to tell you how fast to run—or he might not. Coaching remains somewhat of a guessing game; it's more art than science. People differ in their abilities, and they also differ in their ability to train hard on the track. Someone new to interval training certainly would find it more stressful than an old warhorse like myself. And not every day is equal to every other day. Outdoors, weather can affect workouts. It could be hot or humid or cold or windy. You might arrive at the track fatigued from a hard day of work or too little sleep the night before because one of your kids was sick. What you ran the day before, whether hard or easy, also can affect your training. As a result, it's sometimes difficult to compare one week's workout with the next—although over a period of time, a pattern usually does emerge.

Jim Huff, a coach who works with members of the Motor City Striders in Detroit, warns against setting too-precise goals for interval workouts. "Runners get frustrated if you say run a certain speed and they can't accomplish that, so any time set has to be realistic," he explains. "You can't just read what other people do and try to copy their workouts."

Dr. Owen Anderson suggests in his publication *Running Research News* that interval training be carried out at an intensity of 90 to 100 percent of your MHR—about the same intensity as a 10-K race. Thus, a good starting point for most people beginning interval training is to train at a slightly faster pace than you run in a 10-K race, or at about the same pace you might run a 5-K. Some coaches also suggest that if your racing goal is a 5-K, then you should train at your speed for the mile or 1500 meters. Milers should train at half-mile pace, and so forth.

Dr. Snell advises against running interval 400s at faster than race pace. "It is tempting to run fast during your workouts," he says, "but remember that you're not going to be able to run that fast in a race. If you run too fast during workouts, you'll get too fatigued to do good training, and you'll also get out of your race rhythm. Too much speed is more damaging than too much distance."

Training at race pace does have another important advantage. You develop pace judgment. During the phase of my running career when I ran a lot of intervals, I could almost tell how fast I had run each 400-meter lap without even looking at my watch or waiting for the coach beside the track to call my time. On occasion, I've participated in "prediction miles," where the winner is not the fastest runner but rather the one able to predict his or her time. The enviable purpose, of course, is to allow less experienced runners to win a few trophies in an event where speed is not a factor. Inevitably, the fastest runners still win, because they are most likely to have honed their pace judgment through interval training. In one prediction mile, I embarrassed myself and got all the other contestants upset with me by selecting a time somewhere around 9 minutes, finishing well behind almost everybody who entered, yet still winning because I nailed my time within a few seconds. One year, I led a pacing team for *Runner's World* magazine at the Walt Disney World Marathon and hit five of my mile splits within 1 second of perfect while bringing a group of several hundred runners home almost exactly on time.

My ability to tell you exactly the pace I'm running has recently faded somewhat because I more often run even my interval training away from the track. But I still possess a well-developed ability to sense pace changes of even a few seconds per mile by others running around me in races. This is an important skill because running at a consistent speed is one way to conserve energy.

SETTING REALISTIC GOALS ■

When he coached at the University of Oregon, Bill Dellinger utilized a system of interval training that he borrowed from his predecessor, Bill Bowerman. The system revolved around "date pace" and "goal pace." Date pace is the pace at which you can currently run your race distance. Goal pace is the pace at which you hope to run that distance toward the end of the season—that is, in the important meets. For top University of Oregon runners, that meet was the NCAA championships. My most important race of the year is the World Veterans Championships, where I often run the 5000 meters, or sometimes the 2000-meter steeplechase. To fine-tune my speed for those distances, I would also do several 1500-meter races leading up to that meet. So in doing interval training, I need to work at paces I would be running in races between 1500 and 5000 meters.

When I threw those two fast 300s into the middle of my workout in Indianapolis, I actually was following a variation of the University of Oregon interval system. I was running the reps at a pace near what I felt I could accomplish at that time. A 300-meter pace of 61.1 maintained for 1,500 meters would give me a final time of 5:05.6 for that distance. However, if I could maintain the 58.7 I ran in my sixth quarter, or the 56.2 I ran in my final quarter, I could run 4:53.5 or 4:41.0, respectively.

I was far from being in peak shape during that midwinter workout in Indianapolis, but I had run 4:53.3 the previous August at the Masters Track Field Championships in the same city. And at the same meet in San Diego the year before, I had run 4:45.9, placing third. For the coming year, a world championship year, I was setting my pace higher, so that day's training in Indianapolis seemed quite compatible with my plan. And, indeed, later that summer I placed first in the steeplechase at the World Veterans Championships in Turku, Finland. All of that hard work on the Indianapolis track and on other tracks leading up to that meet did pay off.

I should mention again that I did not set out that morning in Indianapolis to run date pace and goal pace. I simply got out on the track and ran, allowing my body—essentially, how I was feeling—to set the effort of the workout. I was able to do that because of the experience from decades of interval training.

Less experienced runners need to set their date and race paces for interval workouts carefully. Bowerman believed that runners should feel exhilarated, not exhausted, at the end of a workout. "Too many individuals," he said, "simply run themselves into the ground and aren't fresh enough to race properly." He felt that if runners overwork, they become less excited about racing.

That's assuming that racing is the most important reason that you run. For the college coach, the race—whether during cross-country season or part of a track meet—certainly is the raison d'être of running. This was particularly true for Bowerman in 1972, the year he served as head track-and-field coach for the U.S. Olympic team. If your end goal is to develop Olympic champions, then certainly interval training provides a very effective means to that end.

But 1972 was the year that Frank Shorter won the Olympic Marathon in Munich, Germany. Shorter's victory was not the only reason for the running boom that followed soon after, but ironically, it played an important part in forcing an expansion of the goals available to runners. Not every runner has Shorter's talent, or even a fraction of that talent. Not every runner is training for an Olympic medal. Life for most runners today is more than an endless quest for one more race T-shirt or trophy. Most of today's runners don't even race, and when they do, they run races more for social reasons than for success. We've redefined our goals since the time that Bowerman was coaching at Oregon, so that the means often may be more important than the end. The workout is more important than the race. Coincidentally, Bowerman was one of the early pioneers in the fitness movement, teaching jogging to housewives as an aside to training elite athletes.

Perhaps I reflect my own philosophy, because I find myself able to secure as much masochistic enjoyment from a single well-crafted workout—a hard run in the park, a set of quarters strung together on the track—as from winning my age-group in a megarace. I still measure myself in megaraces, but hard running carries its own rewards. Interval training, because of the way it can be measured in bits and pieces, can provide a form of satisfaction akin to racing. That is not to say that dedicated coaches are wrong for their emphasis on racing as the end product. There is room within running for many philosophies. But you can enjoy running fast in workouts without necessarily pointing toward an upcoming race.

Nevertheless, there is nothing like competition to provide a level of motivation not experienced in practice. In describing a downhill ski race on television, Curry Chapman, retired coach of the Canadian women's national team, suggested that the viewer should think of a string tied at the starting line and leading through the gates to the finish line. "In training," Chapman said, "there's slack in the string. Race day, adrenalin pulls the string tighter."

REACHING YOUR PEAK ■

Therefore, races provide a goal that can be approached with logical and systematic training. Interval training, of course, lends itself extremely well to progressive programs, ones in which you begin at a relatively low level of fitness and train progressively harder to improve performance. You go from weakness to strength via the overload principle. This can be accomplished in several ways.

Writing in *Athletics Journal*, Donald E. Boggis Jr., a high school coach from Hollis, New Hampshire, discussed manipulation of the five variables in progressively overloading (and strengthening) the system. Boggis cited variables slightly different from those mentioned by coach Gerschler and others, but the effect is the same. As your training program progresses, suggests Boggis, you can increase the number of repetitions, or you can increase the speed you run them. You can decrease the amount of rest you take during the interval by jogging less, or you can increase the distance of the repetitions, maintaining the same pace. A wide variety of combinations present themselves.

Yet blind application of any number-based system can cause problems. Fatigue, poor diet, and lack of sleep all can affect the intensity of your training. An additional variable—one not mentioned in most coaching articles—is weather. Cold, heat, wind, and rain can affect how fast or how far you run during any given workout.

Nevertheless, the advantage of training using an overload program is that it does provide a strong psychological carrot as you peak for a specific race. It's like runners in training for a marathon, who progressively increase the length of their weekend runs over a period of 18 weeks (if they use one of my schedules that utilizes that time period) to where they finally can cover 20 miles comfortably the last month before they are asked to race 26. It's like the countdown before the launch of a space shuttle. After the long runs to develop endurance, after the fast runs to develop strength, you use a shot of speed training featuring intervals to fine-tune your speed. Because it lends itself to progressive manipulation (as suggested by Boggis), interval training offers an effective way of peaking.

Because it lends itself to progressive manipulation, interval training offers an effective way of peaking.

Maintaining that peak is another matter. In discussing the benefits of interval training, Gerschler and Dr. Reindell commented, "Interval training saves time, is a good stimulant, but its disadvantage is that the achieved condition is not maintained for a long period."

Magic workout, no—but if you expect to run fast, you probably need to include some form of interval workouts in your regular training regimen.

INNOVATIONS THAT MAKE CHAMPIONS ■

I first discovered the advantages of interval training while living in Germany in the mid-1950s. Gerschler was still training runners in that country at that time, but our paths never crossed. I knew him only by reputation.

I was a member of the United States Army, stationed in Germany from May 1955 to November 1956. I ran every day, not always with the Army's permission. While a member of the 63rd Tank Battalion in Kitzingen, I sometimes would crawl under a barbed-wire fence at the end of the day to run in a nearby forest. Later, while working as an ordinance draftsman at Seventh Army Headquarters in Vaihingen, outside Stuttgart, I would appear at the camp exit at 9:00 P.M. dressed in my running gear. The guards at the gate probably thought I was crazy, but they waved me through when I showed them my pass. I remember those runs through what was truly the Schwarzwald ("dark forest") as among the most enjoyable workouts of my career.

ACHIEVING MAXIMUM PERFORMANCES

Portland, Oregon, coach Bob Williams claims that running interval workouts can improve your economy. "You learn how to tolerate race pace and how to accept the discomfort necessary for maximum performances," says Williams.

He warns, however, that runners should use speedwork only after developing a sound training base, and then only sparingly. He says, "If you spend several months gradually building your mileage—and fitness— you'll be able to survive the intense stress that speedwork, specifically interval training, places upon your body."

The downside of this training regimen can be both physical and mental fatigue, plus an increased risk of injury if done too often or too fast. To avoid this, Williams advises runners to limit their speed sessions (on or off the track) to once a week, and not year-round. "Interval training," he says, "is best used when peaking for a specific race or series of races where you want to set a Personal Best and maximize your performance."

On other occasions, usually on weekends, I would drive into town to train on the track of the VfB Stuttgart, a local sports club. Accompanying me was another soldier stationed at the post, Dean Thackwray, who made the 1956 U.S. Olympic team in the marathon. Our frequent training partner was Stefan Lupfert, who won several German indoor championships at 3,000 meters and also competed on the national team in the 3000-meter steeplechase.

Dissatisfied with my previous training methods, I already had begun to increase the number of repetitions. But while training with Lupfert, I saw how he ran somewhat slower reps but jogged much faster between those reps, typically at about an 8-minute mile pace. A standard workout for us was 12 × 400, with a 400 jog between. The fast 400s were done in around 65 or 70 seconds, the slow 400s (or intervals) in 2 minutes.

Also in Germany at that time was Frank McBride, whom I had run against in college when he competed for South Dakota State. McBride placed seventh in the 1500 meters at the 1952 U.S. Olympic Trials, and he later achieved success as a masters runner. But at this period in his life, McBride was serving as a coach of Army runners stationed in Germany, first as an officer, later as a Department of the Army civilian. McBride was familiar with the theories of Gerschler and Dr. Reindell, and he encouraged me to use interval training. I found it to be a worthwhile program that cut more than a minute off my time for 5,000 meters and several minutes off my time for 10,000 meters.

In all honesty, a major reason for my improvement was that in the previous year or two, I had doubled the volume of my training to 100 miles a week. All those nighttime runs in the Schwarzwald were having an effect. (That underlines the importance of building a good training base before beginning speedwork.) Nevertheless, interval training definitely was the key to my success. It was my magic workout.

GAINING AN EDGE
WITH SLOW QUARTERS ■

Later, after my discharge from the Army, I returned home and began training at Stagg Field, the University of Chicago's track. It was also used by nonstudents, members of coach Ted Haydon's University of Chicago Track Club (U.C.T.C.).

Most runners training at the track—varsity and track club members—were more familiar with fast repeats. Like most American coaches, Haydon trained his runners in this manner: You ran a hard quarter around the track while the coach timed you. You then slowly walked or jogged once more around the track and waited until you caught his eye, so he could time you again for another hard quarter.

Interval training had only begun to penetrate the consciousness of the American distance runner. Other runners who decided to run quarters with me would sometimes become edgy about my seemingly slow pace and sprint ahead. By the end of the workout, they struggled to keep up—if they lasted to the end. They had not anticipated the stress imposed by the interval aspect of the workout. What tripped them was not the fast reps, but the (relatively) fast interval jogging laps between the reps. Sooner or later, the others became accustomed to this style of training—or found different training partners.

One Chicago runner who shared my enthusiasm for interval training was Gar Williams, who also had recently returned from service in Germany. Haydon used to chuckle at Williams constantly running all those slow quarters.

Another U.C.T.C. member had placed high in the NCAA championships several years earlier. He trained in the old style, mostly fast repeats. I told Haydon that Williams would probably defeat the other runner later that season when we ran at the National AAU Track & Field Championships. Haydon refused to believe me. Sure enough, Williams did what I had predicted.

Eventually, Haydon and other American coaches came to appreciate the value of slow quarters. (Williams later won a National AAU marathon title and served a term as president of the Road Runners Club of America.)

The advantage of interval training—and one reason for its appeal to track coaches—is that it allows total control over the workout. It is very systematic, very precise. It is also a good means of charting your progress from week to week. If you record workouts in a training diary (or log), you can see that this week you ran your quarters in, say, an average of 75.3 seconds, compared to 76.1 last week, or 85.7 a couple of months ago. Don't discount the value of such record-keeping. One reason you succeed with your running is confidence: a belief in yourself and a belief in your training. Interval training on the track can be an important confidence builder.

Certainly, interval training appeals to the computer-like mind, since by juggling Gerschler's five variables, all sorts of training possibilities present themselves. It is an excellent way of adapting the body to stress, since you push, back off, push some more, back off. It also permits you to train at race pace, and it is an excellent way to learn that pace.

After my introduction to interval training in Germany, I experimented a lot with different patterns. My most frequent workouts were 400s (jogging 400s between) or 200s (jogging 200s between). They could be done very neatly on a 400-meter track outdoors or a 200-meter track indoors. (Of course, back then the tracks and repetitions were linear—thus 440 or 220 yards.) Sometimes, I used long repetitions and short intervals, such as 1,000s with 200s between, or miles with a quarter-mile jog (or 2-minute walk) between. The latter workout I sometimes did with Tom O'Hara, who set a world record for the mile indoors and ran the 1500 for the United States in the 1964 Olympics. It was a workout that O'Hara often did on his easy days.

TOO MUCH OF A GOOD THING ■

At one point, I experimented with megadoses, where I ran 70 × 300 with a 100 jog or 50 × 400 with 30 seconds between. But I found that sometimes the achievement in the workout outweighed achievements in competition.

Eventually, I realized that runners who do too much interval training suffer injuries, possibly from constant stopping and starting and the stress of going around tight turns on a track. Mental fatigue often was as much a problem as physical fatigue. This was during a period when I, and most other distance runners, did all our training on a track. The person who did most to influence us was Mihaly Igloi, the Hungarian coach who defected after the 1956 Olympics and guided the careers of a group of top Americans, including Jim Beatty, Jim Grelle, and Bob Schul. (Beatty and Grelle were among the top milers in the world in the early 1960s; Schul won the 5000 at the 1964 Olympics.)

Igloi was a gifted, extremely dedicated coach who nevertheless had a reputation (whether deserved or not) for destroying as many runners as he helped with his intensive training methods. Every workout was an interval workout.

Although I had made major improvements by using interval training, I also was prey to overtraining. Today's system of running away from the track—on roads, in the woods—is superior to what I did 4 decades ago in a frantic effort to succeed.

"The first rule of practice when using genuine interval training," says Brian Mitchell in his article in *Athletics Weekly*, "is don't use it too often, and don't think it will produce all the goods."

I continue to enjoy occasional interval workouts. My rule now for intervals is never more than a dozen, because the purpose for doing such workouts is speed as much as stamina. Now, a typical interval workout for me would be 10 × 400 with a 200-meter recovery jog between each. Finish refreshed. Save the heroics for race weekends.

QUESTIONS AND ANSWERS ■

Here are some commonly asked questions about interval training and their answers.

Q. What distance should I use for my repeats?

A. The longer the interval, the greater the development of your aerobic system, which is important for endurance. (Remember, interval refers to the rest or pause in the workout.) The shorter the interval, the greater the development of your anaerobic system, which is important for speed. You need to develop both systems to run fast.

Interval training normally encompasses distances from 200 to 800 meters, although some runners favor longer repetitions. Exercise physiologist Dr. Jack Daniels described having members of his cross-country team at the State University of New York at Cortland doing what he called cruise intervals. These were repetitions as long as 2 miles at slightly slower than race pace, with rest intervals of only 30 to 60 seconds. Regardless, the most commonly used distance is 400 meters, because it's convenient—one lap on a track. Start with 400 meters for your repetitions, and vary the distance as you become more comfortable with interval training.

Q. How long should I walk or jog during the rest interval?

A. Gerschler controlled the length of his intervals by measuring pulse rate. A runner whose pulse reached 170 to 180 (90 percent of his MHR) during the repeat would run again when it dropped to 120 to 130 (70 percent of his MHR).

Very fit runners can turn around and start the next repeat within 30 seconds of stopping. I watched British star Sebastian Coe (two-time Olympic gold-medal winner and former world record holder) do just that in a workout. In a session I witnessed, Coe ran 20 × 200 in 27 to 28 seconds several weeks before winning the 1500 at the 1984 Olympics. But a more frequent pattern is to jog the same distance during the interval as you run during the repeat. For someone running 400-meter reps, this would mean doing 400-meter jogs in between. After you become more comfortable with this form of training, you may want to cut the distance (thus also the time) of your intervals.

Q. How many repetitions should I run?

A. There are various formulas comparing total volume of running to race or training distance. Ecker suggests $1\frac{1}{2}$ to 3 times race distance (which probably makes more sense for middle-distance runners in track than for distance runners whose race distance is 5-K or longer).

Dr. Daniels suggests a cap of 8 percent of weekly training mileage for cruise interval days: $1\frac{1}{2}$ miles if you run 20 miles a week; 4 miles if you do 50. Both men are correct, and both are incorrect. Don't put too much faith in formulas—including the one I am about to give you.

A good starting point for runners choosing 400 as the distance for their repetitions is 5. If you can't run 5 reps, you're probably training too fast. A good end point is 10 reps. If you can run more than that, you're probably training too slowly. Runners choosing 200-meter reps will want to do slightly more; runners choosing 800-meter reps will want to do less. But begin cautiously. Dr. Costill warns that too many runners push hard to make themselves tougher, but instead they push themselves right to the failing point. "The danger," he says, "is that they begin to develop poor technique."

Q. How fast should I run my repetitions?

A. Race pace is a convenient and safe measuring point for those of us writing books and articles, because it compensates for the fact that those reading our words and following our charts vary greatly, both in ability to race and in ability to endure hard training. The best judge of training pace is an experienced coach standing beside the track, and even that coach is probably guessing some of the time. So begin at a pace comfortably slower than race pace, progressing to that point and somewhat faster.

One frequent recommendation is to choose a pace you would use in a race one-half the distance of the event you're training for. If, for instance, your goal is a fast 10-K, train at a 5-K pace; 5-K runners train at a 3-K pace, and so forth. Scientists claim that training a bit faster than race pace develops the anaerobic system's buffering capacity—that is, its ability to resist stress. Regardless of scientific explanations, slightly faster than race pace is a good end point for interval training. For those using 400s in their interval training, this would mean running up to 5 seconds per quarter faster than you would in a race.

Q. What form of rest should I use during the intervals?

A. There are three types of rest: jogging, walking, or total rest. I once told one of the high school runners I helped coach that he had the fastest move of anyone I had seen from the finish line to a seat in the bleachers beside the track: one and a half strides. He was the Michael Jordan of interval resters. Absolute rest doesn't make sense for interval training. You recover too completely, which defeats the purpose of trying to maintain your pulse rate at a continuously high rate (70 to 90 percent of your MHR) during the workout.

Walking is an effective means of rest for those beginning to use this method of training, although some highly trained runners use very short walks between very intense runs. I sometimes walk 100, jog 200, and walk 100 while between repetitions. The group at The Bolles School follows this formula, but the most popular (and effective) form of interval rest is jogging the full lap.

Regardless of which kind of rest you choose, be consistent throughout the workout. Don't begin by jogging at a fast pace between repetitions and finish by having to walk. If that happens, you're jogging too fast or running too many repetitions.

Q. What can I expect from interval training?

A. In an article in *Runner's World* magazine, Ohio State University's David R. Lamb, Ph.D., suggested that the biggest benefit was improved running economy. "If you want to improve your economy at your race pace," Dr. Lamb wrote, "you must (train) at or near that pace." Practically every coach would agree with Dr. Lamb.

Interval training also can improve your speed, your endurance, and your pace judgment. But an important, though often overlooked, benefit from interval training is that it improves your ability to concentrate. Because it is very difficult to run consistent times on a track while allowing your mind to drift (as often happens during long runs), you learn to focus your attention on the task at hand. This improved concentration will help with everything you do as a runner.

When I begin running interval sessions in the spring, I frequently find my mind drifting on the backstretch during 400s, as though on a long run. And usually, I fail to run fast times. As the training period progresses, I discover I can concentrate for longer periods of time, until finally, I remain focused for the full lap. And my times improve, both on the track and in races. I sometimes wonder how much of that improvement is the result of better conditioning and how much is simply from improved concentration.

Q. How much interval training should I do?

A. Dr. Daniels permits his runners to do no more than one interval session a week. Once a week seems to be a good rule.

Those of us from previous generations who did interval training more frequently found it difficult to maintain such an intense level of training without injury. Today, there are too many other interesting and effective training methods available to distance runners, so why train only one way?

Q. Is there a best time of year, time of week, and time of day for interval training?

A. Yes. More specific answers depend on your goals and level of ability and conditioning. Interval training works very well when you are getting ready to peak for competition, so if you're seeking fast summer times, early spring is a good time to begin. Weather, of course, may dictate when you can interval train. So will availability of training facilities. If you run long (or race on the weekend), you may want to plan your interval session as far from that effort as possible, thus midweek. Interval training also requires at least a 15- to 20-minute warmup (plus a cooldown at the end of the session) and often takes more total time than a distance run. Most runners probably would fare better running this workout in the late afternoon than in the early morning. Do whatever works best for you.

Q. Where should I do interval training?

A. The best venue for interval training is the track. Four-hundred-meter tracks are convenient because they usually are marked in 100-, 200- and 300-meter segments that make it easier to systemize your training. Tracks certainly are the best choices for those new to interval training. But tracks also offer a form of ambience, since going to the track—driving there, warming up, changing your shoes—signals to your body, "Okay, today's the day we run fast!" Also, training partners often are more easily available at the track. But once you learn the basics of interval training and discover you can measure your level of effort by time, by pulse, or even by your perceived exertion, you can move interval training anywhere: roads, woods, wherever. At some point, such training blends into fartlek (which I'll cover in chapter 9) but don't worry about that yet.

Q. How can I guard against overtraining and injuries?

A. Coach Dellinger states that you should be able to run the last repetition at the same pace as the first—or faster. "If it's a real struggle," he warns, "you should start your next workout at a slower pace, or increase the recovery." Dellinger also suggests that runners use training flats, not track spikes, even for running on a track. (The one exception to this would be on a rainy day, when a wet track might be slippery.) There is no foolproof way to avoid overtraining or injury, but if you approach your interval training with the idea that it should be a challenging workout—but not a punishing one—you will find this form of training both more enjoyable and successful.

Finally, although interval training is a very precise and scientific means of improving your running ability, don't become bogged down with numbers. "Vary the program," advises Dellinger. "Do different sets of intervals, different distances, and experiment with recovery times." Great advice from a great coach. Although all the experts agree that interval training may be the most effective type of training devised, it is not the only type, or even the best. Use it judiciously if you want to become a fast runner. ■

SPEED PLAY

FARTLEK AND TEMPO TRAINING

A woman once passed me toward the end of a 5-K race wearing a T-shirt that had on its front, "Fartlek." And on the back, "It's a runner's thing."

Indeed it is, and assuming the woman used that method of training, that's probably why she sped by me in the closing minutes of the 5-K. Fartlek not only is a runner's thing, it also is a Swedish thing. *Fartlek* is a Swedish term that roughly translates into "speed play." It was devised more than a half-century ago by the Swedish Olympic coach Gosta Holmer. If you took repeats, repetitions, intervals, strides, and sprints and dumped them in a bowl and mixed them all together, you would have fartlek. It is a very effective and satisfying form of training when done properly. It's also fun. And although novice runners might be intimidated by a form of training used by Olympic athletes, fartlek actually is quite easy to master. It's user-friendly.

In an article in *Athletics Journal*, Paul A. Smith described fartlek as "a continuous overdistance run with numerous faster paced interval runs interspersed, until the runner feels tired but not exhausted." Smith claimed that because fartlek existed in the mind of the runner as a form of play, it deemphasized the feeling or perception of fatigue.

Although novice runners might be intimidated by a form of training used by Olympic athletes, fartlek actually is quite user-friendly.

Fartlek was first used successfully by the two great Swedish milers of the 1940s, Gundar Hägg and Arne Andersson. It consists of fast, medium, and slow running over a variety of distances, depending on the terrain.

In a typical fartlek workout, you pick some landmark such as a tree or a bush and sprint to it, then jog until you've recovered. Select another landmark a shorter—or longer—distance away, and run to it at a faster—or slower—pace. The distance and pace are up to you. The most important skill for this drill is listening to your body. Sometimes you may want to jog more. Add some sprints or strides, and maybe even walk, as your mood develops. "An athlete runs as he feels," says coach Bill Dellinger. "A fartlek training session can be the hardest workout a runner does all week, or it can be the easiest." It depends on how you structure the workout and how long you stay out. Coach Dellinger calls fartlek instinctive.

"In order to be a good distance runner," he adds, "you have to build strength and endurance, learn race pace, and practice race tactics. Fartlek training can incorporate all of these essential elements into a single workout."

FAST RESULTS, FEW INJURIES ■

In a *Runner's World* magazine article, Dellinger described a study on the benefits of fartlek versus the benefits of interval training. It included 30 distance runners and was conducted by a graduate student at the University of Oregon. One group ran fartlek, a second group did interval training, and a third group did a combination of both workouts. After a year's training, during which time the runners were tested every 2 weeks, the fartlek group got into shape the slowest and had the poorest early results. But the runners benefited from fewer injuries. The interval group, on the other hand, had the best early marks but also suffered the most injuries. Perhaps because they suffered fewer injuries—and therefore trained more consistently—the fartlek runners began to outperform the interval group toward the end of the study.

But the lesson to be learned came from the third group. This group's performance shone because the runners combined interval training with fartlek. They had better results and fewer injuries.

Clearly, fartlek can play an effective role in almost any runner's training, particularly in the area of speedwork, if it's combined with other methods.

CHANGING TEMPOS

Fartlek is a form of speed training where you alternate fast and slow running at a variety of distances, almost by instinct. Olympian Bob Kennedy recalls fartlek workouts at Indiana University where four or five runners would run together. Over a distance of 5 miles, each would take a turn dictating pace so the others never knew what to expect. "The pace shifts made you really focus," recalls Kennedy. "The workout simulated what happens in a tough race."

After he graduated, Kennedy had less opportunity to train in a group, but he continued to use fartlek in his training. He suggests that the key to fartlek for individual runners is to have a plan, whether you're running short or long repeats, sprints, or tempo. "Know what you're doing," says Kennedy. "If you make your workout up while you're running, it's too easy to sell yourself short." Kennedy believes that the change in tempo is what makes fartlek a valuable workout for building both endurance and speed.

FARTLEK FOR EVERYONE ■

Holmer felt that fartlek, done correctly, could be practiced three to five times a week. He recommended running uphill no more than twice a week, preferably on Mondays and Thursdays. "Fartlek brings us back to the games of our childhood," said Holmer. "The runner is forced to explore."

The Swedish coach operated in an era when competitive runners were only young and highly skilled athletes. (The 5-K as a sport-for-all phenomenon hadn't even been invented yet.) Times have changed, but runners of varied abilities can benefit by including occasional fartlek workouts in their training programs.

Beginners. Can today's runners of average ability benefit from Holmer's fartlek training?

The answer is yes. The Atlanta Track Club, with 60 volunteer coaches, offers a special program for its members—any member of the club can obtain qualified coaching by simply requesting it. Among the volunteers is Mary Reed, who prefers to work with beginning runners, usually women, on a one-to-one basis.

Once her students have reached the point in their training where they can benefit from speedwork, Reed, instead of taking them to the track, teaches them how to do fartlek. Utilizing a ³/₄-mile loop around a reservoir, she has them alternate between running slow and running easy for nonspecific distances and times.

"I find that many beginners, who didn't participate in sports in high school, are intimidated by the track," says Reed. "The track, they think, is where only fast runners go. They're afraid that they'll be the slowest runner and intimidated by being left in a cloud of dust. Instead of going to the track at 4:30 A.M., when nobody else is there, we simply do fartlek."

Reed uses fartlek to convince the beginners that their running can benefit from speedwork. First, she has them run a 5-K race. Then, they use fartlek in their training regimen for 3 or 4 weeks before they measure themselves with another 5-K race.

"With beginning runners," says Reed, "they'll often improve from race to race just because they've had another month of training. But when you mix in fartlek, the improvement often is dramatic."

Team members. Different coaches, of course, interpret fartlek in different ways. At the College of the Holy Cross in Worcester, Massachusetts, W. H. "Skip" O'Connor designed a program based on time rather than miles that included what he described as bursts, lifts, steady strides, specific hill attacks, fast openers, fast closers, passing pickups, and bolts. Bursts were 50-yard sprints on a flat area, a half-dozen or so within a 6-minute time span. These were prearranged sprints performed by his entire team at a signal from the leader. Bolts, however, were sudden and unexpected sprints by various individuals, who had been instructed by O'Connor to uncork them several times during the workout.

The self-coached. Russian coach A. Yakimov, writing in *Track Technique*, said he felt that the length of the fast runs, along with the length and form of rest, should be determined by the athlete, according to how he feels physically. The important ingredient is constant change of pace. Here is Yakimov's formula.

1. Light running for 6 to 10 minutes as a warmup (A fast, even run for 1 to 2 kilometers)

2. A brisk walk for 5 minutes

3. Light, even running with short accelerations (50 to 60 meters) until you sense some fatigue

4. Light running with the occasional inclusion of four or five fast strides (these are like sudden surges in a race)

5. Fast uphill running for 1 minute

Yakimov stressed that at the end of the workout, you should feel not fatigue, but rather enthusiasm. "Fartlek is not a 'carefree' system as is sometimes thought. It is not to be used only as a rest from hard workouts. It demands no less of physical and psychological strength than any other method."

RUNNING FREE ■

To simply copy the formulas of Holmer, O'Connor, or Yakimov (or any other coach) would rob fartlek of its greatest advantage—its spirit of free play. Coach Dellinger believes that it is the intentional vagueness of fartlek that makes it less stressful than other forms of hard running.

Merrill Noden described fartlek in an article titled "Playing on the Run" in *The Runner*. "In any interval session—on or off the track—you are measuring two variables: the distance you run and the time it takes," he wrote. "Real fartlek always leaves one or both of these variables unmeasured." As a result, said Noden, you make it impossible to pass precise judgment on your effort.

As such, fartlek lends itself to the cross-country setting, because training venues away from the track are almost always unmarked and undefined. Yes, courses on which runners race frequently come accompanied by mileposts that cannot be totally ignored; but typically, when runners run off-road, whether through the woods or over a golf course, they run free. It becomes easier, then, for terrain to dictate training. A hill encountered becomes an excuse for a short sprint. A smooth straightaway offers an opportunity for a controlled fast run. Soft footing makes it necessary to slow down.

The principles of fartlek do not need to be reserved for special days. You can work fartlek into almost any workout. On your distance days, you can throw in surges or sprints when the spirit moves you.

One winter's day, for example, I was running with Liz Galaviz, the top runner on my cross-country team. Snow was on the ground, so we ran a 5-mile course through city streets at an undefined pace.

Galaviz was feeling strong, so midway through the run, I found myself hanging on to her fast pace. At an intersection where we normally would have turned right, I pointed her straight up a hill that was 100 to 150 meters in length. We ran the hill side-by-side, and I could hear her breathing become labored. When the hill leveled off and started down, we eased the pace to recover.

You can work fartlek into almost any workout.

"I just did that to be mean," I said.

Galaviz smiled, "I know."

But I did that, as she realized, to toughen her for running short track races later that spring. It was a classic fartlek move, but one that had been inserted within the framework of what had started out as a relatively easy distance run. It was the perfect "speed play."

Tempo Training

Another form of speed play that began to gain increased acceptance in the early 1990s has various titles, the most popular being tempo training, or the utilization of tempo runs. Unlike fartlek, a tempo run usually consists of a single, continuous surge in the midst of a medium-distance run.

Tempo runs are associated with no specific coach, although the one who probably did the most to publicize this form of training is exercise physiologist Dr. Jack Daniels, who coaches the track and cross-country teams at the State University of New

TEMPO TIPS

Here are some tips for boosting your anaerobic power with tempo runs.

1. Hang loose. Structure your tempo runs according to experience, not formulas. Formulas can offer only broad guidelines. Begin by taking a period of time to warm up, and at the end of your workout, take a nearly equal period to cool down. In between is the heart of your workout, which should be 20 to 40 minutes.

2. Run tough. Pick a pace that is comfortably hard. Dr. Daniels and others recommend a pace that is 15 seconds per mile slower than your best 10-K time.

3. Run solo. You may have difficulty finding another runner whose anaerobic threshold matches yours. Even when you can, you should be cautious and run according to your ability. It's too easy to become competitive and push the pace too hard, even in noncompetitive situations.

4. Forget time. Don't measure your level of intensity by your watch. It's too easy to fool yourself into thinking you're improving because you did this week's wind run faster than last week's. The overload principle works with some forms of training, but not here. It's too easy to cheat by running the warmup and cooldown sections progressively faster, which defeats the purpose of the workout. By jogging easily at both the beginning and end of each tempo run, you eliminate any danger of comparing one workout to another.

5. Run anywhere. The road. The track. The woods. Even on a treadmill in a health club. The important factor is intensity, not how (or where) that intensity is achieved.

6. Stay smooth. Maintain a steady effort, not a steady speed. If you run out into a headwind, you'll find yourself returning with the wind at your back. Your actual pace should increase, but not your effort. The same is true on hilly courses, where your pulse actually may rise or drop depending whether you are going uphill or downhill.

7. Concentrate. You'll find you are able to run more effectively if you focus on what you are doing. Because of the speed at which you will be moving, tempo runs offer a good opportunity to pay attention to how you can maintain good running form. This body awareness will help you improve your racing later.

York in Cortland. Dr. Daniels wrote an article on what he called tempo running and cruise intervals that appeared under the title "Cruise Control" in *Runner's World* magazine. The popularity of that magazine being what it is, you could not have a discussion with a serious runner in the several months after the article appeared without that topic entering the conversation.

Different coaches and exercise physiologists have used different terms to describe this form of training. It has been known as anaerobic threshold training, steady state running, or A.T. running (I used that term most often in the first edition of this book). Dr. Peter Snell, the Olympic champion turned scientist, prefers to call it lactate threshold training. John Babington, coach of three-time world cross-country champion Lynn Jennings, refers to it as up-tempo aerobic running. Ron Gunn, coach at Southwestern Michigan College in Dowagiac, describes such workouts as FCRs, for fast continuous runs. In international circles, you may have heard the term *Conconis*, after Francesco Conconi, Ph.D., the exercise physiologist from Ferrara and adviser for many of Italy's top distance runners. Today, the term *tempo training* (and tempo runs) seems to have achieved ascendance.

Regardless of what you call the workout, it refers to a type of training where you gradually push your pace to a high degree of difficulty and hold it there before relaxing and finally cruising home.

Charting your pace on a graph, you would have a line resembling the classic bell curve that rises, hits a plateau, then declines. The plateau is where the peak training occurs and also where you reach what Dr. Snell identified as your lactate threshold.

Dr. Robert Vaughan talks about this as the deflection point—the mythical dotted line around 90 percent of maximum heart rate (MHR) where body systems begin to deteriorate. If you run above that dotted line, say at 91 percent, lactic acid begins to accumulate in your muscles and inevitably causes you to crash. But run just below that dotted line, say at 89 percent, and all sorts of marvelous things happen to your level of conditioning.

When Dr. Daniels wrote about this effect in *Runner's World*, the magazine promoted his article on the cover as "The Biggest Training Discovery in 50 Years." On reflection, this was only a slight exaggeration.

SECRETS OF THE ANAEROBIC THRESHOLD ■

Let's talk about anaerobic threshold, what it means, and where it exists as a function of human performance. Former Ball State researcher Dr. David Costill has described anaerobic threshold as the point during exercise when the metabolism supposedly switches from an aerobic to an anaerobic state, when the body's demand for oxygen exceeds its ability to produce it. "Since lactic acid tends to be produced by the muscles when they are unable to acquire sufficient oxygen to produce energy aerobically, its accumulation in the blood is considered to be a good indicator of the pace that the runner can tolerate during long runs," says Dr. Costill.

The term anaerobic threshold apparently was coined in 1972 by California physiologist Karl Wasserman, Ph.D. He measured the blood acidity of individuals undergoing progressively intense exercise and noted that at a certain point, the blood acidity increased suddenly. Dr. Wasserman suggested that this was the anaerobic threshold, the point at which anaerobic metabolism was initiated.

Not all scientists would agree with this assessment today, although in drafting training plans, it becomes convenient to assume that there exists a dotted line above which you do not stay for long if you plan to continue running.

The biochemical mechanisms that produce glycogen, which

fuels the muscles, are complex and require various fuel sources. When exercise is moderate, aerobic metabolism predominates. Glycogen is broken down completely. Oxygen combines with freed hydrogen ions to produce water and carbon dioxide, which are easily carried off.

Aerobic is defined as "in the presence of oxygen," meaning that sufficient oxygen is delivered by your cardiovascular system to maintain a steady state of energy production through the breakdown of glycogen. Aerobic activity generally is associated with slow speeds, jogging, or running long distances.

But a new system kicks in after exercise increases in intensity, so the demands for energy exceed the rate at which oxygen can be delivered. Glycogen is broken down anaerobically, but the process is not complete. Lactic acid accumulates, along with free hydrogen ions.

Anaerobic is defined as "without oxygen," meaning that your level of exercise is so intense that your cardiovascular system cannot provide sufficient oxygen for efficient energy production. The waste products cannot be carried away rapidly enough. Consequently, lactic acid accumulates in your muscles and bloodstream and eventually makes it impossible to run farther. Anaerobic activity generally is associated with sprinting or running distances shorter than 1,500 meters.

So when does aerobic activity become anaerobic activity? When does a jog become a sprint, at least in perceived effort? Where is the dotted line in running? How can you identify and use this line—or anaerobic threshold—to plan your training runs?

RUN ON THE DOTTED LINE ■

Presumably, if you were capable of determining your anaerobic threshold, you would have an advantage both in training and in competition. You could train at a pace just below that threshold, permitting you to maximize your effort and energy without suffering from the accumulation of lactic acid.

Could that knowledge also be applied in a race? I'm less convinced of that, since in races between 5-K and 10-K, well-trained runners eventually must enter the twilight zone above the dotted line to achieve peak performance. If you're doing your job right, you should be near 100 percent of your MHR when you cross the line. An ability to monitor your anaerobic threshold is most useful in practice. But certainly anything that increases body awareness—training or racing—makes you a better runner.

Unfortunately, theory (and what scientists perceive in the laboratory) does not always match reality. In talking about an anaerobic threshold, many runners probably think there is a certain speed (or pace) below which all activity is aerobic and above which all activity is anaerobic. They might visualize 400 meters run in 120 seconds (8-minute pace) as aerobic and in 60 seconds as anaerobic, with the threshold somewhere in between.

This is not true, as Dr. Costill quickly points out. "In reality, there exists a continuum between aerobic and anaerobic activity. Pure aerobic activity probably does not exist in athletics. It is achieved only at rest or during mild walking. Even in golf, the explosive golf swing is anaerobic."

And even while functioning at a very low energy level— say 50 percent of your MHR—you are exercising both aerobically and anaerobically. You provide oxygen, but not as much as the system demands. As you increase your exercise intensity—going from 60 to 70 to 80 percent or more of your MHR—more of your energy conversion becomes anaerobic. Eventually, you reach that point of muscular breakdown where you can run no longer. Scientists induce this in the laboratory by running a subject on a treadmill, gradually tilting the angle until he no longer can keep pace. For a sprinter struggling down the straightaway in the 400 meters, it certainly does seem as though the track is being tilted just before the finish line.

Scientists have studied aerobic energy production since the early 19th century. Since then, aerobic capacity has become relatively easier to measure by standard laboratory techniques, including analysis of blood and gas exchanges. Although scientists recently have begun to give more attention to anaerobic energy, it is less readily measurable.

One problem with drawing conclusions about the so-called anaerobic threshold from blood and gas measurements is that not all of the action takes place in the blood or immediately affects the oxygen transport systems. The real action occurs in the muscle, and the increase in blood acidity occurs after the fact—how long after, we do not know. It is the acid level in the muscle that affects the muscle's capability to contract—and your ability to run.

The point of this is that the term *anaerobic threshold*, as it is currently being used by many exercise physiologists and interpreted to the public, is probably a misnomer. To obtain precise measurement, we would need to monitor the acidity within the muscle, no easy task even with the new noninvasive measuring devices available to exercise scientists today. Even the pulse watch I sometimes wear in training allows me to make only an educated guess as to when I am approaching my anaerobic threshold. I assume that dotted line to be at 90 percent of my MHR, 133 out of a max of 150. But my anaerobic threshold could be somewhat higher or somewhat lower. One factor is my relative fitness level. The anaerobic threshold for an untrained person might be below 50 percent; someone highly trained could redline above 90 percent, although probably not too much beyond.

After a race in Minnesota, I spoke with a runner of average ability from Minneapolis who had visited a fitness center to have his anaerobic threshold tested. Preparing for an important ultra-marathon race, he was sparing no expense. The test involved having him pedal on an exercise bicycle while having his air volume and blood lactate monitored. The tester eventually informed the runner that his anaerobic threshold was 130 beats per minute.

That value, 72 percent, seemed rather low for a well-conditioned runner, since he reported his MHR at 180. But the center testers had failed to measure that value; they had merely estimated by using a standard formula. Formulas are fine for predicting average values, but not everybody is average. I told the runner that this was a classic case of "garbage in, garbage out." Although the fitness center seemed to be utilizing the latest space-age measuring devices, they lost any chance of a careful measurement of his anaerobic threshold by utilizing a probably flawed estimate of his MHR. Their expensive device was little more than a marketing tool.

I quizzed the runner further about his training, which he monitored with a pulse watch. He and his regular training partner frequently go for 2-hour runs, maintaining a steady pulse rate of 140 to 145, which would mean around 80 percent of maximum. "Then your threshold is probably somewhere around 150," I suggested. I ended by telling the runner he should quit trying to be too scientific and simply train the way he feels.

PULSE TRAINING ■

Nevertheless, I must confess that it's often fun to imbue your training with at least a certain level of pseudoscience. And measuring your training can provide motivation. At various times, I use a pulse monitor to measure my training, specifically my cardiovascular response to stress. A pulse monitor consists of a strap that fits around your chest. The strap contains a radio transmitter that beams signals from your beating heart to a receiver watch. As you run, you can glance down at your watch and obtain an instant pulse reading. More expensive models allow you to review the pulse record of any workout after you return home—sort of an instant replay of how your heart performed. With the proper software, you can even download this record onto a computer and generate charts to serve as additional motivation.

While I consider pulse monitors to be very useful training tools, most experienced runners probably can tell how well they are running by perceived exertion—by noticing how they feel and by listening to their bodies. Another way to measure effort, of course, is by running over a measured course, but this ignores variables. External factors can render time measurements inaccurate. Hot weather, cold weather, wind, hills, surface conditions—all can make a 1-mile run at an 8-minute pace equal to a much faster effort, even 7:30 or 7:00. One individual coached by Roy Benson had a job with Delta Airlines. She lived in Denver, Colorado, but flew out of Atlanta to Puerto Rico. One day she might be running in dry 40-degree weather at 5,000 feet and the next day running in humid 80-degree weather at sea level. For her, a pulse monitor served very effectively to monitor stress.

MAXIMUM GAIN ■

What are the benefits of lactate threshold, or tempo, training? You get maximum gain for minimum damage. According to Dr. Daniels, "Threshold pace training is individualized and adaptable to changes in fitness. It won't cause you to overtrain. It will build your confidence with each workout. And it will produce results, whether you're at the back of the pack, in the middle, or way up front."

How does this training pace compare with race pace? In an article on 10-K training in *Running Research News*, Dr. Owen Anderson identified 5-K runners as racing at 95 to 100 percent of MHR, 10-K runners at 90 to 92 percent of MHR, 15-K and 10-mile runners at 86 percent of MHR, and marathoners at 80 percent of MHR.

Dr. Anderson further suggested that interval training (an intense workout covered in chapter 8) occurs at 90 to 100 percent of MHR. Dr. Anderson concluded that a good pace for A.T. training might be a pace just a bit slower—about 10 to 15 seconds slower per mile—than 10-K pace. Dr. Daniels suggests that in tempo runs, you run at the same pace you would run if in a race that lasted, for you, approximately an hour.

Dr. Daniels also defines lactate threshold training as a steady, controlled tempo run that lasts about 20 minutes at threshold pace.

20-MINUTE FIX

Twenty minutes is the ideal length of time for the middle segment—the quality part—of a tempo run, recommends Dr. Jack Daniels. Do your normal warmup: 1 to 2 miles jogging, some strides, some stretching. Then, run 20 minutes at a steady pace that Dr. Daniels describes as "comfortably hard." The pace should raise your pulse to about 90 percent of its maximum, about as hard as you might run in a race that lasts an hour. Cool down with a 1- to 2-mile jog.

Dr. Daniels says that the workout achieves two purposes. "First, it gives you the feeling of mentally concentrating on an effort for a prolonged period of time. You learn to endure discomfort. Second, it benefits you physiologically. Your body becomes better at clearing lactate." Since you adjust the pace depending on your ability, the tempo run is adaptable to all runners. "Everybody has their own threshold pace," says Dr. Daniels. The tempo run can be done on the track or, preferably, on road or trail courses.

He considers a steady intensity of effort important. "Going too fast is no better than going too slow," he says. "A tempo run is hard but controlled. What's important is the intensity, not the time or speed, which can vary depending on the course, the environment, and whether or not the runner is fatigued or well-rested."

One important bonus of such running, according to Dr. Daniels, is that it helps improve the runner's ability to concentrate. You don't float along between 80 and 90 percent of your MHR—at least for any appreciable distance—without being well-focused on what you're doing.

Dr. Daniels's recommendation for structuring the workout involves 20 percent of the total time spent as a warmup, 70 percent of the time (20 to 30 minutes) featuring good, hard running, and 10 percent of the total time for a cooldown.

When I include tempo runs in my training schedules for various distances from the 5-K to the marathon, both on my Web site and in articles for *Runner's World* magazine, I usually suggest running easily during the first (warmup) phase of the workout, gradually accelerating to near 10-K pace—and holding that pace—during the second (threshold) phase, then decelerating back down to easy pace for the third (cooldown) phase. During a typical 45-minute tempo run, the warmup phase might last 10 to 15 minutes, the threshold phase 20 to 25 minutes, and the cooldown phase 5 to 10 minutes. I cite ranges, rather than precise times, for the phases, because tempo runs are best done in the woods or on the roads, where precise distance measurements are not always possible.

Although in a progressive training program I might prescribe tempo runs of 30 to 60 minutes in length from the start to the end of the program, 45 minutes seems about the right length of time for a tempo run, regardless of your relative ability. To do less than 30 minutes doesn't allow sufficient time to squeeze in all the increments. To do more than 60 minutes turns the workout into more of a long-distance run. Forty-five minutes fits well between these two time limits.

One of the appeals of tempo runs is the deliberate vagueness. You don't get too precise with time, length, or pace. In this respect, the tempo run resembles the fartlek workout described earlier in this chapter. You allow your body to dictate the workout. Admittedly, it does take some experience to read your body signals.

Benji Durden uses a different form of this training method while working with runners, both fitness and elite, in Boulder, Colorado. In a very sophisticated 84-week program he designed for my book *How to Train*, he prescribed tempo runs that involved both hard and easy runs in the middle of the workout. In one workout that he described as "18 wup/cdn, 2 (5 crisp/3 easy)," he had his runners warm up with 18 minutes at easy pace, run 5 minutes at a crisp or a harder pace, back off for 3 minutes to an easy pace, then run 5 more minutes at a crisp pace before a final 18-minute cooldown. Okay, it sounds complicated, but Durden's runners soon figure out what he's talking about. With workouts of this sort, the difference blurs between fartlek and tempo training, but what counts is what works for you.

One of the appeals of tempo runs is the deliberate vagueness. You don't get too precise with time length or pace.

Dr. Costill notes that neither form of workouts serve as the be-all and end-all of training for all runners. "All they are," he says, "is a semiquantitative way to have somebody run at a point where they are at a high level of aerobic training."

Regardless of what you call it, I find tempo running, along with fartlek, an enjoyable and effective way to do speedwork. ■

CHAPTER 10

PURE SPEED

IMPROVE YOUR KICK

Does a competitor in 5-K and 10-K events need to worry about pure speed, flat-out speed, absolute speed—or whatever you want to call sprinting as hard as you can? Forget victory at all costs; what about someone whose goals are more modest? If you're only interested in shaving a few minutes off your times for those distances, not winning races, should you really care how fast you can sprint? Maybe you should; maybe you shouldn't.

After all, in races 5-K and beyond, victory often goes to the runner capable of controlling and maintaining his speed over the full distance. Milers may rely on their kick to win, but 5-K runners more often achieve victory by pushing hard in the middle of the race, working at maximum effort and sustaining a tough pace to the end. And most runners back in the pack compete against only their own previous personal achievements as they reach what might be called the kicking zone, or the last 100 meters.

Regardless of position in the pack, almost any runner who

has entered the last stretch and glanced above the finish line to see the digital clock relentlessly ticking away—55 . . . 56 . . . 57 . . . 58 . . . 59—certainly hopes at that moment to have a kick.

Regardless of race position, we'd like the ability to take it out of cruise control and steam past some guy we've been trailing for the last 10 minutes.

At the Berlin Marathon one year, I saw exactly that sort of countdown as I neared the line. A quick spurt brought me across in a precise 3:09:59. That's far below my PR. I finished 3,711th overall, 49th in my age group. Big deal, you say. Okay, but when the results booklet eventually arrived by mail, I took pride in the fact that I was the last runner listed among the block of runners finishing between 3:00:00 and 3:10:00. I'll take my victories where I can get them, thank you.

If working a little harder—or at least fine-tuning your training—might make the difference between clocking 30:00 and 29:59, would you do it? Sure you would.

Let's face facts: We'd all like a better kick. Regardless of race position, we'd like the ability to take it out of cruise control in the final 100 meters, put the pedal to the metal, and raise a cheer from the crowd as we steam past some guy we've been trailing for the last 10 minutes.

Of course, grumblers will say that if you had properly paced yourself during the full length of the race, you would have fully utilized your energy and not have had anything left for a kick. The goal, it seems, is to finish each race totally spent, knowing that you could not possibly have obtained one more stride from your depleted muscles.

That may be a noteworthy goal for those seeking Olympic medals, but most of us finish races having not quite squeezed the last drop from the lemon. Even the best of us operate somewhere around the 98th or 99th percentile when it comes to extracting energy. During a career that has spanned a half-dozen decades, I figure I've had maybe three or four perfect races, when I couldn't possibly have run a tenth of a second faster. Usually, some reserve remains, both psychological and physical. Most of us can reach down and find an untapped reserve. By driving our arms, by lifting our knees, we can move fast at the finish. In doing so, we are not necessarily utilizing energy or activating muscles that might have better been used earlier. We are actually tapping different energy systems and utilizing different muscles—sprinter's muscles—that otherwise go unused.

REACHING TOP SPEED ■

Apart from any advantage in having pure speed to utilize in the kicking zone, such speed is important to use throughout the length of your race. If you can teach yourself to be a better sprinter and to be a more efficient and economical runner, you will run fast all through the race, not just at the end.

One way to improve pure speed is to start with the three Ss: sprints, strides, and surges. Let me explain these terms.

Sprints. A sprint usually means just that: an all-out sprint for as long as you can hold it, or want to hold it. Sprinters usually reach top speed at about 60 meters into a 100-meter dash, then merely maintain that speed until they hit the finish line. Among 200-meter runners, the winner is not always the fastest, but rather the one who slows the least after reaching top speed. That was Carl Lewis's skill. Scientists suggest that 300 meters is about as far as humans can sprint at full speed without beginning to slow down significantly. If you watched Michael Johnson set the world record of 43.18 for 400 meters at the 1999 World Track and Field Championships, though, you might question that scientific opinion.

Strides. A stride is somewhat slower than a sprint, usually faster than race pace but nowhere near top speed for the full distance. Some strides can be very fast, where the runner gradually accelerates and actually reaches top speed during at least a brief portion of the distance. Other strides can be relatively slow, since you can run no faster than your marathon race pace and still call it a stride. Sprints and strides, at least, are variations on the same theme. Different coaches might define them differently, but both are runs of short distances: a straightaway on a track or a short fairway on a golf course (about 100 meters). One is simply slower than the other.

Surges. A surge is a fast burst—a sprint or stride thrown into the middle of a distance workout. Fartlek, described in chapter 9, consists of a series of surges. Tempo runs, however, would not qualify under this category, because usually there is only a single (and gradual) acceleration. Top runners often use midrace surges as strategic strikes, launched in an effort to break away from the competition.

Are you confused? That's understandable, because the dif-

INTENSITY

Kenneth Sparks, Ph.D., an exercise physiologist at Cleveland State University, believes that the key to success in any training session is intensity. "The important Swedish research with the Kenyans suggests that's one reason why they run so fast: They train at a higher percentage of their capacity.

"The L.S.D. (Long Slow Distance) movement hurt us. People got the idea that they could go for long, slow runs and benefit. I don't think that's true. I do long runs at a quality pace—or shorten the runs to 9 to 10 miles. It does take more out of you, and you have to be more careful as you get older, so you program in plenty of rest. But keep the quality up."

ference between the three Ss is not great. They're all variations on the same speedwork theme. Let's discuss sprints, strides, and surges at somewhat greater length.

STRESSING THE MUSCLES ■

A subtle difference exists between sprints and two forms of speedwork covered in previous chapters: repeats and interval training. When I run repeats, I run nearly flat-out, fully anaerobic, but with maximum rest. In doing interval training, I usually run under control but with less rest, doing a mixture of anaerobic and aerobic work.

"The real advantage of running faster is that you get stronger," says Dr. David Costill.

A sprint is running flat out, but over a shorter distance, so as to stress (and train) the muscles more than the cardiovascular system. Sprints, like repeats, are totally anaerobic, although if enough of them are run with jogging in between, the effect may be similar to that of interval training. At one point in my career, I ran sprint workouts that hit a peak at 50 × 100 meters. But that defeated the purpose of sprints, which, at least the way I now do them, occupy a middle ground between repeats and intervals.

What's the scientific rationale for going faster in practice than you would in a race? I asked that question of former Ball State researcher Dr. David Costill.

Dr. Costill mentioned technique—the ability to run efficiently at a very fast pace—then added, "I've never been convinced that you develop greater energy production for the anaerobic system by doing anaerobic training. That system can be taught to work quite well when only moderately trained, such as through interval training. The real advantage of running faster is that you get stronger."

Most track athletes run sprints on the track. They sometimes call them straightaways, because a convenient way to do them is to sprint one straightaway, jog easily around the turn, and then sprint the next straightaway. Other runners prefer to walk between sprints. They will walk, stop, turn around, walk, jog, and sprint back in the other direction. Or they walk back to where they started and sprint back in the same direction. When I include sprints in my warmup before a track race or even a road race, I usually stop and walk back halfway, then jog to where I start my next sprint. It's a matter of personal preference and convenience as to how and where you run your sprints.

Usually, I prefer running sprints on soft surfaces. If the track is hard asphalt, similar to that at most high schools, you may be better off running your sprints on the grass inside the track. But test the softness and smoothness of any surface before you run hard on it. Football fields often take a lot of abuse. For sprinters, an uneven surface can be a turned ankle waiting to happen.

More often, I use the fairway of a golf course. I live a half-mile from Long Beach Country Club, a private club that, fortunately, does not have a fence around it. During summer months, I arrive early in the morning before the golfers, sometimes even before sunrise. It's a cool, pleasant part of the day. There are several fairways that I favor for sprints, depending on where the greenkeepers are mowing that morning.

I run from tree to tree rather than any specific distance. Distance is irrelevant. Time doesn't matter. Regardless of where you run your sprints, on a golf course or at the track, I consider it useless to time yourself for any distance shorter than 200 meters. Time differences in tenths of a second from one sprint to another mean little. If you're timing yourself, you're diverting your con-

DOES SPEEDWORK INCREASE INJURY?

At the University of Otago in New Zealand, William G. Hopkins, assisted by David G. Hewson, studied 350 runners (118 female, 232 male) over a period of 2 years. The runners ranged in ability from elite to average.

By means of questionnaires, Hopkins and Hewson looked at four phases of the runners' training: buildup, precompetition, competition, and postcompetition. They then compared that with how often the runners lost days due to overtraining, injury, or illness.

What caused runners to lose time due to injury? Whether or not they stretched or the training surfaces on which they ran had no effect. Neither did age, sex, or best race times. Those getting hurt most often were those who did extra strength training during the precompetition phase and the most long running at a pace slower than race pace during all phases of their training. Those hurt least were those who included fast running during their buildup as well as precompetition phase.

Hopkins deduced that it was unwise to skip speedwork for fear of injury. In fact, he recommended that you keep your training pace race-specific. "The take-home message," says Hopkins, "is to cut back miles, but to retain high-intensity work."

---

centration by clicking your watch on and off. Focus your attention on running as swiftly and smoothly as you can for as far as you can, and worry about times at some other point in your training.

GETTING SPRINTS AND STRIDES RIGHT ■

How far should you run your sprints? I recommend confining yourself to 50 to 150 meters—about the length of a track straightaway, or a fraction of a golf fairway. If you run much farther, you're training for something other than pure speed. You begin to train for speed endurance, the ability to maintain speed rather than to increase it. Each form of training has a place in a well-balanced training schedule.

When I was coached by Fred Wilt, he told me that distance runners should run sprints at least once a week for three reasons.

WHY SHORT SPRINTS?

When you say "speedwork," the very word scares a lot of runners, but this important form of training doesn't need to be too fast, nor too hard. Particularly for adult runners, coach Roy Benson recommends what he calls aerobic intervals.

Benson identifies these as short pick-ups or no more than 20 seconds that you incorporate into your training program at various times of the year. "If you do only slow distance, particularly during your base training phase," says Benson, "you lose biomechanical efficiency. Short sprints can help you balance strength and flexibility and improve leg coordination."

The effort should be fast but easy. "Think legs, not lungs," Benson advises. "The idea is to use as big a range of motion with as rapid a turnover as possible, but for a short enough distance so that you never huff and puff. If you do pick-ups longer than 20 seconds, they should be run at no more than 80 percent effort."

Research suggests that lactic acid buildup in the muscles is insignificant in the first 20 seconds of fast running, but it almost quadruples between 20 and 30 seconds. That causes eccentric contractions to begin and forces your muscles to extend while still tight. "You tie up, and that's what we try to avoid by stopping short of maximum effort," says Benson. "Speedwork can be easy if you do it correctly."

A simple and effective way to do this workout is at the track: sprinting the straightaways, jogging the turns. Or do stopwatch fartlek: Run hard for 20 seconds on your beeper watch, then jog for the remainder of the minute. You go 20 seconds hard, 40 seconds easy.

Or, you can throw speed bursts into the middle of your long runs. About two-thirds of the way through a 6-mile run, start doing pick-ups. Cover 1 to 1½ miles this way. "But keep the effort easy," warns Benson. "Don't force yourself, or you defeat the purpose."

1. To develop muscular strength

2. To accustom the cardiovascular system to tolerate a much higher level of effort than normally encountered at race pace

3. To develop anaerobic endurance

I still consider Wilt's reasoning to be sound. Of the three reasons he suggested, I consider developing strength to be the most important. Dr. Costill agrees. "Strength equals speed," he says.

When sprinting, one variation Wilt suggested was to gradually accelerate to top speed at around 50 or 60 meters, then to gradually decelerate. You can do this when running either sprints or strides. Try it and see how it feels.

I use strides as therapeutic repair work, sometimes after a long workout or on what I would classify as an easy day. To me, strides are another form of stretching. I also use strides as part of my warmup before racing or before serious speedwork sessions. Before running repeats or interval training, I do sprints or strides, more often the latter. If I'm running eight straightaways as part of a warmup, the first three or four will be strides (gradually increasing in tempo), with one or two sprints before closing with one or two strides.

A DRILL FOR RECOVERY ■

Many distance runners include long runs as part of their regular training. Often, running a long, slow distance leaves your legs stiff and tight. That's one reason why distance runners lose flexibility, an essential component for running fast. As part of my recovery from long distance, I often breezed through a short, second workout later in the day that consisted mainly of strides. Now that I'm older (and perhaps wiser), I'll run a workout of strides later in the week as well.

One of the main reasons I run strides is to undo some of the damage, such as stiffness, that results from my long or hard workouts and to prepare myself for further fast training.

Remember that while sprints build strength and speed, strides serve best for recovery. A session of easy-flowing strides will set you up to run harder, faster workouts in the days or weeks to come. And those designated tough workouts will build strength and speed.

For me, a typical recovery workout featuring strides would be to jog from my home to the golf course, taking a slightly extended route so that I arrive there after covering about 1 mile. I stretch under an evergreen tree beside the first fairway, dangling from a low branch as one of my stretches. Then, I jog over to the 18th fairway, where I stride through eight or more 130-yarders (tree to tree). Following that, I jog home by a slightly longer route. This gives me a workout of maybe 3 miles. It doesn't look overly impressive in my training diary, but it's good for my body.

Generally, the first stride is little more than a bowlegged shuffle as I work out the kinks from my previous hard workouts. More often, I walk rather than jog between. By the time I have completed eight strides, I usually am able to run a respectably fast pace, though still not a sprint. I avoid punishing myself and quit while I still feel good. Usually, as I jog back home, I run much more relaxed than I did on the way out. I enjoy the sunrise. I wave at the greenkeepers, who wave back. I finish refreshed. There's nothing scientific about the workout, but it feels good.

A GREAT WARMUP ■

Strides also form part of my prerace warmup, which usually begins with a mile or two of jogging. After some relaxed stretching, I run two to four strides of 75 meters or so at a pace that seems to feel comfortable. After more jogging, I am ready to race. This warmup is a holdover from my track days, and it works for me.

Dr. Jack Daniels is among the respected coaches and physiologists who recommend strides as an important element of training on so-called easy days. Dr. Owen Anderson, discussing Dr. Daniels's training in his publication *Running Research News*, described a method of doing strides.

"Midway through or at the end of your easy run, run for about 100 meters at close to your mile pace. (Don't sprint; try to run comfortably.) Following each stride, jog lightly for 15 to 20 seconds before commencing the next stride. After five strides have been completed, walk around for a couple of minutes until you feel completely rested and recovered, and then do a second set of five strides to finish your striding for the day. The purpose for strides is to reinforce the mechanics of race pace (you get 10 chances to run at race speed) and perk up what might be a boring training day. At first, try doing strides on one or two of your easy training days each week; if all goes well, you can increase the number of days you do strides."

I will also use strides as part of my prerace taper, particularly if the race is a marathon. In designing tapering programs for the marathon, I usually recommend that 2 of the last 3 days involve complete rest with about 2 miles of running on the remaining day. Because we all are creatures of different habits, I say that I don't care on which days you rest and on which days you run. My preference, however, is to run easily on the day before the marathon. In other words, rest Thursday and Friday and run Saturday before a Sunday marathon.

Many runners are surprised when they see my schedules with a 2-mile workout on Saturday. "Won't that tire me out?" they ask. Possibly, but more important, an easy run of about that length will help loosen you up, particularly if you spent the day before cooped up in an airplane or car. And what is at the heart of that recommended 2-mile workout the day before? You guessed it: strides! Before the Boston Marathon, I usually jog from my hotel near the finish line to the Charles River (a distance of about a mile), do 3 or 4 strides on a grassy area, then jog back. It's what I need to get race-ready.

Learning to run strides is simple. It took about 15 seconds of instruction for me to teach a new member of my cross-country team how to run strides. Experiment with this form of speed training and see how easy it is.

BREAK AWAY FOR BETTER PERFORMANCE ■

"Surges" may be the third "S," but they fit uncomfortably beside sprints and strides. Some runners might argue that surges do not qualify as pure speed, and they probably are right—except that while you are surging, you usually are moving at a very fast pace.

What are surges? They are fast sprints thrown into the middle of a long run. Coach Ron Gunn at Southwestern Michigan College in Dowagiac used to refer to surges as break 'em drills, since by surging in the middle of a race, you often can break away from your opponent. He had his runners wait until the final third of a workout before doing surges. "If they do them too early, you'll lose them for the rest of the run," says Gunn.

I often include surges in the middle of a hard, fast run. For example, while doing a fast 6-miler, I might begin at a 9-minute mile pace. But after a few miles of gradual acceleration, I'll reach a steady pace near 8 minutes, holding it for several miles. During the middle of this workout, if I'm feeling strong, I might attempt several surges—I pick up the pace to faster than 7 minutes, hold it for several hundred yards, then ease slightly, only to surge again. Usually by the sixth and final mile in such a workout, I have slowed to 8 or 9 minutes, although not necessarily by choice. Obviously, the pace increment for different runners would vary according to ability. A world-class runner might surge to near 4-minute-mile pace; most of the rest of us would be surging considerably slower.

On other occasions, I will run long surges, changing pace several times during a run of anywhere up to an hour's duration. One example is when I used to run with my high school cross-country team in the In-

Many forms of speed training overlap. They lead into each other. They complement each other.

diana Dunes State Park over a figure-eight course that included what we called the ridge trail, a wooded bluff high over the beach. We would begin by running about 10 minutes to a point in the woods where we would stop and stretch, then head up onto the ridge. The trail wound back and forth, dipping and diving, forcing runners to make constant surges, a series of sprints or strides thrown into the middle of what is essentially a long run. At the end of the ridge, we would relax, coast, regroup, and let gravity carry us down a sand dune. We would back off the pace for a mile or so before turning onto a trail and board-walk that crossed a swamp, which coaxed us into a long surge before returning to our starting point.

Wait a minute, you say. Weren't you training speed endurance rather than pure speed? Many forms of speed training overlap. They lead into each other. They complement each other. In actuality, we trained using a blend of repeats and interval training. The easy run between ridge and swamp served as our interval. It's also a form of fartlek. Don't get hung up on terms. Sometimes, you want to go out and try different forms of speed-work just for variety and to feel the wind in your hair without worrying about whether it improves your performance.

If you're a Bob Kennedy trying to break your rival in the middle of a 5,000-meter track, knowing how and when to surge can offer you a tactical edge. And a surge can also assist a high school cross-country runner trying to move from 57th to 56th place at the state championships.

So, do surges make sense for adult fitness runners? Granted, if you surge more than once or twice in the middle of a marathon, you may never make it past 20 miles. But surges and the other forms of speedwork described in this chapter make sense for two reasons. One, practicing surges will improve your basic speed, which can translate to improved performance. Two, being able to change pace midrace can help get you out of a rut, or back on pace, which can result in faster times. Don't overlook the benefits of learning how to run fast.

And when you see that digital clock over the finish line relentlessly ticking away—55 . . . 56 . . . 57 . . . 58 . . . 59—you'll be glad you have a kick. ∎

DYNAMIC FLEXIBILITY

SPEED IN MOTION

Roy Benson, an Atlanta fitness consultant and former University of Florida track coach, stands before a group of several hundred teenagers jammed into the bleachers of a gymnasium in Asheville, North Carolina. They are high school cross-country runners spending a week at his summer running camp. They have come to camp to become better runners. With the week of hard training at Benson's camp, plus the knowledge gained, they hope to return home with skills not possessed by their rivals.

You may wonder what you can learn from a group of high school runners. Plenty. Benson's advice applies to any runner looking for speed.

Today's lesson is *dynamic flexibility*—although Benson does not call it by that name, or by any other familiar terms like *plyometrics*, *ballistic stretching*, or *speed drills*. Dynamic flexibility is a form of stretching—a means of getting loose—that involves continuous movement, as opposed to the static nature of regular stretching.

At his camp, Benson offers what he describes as "learn-by-doing drills." He promises the runners, "These drills are going to teach you how to get stronger, how to be more flexible, how to be more coordinated." Soon, he has them out of the bleachers and lined up facing him on the wide side of the gym.

Benson concedes that one way for runners to improve their speed is to increase their running distance. "If you're running 20 miles a week, I'll guarantee that if you can move up to 40, you'll run faster." But one problem as runners increase distance, he continues, is that they often decrease flexibility. "The first thing that happens is that your hamstrings get tight, because you're using this short stride. Your calves get tight, your shins get tight, your quads get tight. You develop inflexibility, resulting in a shorter and shorter range of motion, and pretty soon, you can't run as fast." Benson states that runners must continue to fight this tightening process by using flexibility drills.

Dynamic flexibility is a form of stretching—a means of getting loose—that involves continuous movement.

Another factor, Benson explains, is that by not working the muscles used when you run fast, those muscles weaken and compound the problem. Finally, says Benson, runners who run long also run very erect, landing toward the rear of their feet, on their heels. That may be an economical way to run distance, but not to run fast. For speed, runners need to learn to land further forward on their feet—more midfoot, toward their toes.

Benson asks those at his camp to run in place. Soon the gym thunders with the sound of thumping shoes.

This is the first step in learning flexibility: employing simple movements that will help you loosen up. There are, of course, different approaches. In fact, a generation of runners has been taught that the best way is to stretch in a static position. "Don't bounce!" is a warning offered by almost every stretching expert, including Bob Anderson, author of a best-selling book on that subject.

Anderson writes, "Holding a stretch as far as you can go or bouncing up and down strains the muscles and activates the stretch reflex. These harmful methods cause pain, as well as physical damage due to the microscopic tearing of muscle fibers."

That's good advice, but static stretching is not the only way to loosen up. Fast running is another way. Simply by sprinting out and lengthening your stride (the sprints, strides, and surges discussed in chapter 10), you stretch your muscles. Of course, you have to be loose to run fast, so it becomes a question of which comes first, the chicken or the egg—the stretch or the stride? The truth is that dynamic flexibility drills do not replace static stretching. Rather, they often work well together.

HIGH KNEES ■

"Stop!" Benson yells out to his class, and he asks how many were landing on their heels. Nobody raises a hand. Benson nods and explains that it is impossible to run in place landing on your heels.

Benson again asks them to run in place—but to now begin moving forward gradually, across the gym. The campers comply and, in so doing, learn one of the first drills, what I call high knees. In this drill, runners thrust their knees upward vigorously, counterbalancing with powerful arm pumps. It's more like sprinting in place than running in place.

As the campers move from one side of the gym to the other, Benson instructs, "Stay up on your toes! Get that feel. Feel yourself coming down on your midfoot, the ball of your foot. That's the feeling you want when you run fast."

To emphasize the high-knee aspect of the drill, Benson next has the high schoolers hold their hands out in front of them, just higher than their knees. Jogging back across the floor, they hit their hands with their knees, gradually raising their hands and lifting their knees to waist height.

"One of the side benefits of these drills is to turn you into better athletes," he says. "We want to make you feel more comfortable and coordinated when you sprint." Benson notes that high-knee drills are good for strengthening the hip flexors, which he identifies as the most important running muscles in your body. "The only way you strengthen your hip flexors," he says, "is to run up hills or stadium steps, or do speedwork—or do drills such as this." He advises running drills when you're fresh, not when you're fatigued from a hard workout.

A variation on high knees is a less dynamic drill I call the drum major. I used it with my cross-country teams. Instead of running in place, it's more like walking in place. The motion is the same. Rise up on one toe, thrusting the opposite knee as high up toward your chest as possible, using a vigorous arm pump to achieve this. But you walk, rather than jog or run. You don't leave the ground, so it's a safe drill if you're recovering from a minor injury. I also recommend the drum major as a good introductory drill for older runners who have just begun to get acquainted with dynamic flexibility drills in an attempt to improve their running.

Some risk does accompany bounding drills, particularly for those with an insufficient training base or those who have passed their 40th birthday. Nevertheless, masters (or beginning) runners can begin with the drum major as a prelude to high knees. But don't abandon it once you've learned the more dynamic drills. It remains a good flexibility drill for all ages and levels.

A complementary static exercise to high knees or the drum

major is the knee pull. Stand in place, and with both hands, pull one knee to your chest, stretching your hamstring. Still another stretching variation is to do this while lying on your back. While warming up before a race, I sometimes use all three drills—high knees, drum major, and the knee pull—to loosen my muscles.

I also use the knee pull while soaking in a hot whirlpool. It's one of my favorite stretches, mainly because I constantly must fight the tendency of my hamstrings to tighten during long runs. Most distance runners have tight hamstrings; they come with the territory. It's one reason why we have trouble touching our toes.

HIGH HEELS ■

High knees is perhaps the easiest flexibility drill to learn and practice. But Benson moves to the next drill, what he calls the fanny-flicker and what I call high heels. Coaches sometimes call it the butt-kicker. I also sometimes refer to it as the glute-kicker, as in gluteus maximus.

Benson begins by walking his group through the drill on their toes. "As you go farther and farther, lift your heels higher and higher, until you're kicking your fanny." Leaning forward makes the exercise easier to learn, although I recommend an upright posture for more practiced butt-kickers. Once Benson's campers learn the movement in slow motion, he brings them butt-kicking back across the gym. "Nice and slowly," says Benson. "Short steps. The minute you try to go fast, it gets too challenging and you fall apart. Short steps. *Flick! Flick! Flick!*"

Benson nudges me and points toward two girls—sprinters, as it turns out. "Watch their kick," says Benson. "They get perfect full extension across the front of their ankles. Their toes point. The classic back kick. That, to me, is the secret of speed."

Indeed, one way to judge a runner's speed is by watching him or her do these drills. On one of my cross-country teams, two runners clearly drilled better than the others. Had you sent that team across the grass in one of the above drills, you would immediately have noticed Don Pearce and Liz Galaviz. Pearce qualified for the state championships in his junior and senior years by running the 800 meters in 1:57. Galaviz, a talented sophomore, was the best half-miler on the girls' squad; that year, she ran 2:32 to qualify for sectionals.

Ironically, Pearce was perhaps the least flexible runner on the team, so static stretching was very difficult for him. And because he didn't like to be seen doing poorly in any activity, he did his stretching routine very reluctantly. If Pearce had a fault (shared by many runners), it was his tendency to rely on his natural ability. Would he have become an even faster runner had he paid more attention to improving his flexibility? I'm inclined to think so, although scientists offer no proof

Benson explains to his class that the high heels drill works well for stretching the hamstrings, but it is particularly effective for stretching the quadriceps. "You have to relax your quads to get that heel up," he instructs.

For older, beginning, or injured runners, walking in place with the high-heel motion works quite nicely. As a complementary static stretch for this drill, try the heel hold. To do it, use one hand to balance yourself on a stationary object and the other to pull one heel up toward your butt.

SKIPPING ■

High knees and high heels are great for beginners. They require relatively little skill or flexibility. Benson's next set of drills, which involves skipping, is trickier. He teaches two variations:

skipping for height, and skipping for distance, the latter in which you try to cover as much ground as possible.

Both varieties are extremely dynamic and involve all of the major muscles used in running fast. Thus, skipping is the heart of the art of dynamic flexibility. In fact, one value of all that goes before—from static stretching to high knees and high heels—is that you become loose enough to do this dynamic exercise. There is no single stretch that complements skipping, although it might be said that all stretches do just that.

Many runners have difficulty learning skipping drills at first, even though most of us skipped naturally as young children. Perhaps it's just a matter of practicing it again. When my oldest son, Kevin, appeared for cross-country practice at Indiana University, he kept getting his legs crossed when coach Sam Bell taught the team the drill. Kevin eventually went behind the dormitory one Sunday morning and practiced skipping until he learned the rhythm. If you have problems learning to skip again, don't feel embarrassed. With some practice, you can master this skill. Kevin did, and it helped him finish the season as the second-fastest runner on the Hoosier team that won the Big Ten title and placed eighth at the NCAA championships. The only runner faster than he was Olympian Jim Spivey.

As Benson sends his campers skipping across the gym, sure enough, one lad keeps getting legs and arms tangled. Arm movements in skipping are like arm movements in running or walking: the left arm comes up as the right knee comes up, and so forth. But the camper keeps getting his left arm and left knee up together, until finally, everything falls apart. Benson sends him back and forth across the floor several times, but the camper just can't seem to pick up the right rhythm.

It's not easy. So Benson instructs his students on the technique of skipping. "To skip, you must be coordinated. You start skipping with high knees, stay relaxed, and slowly bring your arms in like a sprinter. Arms are straight, pointing down the track, not across your body. You want to have straight hands, up about jaw height, so you're pumping your arms, getting up in the air. I want to see you hanging like Michael Jordan! Pump your arms. Elbows go as high as possible in the back. That helps you push harder against the ground with that opposite toe. Then come up in the front with a short punching motion to help you lift in the air. Now let's try it slowly. Everybody together, doing a little skip with your arms up. Get those knees high! Hang up there!"

Admittedly, skipping is not easy to explain—or teach. You just do it. If you think too much about what you're doing, it may confuse you more. One way to learn to skip is to make very slow and short movements at first: Skip a few inches forward on one foot, then the other. Hold both hands in front of you for balance. Gradually let your hands counterbalance your foot movements. Then stretch out. Once you learn to skip, you'll be amazed how simple—and fun—the exercise becomes.

As I mentioned earlier, there are two variations on the skipping drill: skipping for height, and skipping for distance.

Skipping for height is akin to high knees. You move forward gradually, concentrating on getting high off the ground. Accentuate your knee rise. Counterbalance with your arms. As one knee comes up high, the opposite arm thrusts skyward in a palm-open movement. Don't try to cover too much ground. When my team does skipping for height, I yell at any of my runners who try to "win" the drill by moving ahead of the others. Getting up in the air is most important. Indeed, those doing the best job with this exercise are often in the back rather than the front.

Skipping for distance is similar in its movements, only now you try to cover distance horizontally rather than vertically. The knees and arms still come up high, but movement is more forward. I still discourage those who try to "win" the drill, since moving forward too rapidly makes the skipping too difficult to maintain.

Skipping drills are best conducted on smooth, soft surfaces. Football fields are sometimes too lumpy for safe practice of this or any other drill in this chapter. The tracks around them often are too hard. Basketball courts are okay, since the wood floor offers some bounce. The perfect surface is the fairway of a golf course—if you can avoid being evicted by the greenkeepers.

I also enjoy throwing a few skips into my warmups before a race, mostly just for the fun of it. It looks so quirky that other runners smile when they see you doing it. If you have ever raced internationally, you may have noticed that European runners use skipping drills and other similar movements in their warmups more than American runners do. I suspect it's because of the training they get in gymnasium classes during their youth.

> *Skipping is the heart of the art of dynamic flexibility. In fact, one value of all that goes before is that you become loose enough to do this dynamic exercise.*

TOE WALK ■

As his campers skip back and forth across the gym floor, Benson talks to me about speed. "When you go to sprint, you don't care about economy. You don't care how smooth and relaxed you are. You want to be powerful, dynamic. You pump your arms to make your strides go faster. You turn over quicker. That way, you'll really take off."

Benson has one final drill to teach his campers: the toe walk, a less dynamic variation of the drum major discussed on page 152. It's a good exercise for calf muscles—and a simple one. All

(continued on page 160)

FLEXIBILITY DRILLS THAT BUILD SPEED

Here's a summary of drills designed to add flexibility and speed to your run. To avoid sore muscles, you should always warm up before (by jogging and stretching) and cool down after doing any of these drills. When starting a dynamic flexibility program, begin with only one or two drills, and gradually increase your capacity over a period of weeks and months. These drills are best done on your easy days, when you are running short and have more time to concentrate on nonspecific training activities.

They are also best conducted during warm weather, when you can utilize soft, smooth grass surfaces. Living in the Midwest, I used to consider flexibility drilling as more of a summer activity and weight lifting as more of a winter activity. But recently, my wife and I bought a second home in Ponte Vedra Beach, Florida, offering me new and different training options. The flat and firm Atlantic beach, which is only a block from our home, is perfect for most of these drills. Obviously, any training regimen in this or another book must be adapted to fit the realities of each runner's situation.

To do the drills, you need a straightaway 50 to 75 meters long, preferably grass or another soft surface. My son Kevin would do two to four repetitions of each of the drills, in the following order.

1. High knees. Probably the simplest drill, high knees is little more than running in place while moving forward gradually. Lift your knees high and land on the balls of your feet. Point your toes, with all movement straight ahead. Your arms pump high in countermovement to your legs. Coach Sam Bell warns against doing high knees too fast, which may make it difficult to do the movements correctly.

2. Fast feet. The late Bill Bowerman described fast feet as one means of teaching form to sprinters. This drill resembles high knees, except instead of emphasizing knee lift, you concentrate on moving your feet rapidly, almost pitter-patter. Straight-ahead movement with pointed toes is equally important here.

3. High heels. This exercise is easier than the two previous ones, and

Kevin used it at this point partly to catch his breath. Runners new to flexibility drills probably should master this drill before attempting the next two drills. It is simply running in place, like high knees, but you kick your legs high in back instead of lifting your knees. Relax during this drill, and don't overemphasize speed.

4. Skipping for height. To skip, you must push off one foot and land on that same (trail) foot before bringing your lead foot down. It's like the first two jumps of the triple jump. Skipping involves a pause, like the syncopated beat in music. In skipping for height (as with high knees), emphasis is on high knee lift. During the pause, while suspended in midair, focus on getting your knee as high as possible.

5. Skipping for distance. This is the same as skipping for height, except the emphasis is on distance. Remember to keep all movement in a straight line. The two skipping drills require good flexibility, but they also promote flexibility. It could be said that the first three drills help warm you up for the skipping drills.

6. Bounding. This is an elongated running action in which you concentrate on lifting your knees and striding with your arms up. It will become running unless you focus on knee lift. You also might compare this drill to the first stage of the triple jump: the hop.

7. Double leg hop. Not a drill for inexperienced runners. The movement is similar to that in drill 3, high heels. Stand in place and hop, kicking both heels in back. The distance covered is unimportant.

Once you master these speed-improvement drills and can do them without excessive fatigue or postworkout soreness, you can integrate them into different parts of your training week. Try them in the middle of your medium-distance workouts. I sometimes include several of the drills as part of my prerace warmup. High knees, high heels, and fast feet work well to loosen me up.

Also, don't ignore the stepping or standing variations of these drills. They may be more suitable for cold weather conditions or for those for whom too-vigorous drilling raises an unnecessary injury risk.

you need to do is walk forward and accentuate your toe push-off: rolling up and over on the toes of the feet. "Way up on your toes," says Benson. "Don't bounce. Walk. Stay up on your toes. Feel your calves tightening. You're building power, strength, explosion."

Having used nearly an hour to teach four simple drills (high knees, high heels, skipping for height and for distance, and toe walks), Benson releases the group to its next activities. Had he the time or the inclination, Benson could have offered several additional speed drills. One book I own—*Plyometrics: Explosive Power Training* by James C. Radcliffe and Robert C. Farentinos— offers dozens of drills, some involving steps and medicine balls. One illustration shows a coach telling his athlete to jump off a cliff. Going off the edge, the athlete asks: "Are you sure, Coach, this is how to do plyometrics?"

Indeed, beginning runners may feel as though they crash-landed at the bottom of the cliff the day after their first dynamic flexibility drills. Any time you use different or untrained muscles, you probably will feel sore for 24 to 72 hours afterward, and it makes little difference how otherwise well-trained you are as a runner. The same would happen if you switched suddenly to cycling or skiing or tennis. For this reason, introduce bounding drills very gradually into your program. Begin with only one or two drills and minimal repetitions. Do them on your easy days. Gradually introduce additional drills and increase the number of repetitions. You will avoid both discomfort and the increased risk of injury that comes as the price for wanting to run fast.

FAST FEET ■

One additional drill that I used with my teams is fast feet. It's one that I learned from the late University of Oregon coach Bill Bowerman. I consider Bowerman to have been the single most influential American coach in the area of training distance runners. Many other coaches and writers feel the same way.

While giving me an interview for an article, Bowerman described a drill he had learned from the previous Oregon coach, Bill Hayward. The drill is very simple, similar to high knees, except that instead of raising your knees high, you keep them low and move your feet as rapidly as you can: *Pop! Pop! Pop! Pop!* Your arms move equally fast in short arcs.

But that wasn't the only thing I learned. I couldn't help but take advantage of Bowerman's expertise. So I asked him, "What are the secrets of running fast—if that isn't too basic a question?"

"No, it's a good question," he said. "I did an article with somebody once on the secrets of speed. It was published in *Sports Illustrated* in 1968. And basically I was telling what Hayward taught me. It's very elemental: A straight line is the shortest distance between two points. My line mechanics were so bad that my foot would fly out to the side. One of the things that Hayward had me do was lean up against a wall and watch my feet. I would bring my leg through like this to try to get the feel of my leg moving in a straight line. (Bowerman leaned against his fireplace and slowly rotated his leg to mimic a sprinter's stride.) One leg, then the other. I've done this with a lot of people, and it works.

"The second thing was reaction time. (He jogged in place, his feet pitter-pattering at a rapid pace.) You stand like this and gradually speed up your legs. . . . The reaction of bouncing the feet rapidly, then bringing the knees up slowly, trying to keep everything straight ahead, picking up the rhythm—but you don't do it only with the legs. You have to use the arms, because that's the way you're wired. By gradually speeding up the arms, you speed up the legs. Then, use the sprint distances as merely a measure of testing; how much is this fellow improving? We did sprint drills three times a week. High knee, fast leg, and sprint 40 yards. Simple drills: everything straight ahead, reaction time, mechanics of running. If there's some bad habit, work on it. For every action, there's an equal and opposite reaction.

"That was what Hayward did for me. I never knew how fast I was. I couldn't beat anybody; I was the slowest man on the high school team. After Hayward was through with me, the only man I couldn't beat was our university sprinter, Paul Starr, who was third in the National AAU Championships . . ."

"So you were able to improve the speed of your sprinters with these simple drills of Bill Hayward's," I said.

"God determines how fast you're going to run. I can only help with the mechanics."
—the late Bill Bowerman

"And what works for sprinters applies to other runners as well," he explained. "God determines how fast you're going to run; I can help only with the mechanics."

Bowerman's successor as track coach at Oregon, Bill Dellinger, later described the fast-foot drill in an article in *Runner's World* magazine: "The concept behind this is to see how fast you can make your feet move. Unlike the high-knees drill, you barely lift your knees at all. The emphasis is on quickness. Don't stride out. Simply move your feet as if you were running over hot coals. You're teaching your feet to react quickly."

TWO ADVANCED DRILLS ■

There are two additional drills that my son Kevin learned from coach Bell at Indiana University that are worth mentioning. However, I don't necessarily recommend them for all (particularly older) runners, because of the stress they place on the joints. These drills are bounding and the double leg hop.

Bounding is an elongated running action in which you concentrate on lifting your knees and pumping with your arms up. This is not running. You bound. You hop from one leg to the other: left, right, left, right, getting as high off the ground as you can. Focus on your knee lift. Add this to your repertoire of flexibility drills only after you are well-practiced in the other drills and your leg muscles have adapted to what is admittedly a very vigorous exercise.

The double leg hop also is not a drill for inexperienced runners. The movement is similar to that in high heels. You stand in place and hop, kicking both heels in the back. The distance covered is unimportant. My son Kevin would use this final drill only when in top shape. Add this to your routine last. I've already subtracted it from mine; at my age, it's too likely to cause an injury. It's too dynamic. All of the drills in this chapter probably should be offered with a warning label: "Can be injurious to your health."

Edmund R. Burke, Ph.D., an exercise physiologist who works with the U.S. Cycling Team, warns that like any other type of training, bounding drills can lead to poor results if not used properly. "Symptoms of tendinitis and synovitis, particularly of the knee, can result from too much plyometric training," says Dr. Burke.

For distance runners, I don't recommend exercises that involve jumping on and off boxes and sideboards. Drills that promote dynamic flexibility—whether called bounding or plyometrics or ballistic stretching or learn-by-doing—do have their obvious place in the training program of a high school cross-country team.

For one thing, the drills are sort of hokey. The kids enjoy doing them and can show off with the drills during their warmups. The well-trained athletes on college teams, such as those at Indiana and Oregon, also benefit by adding bounding to their program.

But how appropriate are such drills for other runners, particularly those in the masters ranks? The risk of injury may be too great for many high-mileage runners, who aren't used to speed drills and have limited flexibility.

Nevertheless, I believe that any runner can benefit by eventually adding at least some of the drills covered here to his or her training regimen. Benson's experience at his running camps would suggest that this is so, since he has taught speed drills to many adult runners who have attended his camps. ■

HIT THE HILLS

CLIMB YOUR WAY TO THE TOP

The University of Oregon's Bill Bowerman was known for his bluntness. I once quizzed him about whether training on hills could make you a better runner. "When they start putting hills on tracks," he replied gruffly, "I'll have my athletes run hills in practice."

It was a classic remark from a classic coach. Specificity of exercise is important for any sport, which is one reason why I don't over-prescribe either cross-training or strength training. Yet Arthur Lydiard, the New Zealander whom Bowerman admitted using as a source for many training ideas, strongly recommended hill training for those wanting to improve their speed on track or road.

Exercise physiologist Dean Brittenham also believes that one way runners get stronger (thus faster) is to run up an incline. "Most good training programs have one common philosophy—some type of resistance running," he says. "And the best way to achieve that is with hills."

I live just over the crest of a hill that rises about 75 feet above the shores of Lake Michigan. The road in front of my house, Lake Shore Drive, is relatively flat to the west, sloping slightly downward. To the east, however, the road dips more precipitously, losing most of its above-lake altitude within several hundred yards before starting to level off. So right out my front door, I have a nearly $\frac{1}{4}$-mile hill that's perfect for resistance training.

When I run east on the Drive, I must begin downhill, which can be painful on days when I am tight from the previous day's hard workout. Returning, I must cope with this hill in the closing minute of my run.

The "Higdon Hill" was a pivotal part of the 15-K course used for the Michigan City Run, a major local race. (In recent years, that race has been replaced with a 5-K held on a different course.) Runners headed down the hill midway through the fourth mile, made a U-turn farther down the road, and came back up it just before the 6-mile mark. The hill therefore became the break point where many races were either won or lost.

When American marathon great Bill Rodgers ran Michigan City in 1978, I pointed out to him that the hill (which, because of a bend in the road, seems to go on forever) steepens just before the crest. Once over the top, however, he could use the quick drop and the gentle decline that follows over the next half-mile to gain momentum for a long surge to the finish. And that's where Rodgers left the other competitors in the race.

LEARNING TO LOVE HILLS ■

Let's talk about hills. Uphills and downhills. Big hills and small hills. Hills as both aid and deterrent to performance. Hills in training and hills in races. Hills as both a cause and a preventive of injuries. How to run them and how to avoid them. What to do when you don't have them, yet you still have to race on a hilly course. Hills to build strength and hills to build speed. Hills to build courage and hills to discourage. Are they an essential training tool or a gimmick dreamed up by a New Zealand coach out to prove to joggers that they'll never make it as serious racers?

The coach is Arthur Lydiard, who has outlined hill running in his books and numerous lectures as an essential ingredient of his three-step training buildup.

1. Endurance training
2. Hill training
3. Speedwork

Lydiard didn't discover hill training, however, any more than Zebulon Montgomery Pike discovered the mountain peak bearing his name. The Indians arrived at the peak before Pike, and Percy Cerutty was using hills before Lydiard to train Australian runners such as Herb Elliott, 1500-meter champion at the 1960 Olympics. Cerutty used to send Elliott sprinting up sand dunes near his training center at Portsea. Even before Cerutty, there were other coaches and runners who advocated hill running to build stamina, although Cerutty may have been the only coach to claim that running at full pace up a hill could bring "relief from constipation."

Lydiard made no such claims. He was less a discoverer of hill training than one who developed a systemized program that utilized hills as a key training ingredient. Lydiard's runners, including Olympic champions Murray Halberg and Peter Snell, did not merely run hills, they trained on them at specific points in their season to peak for specific races.

Lydiard's hill workouts had a pattern. His athletes would

run a 5-mile warmup, then run up a $\frac{1}{2}$-mile hill, run $\frac{1}{4}$ mile fast on top, run hard downhill, and run $\frac{1}{4}$ mile of quick fartlek at the bottom. They'd do six or eight of these hill loops, followed by a 2-mile cooldown. This was hardly the sort of workout schedule you would suggest to a beginner, but after Lydiard's runners started to win at the Olympics, track fans began to ask, what is it that they are doing differently? The answer was they were running hills.

Although Lydiard's endorsement was unequivocal, the research is inconclusive. Studies related to the specificity of exercise suggest that if you plan to race on hills, you need to train on hills. But whether such training also makes you a better runner on the flats and on the track is difficult to measure in the laboratory. (Apparently, Bowerman's reasoning for not recommending hill training to track athletes was well-founded.) But Lydiard believed that running up and down hills can make you a faster runner—and the achievements of his athletes would seem to support him.

ADVOCATES AND SKEPTICS ■

Exercise physiologist Dr. Jack Daniels's research determined that the addition of hill running does indeed increase the intensity of a training program. A runner's energy cost, he found, increases by 12 percent when running up a 1-degree slope, but only 7 percent of the energy returns when coming down that same slope.

Jack H. Wilmore, Ph.D., supervised a project by graduate students Doug Allen and Beau Freund while at the University of Arizona. They trained two groups of runners, one on the flats, the other running a gradual stadium ramp. At the end of the study, they found no difference between the two groups, at least not in the changes of their max VO$_2$. "That tells you something," says Dr. Wilmore, "although maybe athletes don't want to hear it." Dr. Wilmore and his team did not measure performance by testing the runners on a track or in races, so it is possible that hill training might have some important mental benefits, convincing runners they are tougher.

Former Ball State researcher Dr. David Costill maintains that theoretically, hill training should improve speed. "In order to have good speed," he says, "you must create force through the thigh and hamstring muscles, and hill work develops both." But Dr. Costill has not researched the subject and knows of no other exercise physiologists who have.

"Hill training is another form of resistance," claims Dr. Ned Frederick. "All training boils down to cleverly increasing the amount of resistance that your body can adapt to. So running uphill is one way of tricking the body. But there is no magic to hill training, no special adaptation that you can't get somewhere else."

Bob Glover, coauthor of *The Runner's Handbook*, believes that if you plan to race on hills, you need to train on hills. He offers several reasons, however, why even runners racing on flat courses should consider training on hills.

- Uphill intervals can be used to improve your form. You must concentrate on form to get up the hill.
- Downhill runs can teach relaxation and improve leg speed and stride.
- Hill running is "speedwork in disguise." It can be used in place of grueling track workouts to improve your anaerobic efficiency.
- Hills strengthen your legs, especially your quads, lessening the possibility of knee injury.
- Your mental ability to handle hills in races improves.

Glover adds, "If you live in the flatlands, be creative. Highway ramps or parking garages are possibilities, although they may pose obvious safety problems."

ELITE ADVICE ON HILLS ■

Whether to build strength or to condition themselves for hilly races, most top runners use hills in their training. Bill Rodgers, who in his prime had an excellent reputation as a hill runner (particularly on the descent), was among them. He once told me, "First, as an uphill runner, I'm weak. I've tried to do more hill repeats to compensate for this. Downhill, my success may be just from the way I land, my lightness. But even in high school, my coach emphasized pushing over the hill and not running as hard going up.

There is no magic to hill training, no special adaptation that you can't get somewhere else.

"I don't practice downhill running. The only time I would run hills was before Boston. I started to do more uphill training when I saw how well Randy Thomas and Greg Meyer ran on the uphills."

Rodgers used to train on none other than Heartbreak Hill, the fourth of the Newton hills that comes near the 21-mile mark on the course of the Boston Marathon, which he won four times. Although Heartbreak Hill is not particularly steep, it is about 600 yards long. Rodgers would run on the grass parkway beside the road, doing 6 to 10 repeats in 1:35. Between uphill bursts, he would jog back down, letting the grass cushion the impact of the downhill (an important step in injury prevention). "I see a lot of other runners training on Heartbreak," says Rodgers, "particularly before Boston."

When Joan Benoit Samuelson coached at Boston University, she often took her team there. "The girls on the team enjoyed it," recalls Samuelson. They would do five to eight repeats. Other times, they ran Summit Avenue Hill, several miles from Heartbreak but not on the marathon course. Samuelson notes that it usually took her team 2 to 3 days to recover after a workout on Summit.

"Living in Boston back then, I didn't get onto hills that often," she commented on the training that led her to an Olympic marathon victory in 1984. "During the course of a run, if I came to a hill, I would really charge it." Now living in her native state of Maine, Samuelson has more access to hilly running areas.

Hill running is "speed-work in disguise." It can be used in place of grueling track workouts to improve your anaerobic efficiency.

Herb Lindsay, formerly a number one–ranked road runner, lived in Boulder, Colorado, where the Flatiron Mountains provided "hills" that rise several thousand feet above the city. Canyons feature numerous uphill and downhill trails for training. Lindsay felt that the rolling plains before the front range also offered an opportunity for specific hill training, although he preferred to call it incline training.

"At altitude, one of the negative factors is that you can't get the quality of speed training you can at sea level," Lindsay explains. "You're limited by the thin air, but you can compensate by running on a gentle descent. With gravity pushing you along, you can run as fast (that is, with the same leg speed) as you can at sea level. I did train on uphills, but I probably used downhills with more planning."

ADVICE FOR FLATLANDERS ■

One strong believer in hill training is former American 5000-meter record holder Marty Liquori, which may seem strange when you consider that Liquori lives in Gainesville, Florida, which is as flat as one of coach Bowerman's tracks. As a substitute for hills, Liquori ran the stadium steps at the University of Florida. He says, "My feeling is that if Arthur Lydiard had a stadium in Auckland like we have in Gainesville, he would promote stadium running. Florida's stadium seats 70,000 people and has three levels of incline that get progressively steeper; it takes 35 seconds to reach the top, and nobody can run up it more than about eight times."

Liquori would train there once or twice a week before the track season. In between "uphills," he sometimes would run an easy 4 × 400 on the track to loosen up, then go back up the stadium. "At the end, you're totally rigged," he recalls.

Liquori's "stadiums" can be compared with Lydiard's ½-mile hills, coming as they did during a specific segment of his training year. Liquori ran the stadium in a transition period be-

MAKE UPHILL RUNNING A BREEZE

Here are some tips that will make running uphill easier and more comfortable. Use them the next time you face a tall hill. They will surely give you an edge in both your racing and your training.

Enjoy the hill. Consider the hill an opportunity to relax, change pace, and use different muscles.

Look upward. This helps you keep your body angle perpendicular to the ground, which is best for traction.

Shift gears. Seek a short, quick stride. You want the most efficient tempo for least wasted energy.

Don't push. Hills are hard only if you make them hard. You need not maintain your same speed from the flats.

Run over the top. Cresting the hill, quickly resume your previous pace from the flats. A cyclist would shift into high gear here; a skier would pole off. So should you.

tween distance running and track work. "When you run a lot of distance, your stride shortens," says Liquori. "Your leg muscles are not extending, so they become fairly weak. You go to a hill phase to make a transition, to force you to open up your stride by bounding up hills. You exaggerate knee lift and arm swing, push off with the toes and calves. This strengthens your quadriceps and buttocks muscles before going back onto the track. It's right out of the Lydiard book."

Another important factor, believes Liquori, is that somebody who has limited time for training can fatigue the muscles more rapidly on hills than on the flats. "When I was traveling and knew I had only a half-hour to work out," he says, "I'd look for a hill. I could get more exhausted than doing a 90-minute run."

In a situation where you have neither mountains nor a stadium nearby, yet you face scheduled races on hilly courses, you may need to try another training modification. Fred Wilt said, "If you are not going to run uphill in training, you have to do a lot of running where you go at one pace, then cut loose for 50 yards. The energy requirements for going uphill are so much greater than on the flats, you have to get used to higher energy expenditures in a race."

Still another option is to use a treadmill with an adjustable incline. Many runners now have them in their recreation rooms or belong to health clubs that have treadmills and other exercise machines that develop the same muscles.

USING HILLS TO BUILD MUSCLE ■

Jeff Galloway wrote in an article in *Runner's World* magazine, "Many coaches and strength experts believe hills provide better strength for running than weights or machines. Pushing up the incline builds the lower leg muscles. With power there, you can develop a more efficient push-off, better running posture, and more strength in your legs.

"Weight lifting strengthens those same muscles, but it won't train them for the demands of running. The large and small muscles in the legs must work together perfectly to produce a smooth stride. Hill running builds strength and coordination at the same time."

When Ron Gunn coached distance runners at Southwestern Michigan College in Dowagiac, he often used a 200-meter sloping fairway on a golf course near the campus. There, he had his team do circuit sprinting on the grass following a fast run of 5 to 7 miles. He called the circuit Scando-loops after the Scandinavians.

Here's how Gunn defined the workout. "Go at a faster-than-race pace up the hill, then do a relaxing jog around the top. Run easily the first 75 meters of the downhill that is steep; then when the drop begins to level out, relax and lift up on the balls of your feet, arms vertical, and sprint down the hill. It's what we call going into fifth gear. Get back down to the bottom, then jog some more, sprint again at the bottom, jog some more, go up again. Do about six of those. It develops speed and strength, and it also teaches you to run a hill properly."

Another Gunn circuit on an old country road featured a hill with three levels, where his runners alternated fast and slow running according to the pitch of the hill. Gunn had his squad run hills twice a week for as many as 8 weeks prior to a major competition. Sometimes, the hills served as just one part of a structured program, other times, they made up the entire workout. He says, "Hills also are good for getting into condition quickly without the risk of injury. You don't have to do a lot of running to obtain a quality workout. You don't need as many repetitions."

Liquori adds, "With the caliber of runners we have today,

they can't get tired doing interval work on a track. You could take a workout like 20 quarters in 55 seconds, and today's runners just might be able to do it. But before they finish, an Achilles tendon would flare up, or ligaments would give way. Running hills permits you to do more by doing less. When you get to the point where everybody runs 120 miles a week at a 5:30 pace, you have to find other ways to generate more stress. Hills may be the wave of the future."

One warning, however: Running hills strains the muscles, tendons, and ligaments of your feet, particularly the bottoms of your feet, because in running up an incline you push off from the ball of your foot. This strains the plantar fascia. You'll feel sharp pain on the heel (where the fascia connects) if you get this injury. It feels like a heel bruise, but is not. Hayward, California podiatrist Steven Subotnick, D.P.M., Ph.D., says that plantar fasciitis is a common injury in his area because runners do a lot of their training on hilly courses. If you plan to add hills to your training program, introduce them gradually. Think like a beginner. By moving slowly into hill training, you will decrease your risk of injury.

RUN TO THE TOP ■

Obviously, elite runners turn to hills to add an intensity to their workouts they just can't get anywhere else. But what about mid-pack runners? Coach Gunn can tell you. He has trained just such people in classes at his community college: men and women, young and old, with little background as competitive athletes. "They do circuits on the same hills," says Gunn, "only involving different techniques. As with our college students, I'll have them do some kind of tempo run; then they'll end up in the latter stage of the workout doing hills. They'll start with three to four and build up to seven or eight, running faster than race pace, then turn around and jog down. They don't do the other phases.

"We run on golf courses or forest trails. We've gotten off hard roads now. It's pretty difficult to injure an athlete running up a hill. The time you have to be careful is coming down."

At the Nike Sport Research Laboratory, Tom Clark studied the impact shock of running up and down hills. Ten well-trained runners ran at various grades, from 6 percent uphill to 8 percent downhill, at a 7-minute-mile pace. At the steepest uphill grade, the shock was only 85 percent of that experienced running on level ground. The steepest downhill grade resulted in 40 percent more leg shock—an increased risk of injury.

It may be, then, that hill training—particularly intensive training—and running fast downhill should be reserved for days when you are well-rested and at a point during your workout where you are relaxed from a good warmup but not yet excessively fatigued. "You're more likely to injure yourself when you're tired," says Herb Lindsay of his incline training.

Of course, what goes up must come down—or does it? Marty Liquori claimed one trick he learned from world-class New Zealanders Rod Dixon and John Walker was to not run downhill. "Instead of 4-minute intervals on a track, they would go 10 minutes up a steep hill and get a ride back down," Liquori explains. That suggests the ultimate athletic perk: a satisfied coach standing beside a limousine at the top of a mountain. Even without that, most runners who attempt hill training will find that it makes them better runners.

DEVELOP HILL TECHNIQUE ■

Once you agree that training on hills can make you a faster runner, you should be ready to develop a hill running technique.

One summer, I taught at the Green Mountain Running Camp in northern Vermont. Each morning from our hilltop campus at Lyndon State College, I looked out over a rolling landscape. Fog settled in the valleys; hills above touched the sky. I wanted to run those hills forever.

But as I discovered from observing the runners at the camp, not everybody knows how to run hills—up or down. Their main form fault was not knowing how to lean. They leaned into the hill going up; they leaned backward going down. Actually, they should have been doing the opposite.

Uphills. Let's focus first on uphills, which trouble runners most. Runners can learn about hill running technique from skiers and cyclists. Going uphill, a cross-country skier looks toward the top of the slope. Raising his gaze causes a slight shift backward in weight, anchoring each ski plant enough to avoid slipping. If he leans forward, his skis lose traction. At the end of cross-country ski races, I constantly have to fight the tendency to slump forward from fatigue, which causes my skis to slide backward.

> *Not everybody knows how to run hills— up or down. Their main form fault is not knowing how to lean.*

The same is true in cycling. My first time on a mountain bike, I also learned quickly to sit back in the saddle going up the trail. When I did otherwise, my wheels spun. For best bike traction, you keep weight over the power (rear) wheel. The same is true for running: Learn to lean back when going uphill. Focusing on the top with your eyes will get you to the top.

Also, change your tempo when starting uphill. Just as a cyclist downshifts for more power, runners need to change gears by shortening and quickening stride. But don't push too hard uphill; otherwise, you won't have enough stamina to run fast downhill.

Downhills. Running downhill takes another skill and a different attitude. In the closing miles of the Boston Marathon, people lining Commonwealth Avenue encourage runners by shouting: "It's downhill all the way!" Actually, most runners find it more difficult running down than up. Uphill, you can survive on guts; downhill requires skill and practiced techniques.

I learned about downhill running from Kenny Moore, the 1968 and 1972 Olympic marathoner who writes for *Sports Illustrated*. During the course of researching hill running for a two-part article that appeared in *Runner's World* magazine, I was told by several runners that Moore was their downhill running guru. I contacted him and later received a letter that, even several decades later, is probably worth reprinting in full.

> *I have a recurring dream (it has come twice) in which I plunge blithely over a cliff and run down the face with floating, 60-foot strides. But instead of coming to an abrupt flattening, it happens that the incline gradually becomes less severe. My gravity-assisted bounds shorten to 50, then 40, feet. My speed drops from 125 mph to 80. Eventually, assuming my hamstrings stay relaxed as the hillside rips my feet along under my torso at a rate six times as fast as my muscles can do it by themselves, I emerge safely on the level plain, a couple of miles beneath my starting point, where I ultimately starve to death.*
>
> *I don't suppose it is possible. But it might serve as illustration of the sort of things which facilitate downhill running.*
>
> *Primary, I think, is raw smugness, preferably born of experience, which will let one bolt freewheeling down a slope without any fear of falling. That fear, I'm sure, works against the kind of relaxation necessary. It takes, at first anyway, a bit of nerve to lean forward so the torso is perpendicular to the surface of the hill, and to run with the same action and foot-*

plant one would use on the level. The idea, of course, is to let gravity do all the work, and that can't happen if you're clunking down on your heels or shooting the soles of your feet along the pavement.

Downhill running takes practice as well, to condition the thighs to the intense pounding. And to get the legs used to the much higher rates of stride, even if the backs of the legs and back don't have to do anything but follow along. I find downhill strides wonderful speed training, but that's nothing new. Lydiard has taught it in New Zealand for years, and in 1960, Alan Lawrence ran intervals (440s in 48.0, 660s in 1:14, if I remember correctly) hanging on to the back of a car. He thought it helped him and stressed the need for confidence. I'm sure it was the same sort of thing.

The only other tip I can offer: Don't reach the top of a hill exhausted, or it won't work. I'll give up 5 or 10 yards uphill to anyone and get twice that down the other side if I'm able to save enough energy to keep my knees up.

The main problem in downhill running, as Moore clearly understood, is attitude. Not mental attitude, but the way the astronauts use that term to describe positioning a space capsule. When I interviewed Mario Andretti for a book I was writing about auto racing some years ago, he also talked about attitude when it came to angling his race car into a turn at the Indy 500.

The right attitude for downhill runners is leaning forward. Just as you can learn from skiers and cyclists going uphill by leaning backward and shifting gears, you also can learn from these other athletes on the downs.

Going downhill, a skier keeps weight evenly distributed on his skis, but tilts forward from the waist into a tuck position to minimize wind drag. A cyclist does the same thing. As a runner,

FREE SPEED

You will go faster when you run downhill. It's free speed. But that's not always a welcome sensation if the hill is too steep. Here is a four-step method to cope with increasing speed.

1. Starting downhill, tilt forward, beginning at the waist. How much you tilt depends on the angle of the hill.

2. As you move faster, raise your knees and lengthen your stride to cope with the increased speed.

3. For better balance, particularly on uneven ground, allow your elbows to rise up and out.

4. To cushion the shock of the descent, land more on the balls of your feet rather than on your heels.

Most important, practice! Like technique in any sport, learning to run downhill takes time. Running downhill becomes more difficult toward the end of a long run or race, when fatigue makes the concentration necessary to perform skills such as those listed above difficult. Those people shouting encouragement at the end of the Boston Marathon mean well, but running downhill is no easier than piloting a spacecraft or driving a race car at Indy.

you need not worry as much about drag, but you also should tilt forward to let the hill carry you down. Not only will you go faster, but you minimize pounding by getting off your heels. Braking slows you and wastes the effort you just invested in running uphill.

Here's where attitude comes in, because you want to tilt forward, not merely lean. The tilt begins at the pelvis and is ever so slight. To master this pelvic tilt, you need practice. Find a long downhill—not too steep—and experiment with different tilts as you run, seeing what angle changes do to both your speed and comfort.

Finally, know the courses where you plan to race. In preparing for the Boston Marathon, I always advise runners to practice downhill running as well as uphill running. The four Newton hills—including famous Heartbreak Hill—get a lot of publicity, but the course is more downhill than up with a drop of roughly 450 feet from the start in suburban Hopkinton to the finish on Boylston Street in downtown Boston.

Some of the Boston drop—such as that in the first mile—is noticeable, but other downhills are so subtle that you barely notice them. This is particularly true in the last 5 miles, which is where tired runners have the most difficulty coping with the downward slant. And it's where they do the most damage to their leg muscles because they no longer have the strength to maintain a forward-leaning position on the downhills as recommended by Kenny Moore. They lose form and begin pounding. As a result, they spend the week after the race walking very stiff-legged.

One way to avoid at least some of the muscle damage that occurs is to train for the downhills. In running repeats on the hill in front of my house before Boston, I usually would run one downhill repeat for each two uphill repeats. There is a danger, however, in overdoing downhill training because of an increased risk of injury because of impact.

Nevertheless, training on hills can make you a stronger runner. And when it comes to running fast, strength equals speed—as we will discuss further in the next chapter. ▪

CHAPTER 13

STRENGTH DOES IT

MORE MUSCLE MEANS MORE SPEED

As recently as a decade ago—about the time the first edition of this book appeared—when I used to suggest to runners that they might improve their times by incorporating strength training into their programs, it was a tough sell. Runners just wanted to run. They enjoyed heading out the door and running the roads, or through the woods. Running was fun. Hanging out in a gym and pumping iron was not fun.

Times have changed. The new breed of runners more often realizes the importance of strength training—not only to help them run faster, but also to prevent injuries and improve their general health. This includes increasing numbers of women runners, who are no longer intimidated by walking into a weight room that once was the sole province of muscle-bound men. And the guys now have become accustomed to having a gal pumping iron at the next bench.

So it's no longer a matter of should you strength train, but of how do you do it?

Unfortunately, too many serious runners still ignore, or even avoid, exercises that might strengthen them. And I confess that I'm sometimes guilty of shortchanging my own strength-training program. At the end of a day when I figure I have maybe a half-hour to sneak in a workout before dinner, I usually opt for a run outdoors rather than a workout with weights in the basement. Still, I've become more faithful in recent years because, as an aging runner, I know that strength training is as important to my health as to my ability to run fast in a 5-K.

VERTICAL HYPHENS ◾

Tom Brunick, a consultant with The Athlete's Foot chain of stores, claims that too many runners look like "vertical hyphens." We're skinny, with no upper-body mass. Running develops the lower body, but does little for the upper body. The arm-swinging we do to counterbalance leg motion offers some development, but not much. There's also a question as to exactly how much benefit runners actually get from all the weightlifting and cross-training they might do for supplemental exercise. Will strength training help you run faster, or is it simply one more gimmick to sell exercise equipment and health club memberships?

While some runners find that weight lifting or other forms of strength training do make a difference, many researchers concede that there is little conclusive evidence. The benefits are not easy to document, either on the track or in an exercise lab. It depends partly on your running event, partly on your ability, partly on how much you run. Most scientists concede that documented studies fail to demonstrate any benefit of weight lifting for young, male, elite runners—although they may for individuals in other categories. Studies at the University of Massachusetts in Amherst, for example, have shown strength gains of 10

As an aging runner, I know that strength training is as important to my health as to my ability to run fast in a 5-K.

to 15 percent among older runners who add weight training to their schedules. But Daniel Becque, Ph.D., who conducted the study, admits strength may be more important for sprinters than for distance runners. "For Olympic champion Haile Gebrselassie to suddenly start pumping iron would be fruitless," says Dr. Becque.

I've discussed the subject on several occasions with former Ball State researcher Dr. David Costill. He claims that strength training makes you a better weight lifter, but not necessarily a better runner. "There's no raw, objective data," he says, "that proves you will run faster if you weight train."

POWER UP ■

Still, weight training does have its share of running advocates. Lawrence E. Armstrong, Ph.D., a former colleague of Dr. Costill, believes that power training can help improve your stride length—one element that separates fast runners from slow ones. Dr. Armstrong currently is with the human performance laboratory at the University of Connecticut in Storrs. He did his graduate work at Ball State, where he collaborated with Dr. Costill on a study that attempted to measure the difference between sprinters and distance runners.

The sprinters were more muscular; the distance runners were more lean. Dr. Costill and Dr. Armstrong filmed the athletes during a maximum sprint. They noted that at maximum speed, the sprinters and distance runners had identical body angles: straight up. But they also found a revealing difference—stride lengths. At maximum velocity, the sprinters' stride lengths were longer than the distance runners', although stride frequencies were the same. Apparently, a longer stride is what permitted the sprinters to run faster for shorter distances. It gave them a special "kick."

"Because stride length, and not stride frequency, is paramount to speed production," Dr. Armstrong summarized in his report, "training should focus on the muscles which produce a long, powerful stride, namely the muscles of the hip, thigh, and lower leg." He noted that speedwork develops those muscles. He felt that the study supported those coaches who recommend power drills, such as uphill training and bounding, to improve leg strength, which consequently lengthens the stride. But he also suggested that weight lifting might add an "extra edge" and help to stabilize joints by strengthening the surrounding musculature.

> *"Too many runners look like vertical hyphens," claims Tom Brunick. We're skinny, with no upper-body mass.*

To increase the power output of the hip flexors, hip extensors, knee extensors, and ankle extensors, Dr. Armstrong recommends half squats, leg lunges, hip extensions, and heel raises. He warns that the transition to power training should be gradual to avoid ligament, muscle, or tendon damage.

Here are some weight-training exercises that can strengthen those parts of the body. For best results, lift 50 to 60 percent of the maximum weight you can lift in a set of 12 repetitions.

Half squat. Stand with your feet shoulder-width apart (or wider), with the weight of a barbell resting across your shoulders and behind your neck. Bend your knees and lower your body until the tops of your thighs are parallel to the floor. Dr. Armstrong recommends that the descent be constant, slow, and controlled. The barbell should remain stable—that is, with very little movement forward or rearward. After reaching the bottom position, begin your ascent, keeping the movement constant but rapid. Complete the movement with a forward hip roll. (Deep squats are not recommended because of an increased risk of injury.) This exercise strengthens four muscles: the quadriceps, hamstrings, gluteals, and erector spinae.

Heel raises. Again, stand with your feet shoulder-width apart, a barbell resting on your shoulders behind your neck. Use a support block $\frac{1}{2}$ to 1 inch high. Stand with the balls of your feet on the block and your heels on the ground, but otherwise in the same position as for the first exercise. Raise your heels off the ground so that all your weight is forward, on your toes. Your movement should be deliberate and controlled. Return to the starting position and repeat. Even without weights, this is a good stretching exercise. This exercise strengthens the gastrocnemius and soleus, the main muscles of the lower leg.

Hip extensions. This exercise is best performed using an exercise machine that features cables and pulleys, with a brace on the end of the cable in which you can position your calf. Stand straight, facing the wall or the machine, and hold onto the machine for support. Your legs should be shoulder width apart. Move the braced leg back to a 45-degree angle. Bend your support leg if necessary, but keep your braced leg straight. Return your leg against resistance to the starting position and repeat. Switch legs. With the exception of the quadriceps, this exercise strengthens the same muscles as half-squats.

These exercises surely will improve your leg power and maybe will make you a better sprinter. But would they make you a better distance runner?

The same question troubled me. Concerned by my poor strength performance one year during a fitness test at the Cooper Clinic in Dallas, I returned home and consulted Charles Wolf, director of a physical therapy department in northwestern Indiana. Dr. Cooper's test showed I had little power for the leg and knee extensions, even for my age group. But he was measuring pure power, the kind the makes you a better sprinter or weight lifter. Wolf duplicated the tests, but added one more—a leg endurance test that involved 30 repetitions rather than just four, as used in Dr. Cooper's test. On the 30th rep, I was kicking with almost the same power as on the first. I had endurance.

But what about strength? "As a distance runner, you don't need a lot of strength," admitted Wolf. "You just need a little strength at the right time." The "right time" is the moment that the leg pushes off the ground, propelling the runner forward. That particular action is a functional strength, and it's best trained by running. For distance runners, therefore, weight training may be best as a supplemental activity.

RUNNERS WHO BENEFIT MOST ■

Do you think your running would benefit from weight training? Certain individuals probably benefit more from strength training than others.

Ectomorphs. These are individuals considered to be of the slender physical type—"having a thin body build," my dictionary politely says—the ones Brunick describes as "vertical hyphens." Ectomorph is the opposite of endomorph, someone with more muscle and a heavier body build. You know who you are, you ectomorphs. I'm one of you. I'm effective as a runner because I weigh near 150 pounds. The most muscular part of my body is my legs. The front ranks of any distance race consist primarily of ectomorphs, who, as kids, were among the last picked for neighborhood football games. (The sport of 5-K racing might be called The Revenge of the Skinnies!) Many, if not most, of these front-runners probably need to do at least some weight lifting to maintain their strength and speed—as long as they can do it without significantly increasing their bulk or weight.

Women. One of the main differences between men and women is strength. It's a simple fact of genetics. Exercise scientists frequently cite this strength difference to explain why female athletes in all sports—golf, tennis, skiing—cannot compete on equal terms with their male counterparts. Thus, women probably can benefit more from strength training than men—as long as the extra strength does not equal extra weight, or what some beauty-conscious women might consider "ugly muscle." Because more and more females realize that they need strength, too (which can help prevent osteoporosis, to cite one reason), you see more of them in the weight rooms these days.

Masters. "Strength fades as we age," insisted Dr. Michael Pollock of the University of Florida. (Before his death, Dr. Pollock supervised one of the most comprehensive longitudinal studies on the effects of exercise on aging.) "As strength fades, so does speed." It's easily measurable in the laboratory. As we move through the ages, from 30 to 40 to 50 and onward, we lose strength faster than endurance. That's one reason why older runners have more success in ultramarathons (races beyond 26.2 miles) than in 1500-meter races against younger runners. "As you get older, you need to focus more and more on this (strength) aspect of your conditioning," said Dr. Pollock.

George Lesmes, Ph.D., director of the human performance laboratory at Northeastern Illinois University, notes that he has been able to increase the endurance of men 55 and over by offering them strength training for their legs. "They can stay up on the treadmill longer," says Dr. Lesmes, "and it's simply a matter of strength equaling improved endurance."

Given the above, the person most likely to improve running speed through strength training would be a skinny, female, masters runner. (As a skinny male masters runner, I fit two of the categories, which is one reason I now put more emphasis on strength training.)

Does the above mean that if you are a muscular young male, you need not worry about strength training? Not necessarily. More than likely, the benefits for you will be less, but that's no reason to shun the weight room. As you age (and we all do), the muscle you built while younger will continue to benefit you. In fact, the best time to build muscle mass and overall body fitness, whether you're male or female, is when you're young. Then, hang onto it!

GIVE STRENGTH A CHANCE ■

The rules are set: Muscle fiber cannot be created. Genetics determines how many muscles we have. Muscle fibers, however, can be thickened, an increase in size that is called hypertrophy. Exercise physiologist Dean Brittenham explains that lifting heavy loads (more weight, fewer repetitions) tends to build maximum strength and muscle size. Lifting less weight but with more repetitions develops greater muscle endurance, along with muscle definition.

But competitive runners are not interested in muscle size or muscle definition, the pumped-up look that you see on bodybuilders. Until Arnold Schwarzenegger shows that he is as adept at running fast 5-Ks as he is at making box-office hits, most runners will decline to follow his type of training.

Yet maybe we should give strength a chance. When Gabriel Mirkin, M.D., once wrote in *The Runner*, "There is no proof that (lifting) will in any way improve your times," a reader from New

Jersey replied in strong disagreement. "Dr. Mirkin may be correct for runners blessed with a fair amount of upper-body strength," he wrote. "But I had very little strength to begin with and have found (after 6 months of Nautilus training) that I can now run any race without the extreme fatigue I formerly felt in my shoulders and arms."

It's a good point, but it proves only that strength training benefited that particular runner. It may not benefit all of us. So how do you know if weight training is right for you? Let's consider the subject further.

FIGHTING UPPER-BODY FATIGUE ■

Masters runner Bob Schlau is one who believes that strength training can improve speed. He told me about his own experience for an article on strength training I was writing for *Runner's World* magazine. Schlau claimed that prior to 1980, his arms and shoulders always tired toward the end of a race (usually a marathon). His legs also started moving more slowly, so his pace fell off. "My upper body would just go dead," he told me. "I know it affected my times."

Hoping to improve his performances, Schlau began a strength-training program for his upper body. He developed a 3-day-a-week routine of weight work that included situps, stretching, and free weights. "All upper-body stuff," Schlau said. "Mostly curls and presses. I also take light weights and replicate the running motion with my arms."

Did it work? Soon after starting his strength routine, Schlau found he no longer had trouble with arm and shoulder fatigue. And it improved his 5-K and 10-K times as well. At age 42, he ran a 30:48 10-K. It is the contention of Dr. Becque, of course, that strength training is particularly important for masters like Schlau. "One of the first things you lose as you age is power," he says.

Yet one of the most successful masters runners claims he never weight trains. Norm Green, a minister from Wayne, Pennsylvania, won the 10,000 meters at both the 1987 and 1989 World Veterans Championships. His 10,000 time in the 1989 meet in Eugene, Oregon, at age 57, was a rather incredible 33:00. I say incredible because I got a good look at him as he lapped me. Green is a naturally powerful, well-muscled runner. Yet he claimed to rely only on the basics. He just ran hard in every workout and rarely let his pace lag slower than 6 minutes per mile.

Would Norm Green benefit from strength training? The evidence suggests that Green ran fast enough without benefit of pumping iron. Has Bob Schlau benefited from strength training? It's possible that his fast 10-K times come from other aspects of his training, but I'm not about to suggest that Schlau walk away from the weight room. And I'm not asking Green to join Schlau. They're individuals. Each benefits from different types of training.

SEEKING ALL-AROUND FITNESS ■

To develop an all-around fitness program, Dr. Pollock suggested a minimum of 2 days a week of resistance training. Each session should last approximately 20 minutes and include 8 to 12 repeats on each of the major muscles of the body: legs, hips, trunk, back, arms, and shoulders. This is in addition to a general aerobic program (such as running) that also should include warmup, stretching, and cooldown. "It's important to exercise all major muscle areas of the body," said Dr. Pollock. "Aerobics is good for legs and heart and body composition, but it won't strengthen

CORRECTING IMBALANCES

To both correct and prevent muscle imbalances, Julie Isphording, a competitor for the United States in the 1984 Olympic Games, recommends strength training twice a week for 20 minutes, both lower and upper body, after running rather than before. "Running must remain your priority," says Isphording. "The best time to strength train is after your run, usually on an easy day."

For your lower body, specifically the muscles around the knees, Isphording recommends leg extensions, either on a machine or where you place a weight on your ankle and slowly straighten your leg. Lunges also are good for strengthening the trunk. "With your shoulders back, take a lunging step forward, dropping your back leg toward the floor, then lifting up. Use hand weights to increase the stress," Isphording instructs. (Be sure your front knee doesn't extend over your foot.) To strengthen your abductors and adductors, do side lifts (raising the weighted leg sideways). Hamstrings can be best exercised using machines.

Crunches remain a good stomach-strengthening exercise. For your arms and shoulders, use machines, free weights, or dumbbells, which can be swung to simulate the running motion. In all weight-lifting exercises, concentrate on form. "Ask a strength trainer for help if you don't know how to do the exercise," cautions Isphording.

---

muscles or maintain their strength, so a well-rounded program is very necessary."

Keep in mind that Dr. Pollock was more interested in developing fitness, not speed. Someone hoping to use strength training to run fast might like to try my own routine. Despite relatively low marks in the strength test at the Cooper Clinic, I have always incorporated weight training into my program. And I find it helps.

In 1958, I competed in the National AAU 30-K Championships in York, Pennsylvania, and placed third. The main sponsor was the York Barbell Company, whose president, Bob Hoffman, was an avid fitness promoter. My prize was a pair of barbells.

For several years, I used the barbells on my back porch. This was during a period when I was a contender in every race I ran. (I placed fifth in the 1960 Olympic Trials in the 3000-meter steeplechase.) Untutored, I utilized the three Olympic lifts used in weight-lifting competition: three attempts at each lift to see how much iron I could throw over my head. (Don't even ask!) I also worked out occasionally in the weight room at the University of Chicago. That was rather unusual for a distance runner in those days, but at that time, I considered pumping iron as much a form of play as of serious training.

Eventually, I donated my York barbells to Mount Carmel High School in Chicago, where I coached for several years in the mid-1960s. I drifted away from weight lifting for a decade as I took a hiatus from elite competition, then bought a set of weights for my son. When he went to college, I appropriated them.

In the mid-1970s, I became more and more involved in masters competition. I met Bill Reynolds, an Olympic lifting candidate who wrote *The Complete Weight Training Book*. We were both speakers at a clinic in California sponsored by *Runner's World* magazine. Reynolds was cautious about promising benefits for distance runners, but nevertheless, he taught five basic lifts.

Aerobics is great for the legs and heart and body composition, but it won't strengthen muscles or maintain their strength, so a well-rounded program is very necessary.

Clean and press. This is one of the Olympic lifts. Stand with your feet spread about shoulder-width. Reach down, grasp the bar, and bring it overhead in one continuous movement. Return the bar to the floor and repeat.

Bent-over row. With your knees slightly bent to prevent

stress on your back, reach down and grasp the bar with your palms facing down. Lift the bar to your chest without rising from the bent position. Return the bar to the floor and repeat.

Upright row. Again, with your palms down, bring the bar-

TIPS FOR THE WEIGHT ROOM

Here are some things to keep in mind as you head to the weight room.

Running remains your best strength exercise. Exercise is very specific. To best develop your running muscles, you need to run—and run fast. Hill running is most favored by many runners interested in building strength. Weight lifting and other forms of strength training are important mainly as supplemental activities.

Don't compete with other lifters. The worst thing is to walk into a weight room and try to lift the same loads as weight-trained athletes around you. You wouldn't expect a 230-pound hunk to beat you in a 5-K, so don't expect to outperform him in his sport. And if you're a male, don't be intimidated if that female on the next machine is lifting heavier weights than you just did. She may not be as interested in running as you are.

Balance the benefits of free weights versus machines. Free weights do a better job of exercising the total body because they stress multiple muscles in a single lift. Machines, on the other hand, isolate muscle groups. If you choose to use free weights, be careful. Since they're not connected to a frame and pulleys, they can be dangerous if you're not accustomed to using them. Some lifts—such as squats and half-squats—require proper lifting form to avoid injury risk, so seek out qualified instruction. The late Dr. Michael Pollock of the University of Florida recommended exercise machines for masters because of safety. "As we age, we have balance problems," Dr. Pollock advised. "You're less likely to get hurt using a machine."

Avoid heavy weights. If you're interested in improving performance, as opposed to physique, stay away from lifting heavy weights. They may be hard on the lower joints, or they may cause you to bulk up. Excessive upper-body weight is dead weight in a 5-K Watch your bathroom scale. If your weight-lifting routine causes you to gain bulk, try using less weight with more repetitions.

bell to an upright position so that you are standing straight, with the bar resting against the fronts of your thighs. Letting your elbows go out to the sides, raise the bar to chest height, keeping it close to your body. Repeat.

Don't try to peak as a weight lifter. You'll find that strength coaches at health clubs often advise you to fatigue each muscle to its maximum, increasing weights and varying reps as you improve in strength. This might be on-target for building muscles and bulk, but as a runner, that is not your goal. Over a period of time, develop a strength workout that you can do comfortably and consistently. Stay with it. Don't feel you need to do more.

Vary your lifting. The hard/easy principle works in lifting as well as in running. Lifters typically work one group of muscles one day, then rest those muscles the next day while they exercise a different group. If you're lifting on a daily basis, you may want to do the same.

Lift on your easy days. Coming in from a grinding interval workout and heading for the weight room is not a good idea. Save your lifting for those days when you run at an easier pace. Even after your easy run, rest up a bit before hitting the weights. Exercise physiologist Dean Brittenham suggests doing your strength training at a different time of day from when you run. That way, you'll get more out of each workout.

Lift most during the off-season. Not every runner has an off-season, but the best time of year for strength training is when you are not training hard or racing often. For those of us in the North, that's usually in the winter; for those in the hot and humid South, it may be summer.

Don't overlook the value of calisthenics. Situps, pushups, and pullups remain effective means of developing and maintaining strength. You don't need to buy a high-tech machine or join a glitzy health club. You can include calisthenics as part of your regular stretching routine.

Be your own person. Eventually, each runner should develop a strength routine specific to his own needs. "Whether or not strength training makes you a faster runner," says former Ball State researcher Dr. David Costill, "it makes you a fitter individual."

Curl. This is a basic lift for any weight-training routine. Assume the same position as for the upright row, with the barbell resting against the fronts of your thighs. This time, though, your palms should be facing up instead of down. With your elbows close to your body, lift the bar to chest height. Repeat.

Military press. Perhaps the most basic lift. In the upright position, with your palms down, bring the bar to shoulder height. Raise the bar overhead, fully extending your arms, and repeat.

Following Reynolds's advice, I did these routines with low weights and high repetitions. I stretched between sets of 10 and lifted only every other day—usually during the off-season, when I had no important races. Although I've modified my strength-training routine in recent years, I continue to use these lifts from time to time.

MACHINE DISCIPLINE ■

At one time, my wife, Rose, played tennis at a local health club, so we had a family membership. When the club added a Nautilus center, I moved some of my training there. While Rose was snapping backhands, I pumped iron.

From visits to that tennis club and other fitness centers, I discovered that the first time you appear and ask the attendant (who may or may not know anything about running) what machines to use, he will try to convince you to use all of them, and regularly. That was part of the Nautilus pitch back then, and it still is to a lesser degree. I still recommend selectivity. Frank Shorter once told me he worked only on his upper body, and I did the same. My favorite was the pullover machine, where I sat on a bench and pulled down a bar from overhead to a position in front of me. I liked it because it did a good job of approximating the double-pole motion essential to good cross-country skiing, another sport I enjoy.

In addition to the pullover machine, I worked on the torso, arm, rowing, lateral raise, and overhead press machines. Walk into any fitness center, and the attendant can guide you to these machines or to others designed to improve upper-body strength.

Earlier, I experimented with leg extensions and leg curls, but I found that my knees ached so much the following day that I could hardly run. (For this reason, it's usually a good idea to reserve your strength-training sessions for after you run or on easy running days.) Lighter weights and a more gradual buildup also might have alleviated my sore-knees problem.

One distinct advantage of a machine is that you can focus on a specific muscle group and avoid stressing others. This is important when recovering from injuries. Unless you have some specific muscle imbalance, or you have a strength coach who knows something about running supervising your weight training, you might want to leave your lower body alone. You definitely don't want to develop antagonistic muscles that can interfere with your running stride.

While it's important to have strong quadriceps muscles to get you through the last few miles of a marathon, bulky quads can be a hindrance. If you don't believe me, check the quads on cyclists who compete in the Tour de France. Their quads often are so large, they almost overlap their kneecaps. These athletes are very good at what they do—riding a bike very fast for endless hours—but running can be very painful for them.

Cross-training that includes strength training and other aerobic activities also can be a mixed blessing. Despite their overall athletic ability, few triathletes have great success in running-only races. No Ironman winner has had equal success in any major marathon, despite the considerably higher prizes offered in marathons. For a period of several years, I suffered what I called a "midlife triathlon crisis." As a break from running competition, I concentrated some of my energy on triathlons and was good enough one year to qualify for the Ironman (although I did not compete in that prestigious event). While training for three sports, I discovered that the faster I was able to ride a bicycle, the slower I was able to run. For every minute I took off my bike-leg time, I gained a minute on my running-leg time.

For this reason, I advise runners to be cautious about over-doing cross-training. (Notice I used the word "overdoing.") Despite my own disclaimers, I have begun to do more lap swimming as an alternate fitness activity. As I age, I discover I find it increasingly difficult to run as many miles as I once did. I need more rest days. Yet I enjoy the work break that exercise gives me. I spend too much time in front of a computer in my home office. Some days, if I don't get out to run, I don't get out of the house. Recently, I joined The Lodge & Club in Ponte Vedra Beach, Florida, where we now have a second home, so that I can use its pool. I swim both to strengthen my upper body and to burn calories, whether or not it makes me a better runner. I always thought lap swimming had to be the world's most boring activity, but, surprisingly, I now find that I enjoy it.

Most of my cross-training and strength training is intuitive; very little is scientific. I do it as much because I enjoy the discipline as from any knowledge that it will improve (or maintain) my speed. I feel that extra strength does equal extra speed, but I can't prove it to you. Nevertheless, it's a good enough reason to keep me pumping iron. ■

THE POLISHING TOUCH

BE YOUR OWN BEST COACH

One of the secrets of becoming a faster runner is learning not merely how to train but also when to train—in other words, putting it all together. In 1988, Lynn Jennings proved herself as one of the world's best runners. Self-coached, she placed sixth at the Olympic Games in Korea—no small accomplishment. But as Jennings herself admitted, "I had stalled out." She wanted to run faster.

"My goal," said Jennings, "wasn't just to be the best American runner; I wanted to be the best in the world." To achieve that goal, she began training the following April under the direction of John Babington, an attorney who coached for the Liberty Athletic Club in Cambridge, Massachusetts.

The combination clicked. In January 1990, Jennings set a world indoor record for the 5000 meters at the Dartmouth Relays. In February, she broke the American record for the 3000, winning the national Track-and-Field Championships. In March, she ran 31:06 for an American road record at the Red Lobster 10-K

Classic. And later that month, in Aix-les-Bains, France, she became the first American woman in 15 years to win the World Cross-Country Championships.

As Jennings already had demonstrated, she knew how to train. She also knew her own physiological strengths and weaknesses, having been tested frequently by expert scientists as a member of Athletics West, the Nike-sponsored club. What Babington offered to Jennings was something that all runners need: organization, an objective look at her abilities, and advice on setting goals and peaking for important contests.

"One thing we did at the outset," recalls Babington, "was that we looked at what was her stable and comfortable level of training. It was a ballpark amount of mileage that involved a carefully chosen intensity. We asked ourselves, what components can we upgrade without exhausting her? What additional training margin could she benefit from?

"There's a general principle that says if you want to get better, don't bite off more than you can chew. All changes should be gradual, not abrupt. Our starting point was based on Lynn's lifestyle and time constraints. We asked ourselves, what one or two things can we change, or upgrade, to make her a better runner?"

There's a general principle that says all changes should be gradual, not abrupt.

Jennings and coach Babington observed that her weekly mileage had been relatively low for a world-class runner, between 50 and 60 miles. They decided to push into the 70s. Jennings benefited from this small shift in her training. "That was one of the main differences between Lynn in 1988 and Lynn in 1990," Babington says.

Training adjustments often are achieved most easily with a coach riding shotgun. The instinct of most runners when they want to improve is to do more, but in some instances, they may be better off doing less. Not every runner is like Jennings, who found she needed to do more to develop an edge. As head of the New York Road Runners Club's coaching program, Bob Glover supervises 20 coaches, who in turn supervise hundreds of runners. "At the beginner level," says Glover, "people benefit from being enrolled in a fitness program, because they tend to do too much too soon. For individuals making the transition into racing, a coach can encourage them. The faster a runner gets, the less there is to push. At the elite level, runners have so much drive they don't need a coach pushing them; they need a coach holding them back."

Coach Jim Huff of Detroit's Motor City Striders stresses the importance of planning. "You need to look at your training program, determine specific goals, and develop a program that will help you accomplish those goals, as long as they are realistic. Unfortunately, a lot of runners don't have the basic know-how to progress toward a goal."

THE COACH APPROACH ■

One way you can better plan your training is to obtain a coach— a Babington, Glover, or Huff—who can apply the generally accepted principles of training outlined in this book to your goals. Unfortunately, most runners don't have a coach and never will. I have mostly been self-coached for more than 3 decades. This was not entirely from self-choice. There simply was no knowledgeable coach nearby who I felt could assist me with my training.

Being self-coached, I've found that you don't always need a coach, but you do need to know coaching principles. Just as there are sound physiological principles involving aerobic and anaerobic training that can help you maximize performance, there also are sound coaching and planning principles that can help you succeed. In fact, the latter may be more important than the former.

Putting together your own coaching program just takes a

little planning and the knowledge that you have gained from this book. Here are some suggestions that a good coach might offer you.

Plan ahead. Exercise physiologist Dr. Edmund Burke once said, "Good order is the foundation of all good things."

When coach Babington sought improvement for Jennings, their first action was to sit down and plan her long-range training. I do the same for myself. Flying home from the 1979 World Veterans Championships in Germany, I planned my training for the 18 months leading up to the next world meet. That was the first step to the gold medal I won in 1981.

Each year, I review the previous year's results and plan ahead, determining what races to peak for—even determining whether I want to peak. Some years, I focus attention on short track races; other years, I shift to the roads. I may plan to take a year off, where I run mainly for fun. But it's a conscious decision. You can't get where you're going without a road map.

Look behind. You also can't get where you're going unless you know where you've been. Record your training on a daily basis. In my office, I have a set of loose-leaf notebooks dating back to 1963, when I was fortunate to have the attention of coach Fred Wilt. He asked me to record daily workouts on $5\frac{1}{2}$- $\times$ $8\frac{1}{2}$-inch diary sheets, which he provided. Later, I developed my own training diary sheet, which I had printed in large numbers for minimal cost.

I record items such as the date, time, location, surface and conditions, and distance, along with my weight. I also record what I did to warm up and cool down, and any comments concerning the actual run. There's space to record an optional second workout and boxes for race split times. (It's also a good idea to include space to jot down notes on your diet.) I also developed different diary formats for my cross-country ski workouts and for my high school team, as well as an online diary.

Various running diaries can be purchased at bookstores. Or you can even record your miles on a simple calendar.

There are several reasons for keeping a diary. One, it provides motivation, the same way reporting your workouts to a coach would be motivational. Two, it allows you to learn from your successes and failures. If you ran well, what type of training was responsible for your success? If you ran poorly or were injured, what training error was responsible?

Running diaries are important equipment, almost as important as running shoes.

Define your goal. What do you want to accomplish with your running? Is it continued fitness and the enjoyment of staying in shape? If so, your training plan will differ from one designed to maximize your performance and to run fast times. Most runners choose goals that are event-oriented. They desire to run well in a specific event—a local race, a national championship. Event-oriented goals are helpful because they allow you to tie your training to specific dates.

But coach Mary Reed of the Atlanta Track Club warns against choosing too many goals. "A person who wants to simultaneously run a sub-25 5-K and break 4 hours for the marathon is liable to fail at both goals because they are so diverse." Reed suggests concentrating on one or the other to allow more precise planning. "Pick one goal this season, then go after the other the next," she says.

Be realistic. If your fastest 10-K time after several years of serious training is 45 minutes, you hardly should expect to break 30 minutes and qualify for the Olympic team within a year. Set your goals and plan your training conservatively. If you exceed your hopes, you can always aim slightly higher.

Bruce Tulluh, formerly one of Great Britain's fastest 5000-meter runners, writes in *Running*, "When building your own schedule, the first thing to decide is the volume of training

A COACH FOR MANY DIFFERENT REASONS

Most runners are self-coached, but sometimes, they can improve their ability to run fast by seeking the advice of a coach. Here are 10 services that a coach can provide for a runner seeking improvement.

Motivation. Getting started is important for beginners; keeping going is a necessity for even experienced runners. A good coach can provide the necessary jump-start in the first case and continuous pushing in the latter. Reporting on a regular basis to a coach or mentor—even only once a week or by e-mail or phone—can provide an important keystone to any training plan.

System. "Good coaches are like chefs," claims Gary Goettelmann, who coaches a club connected to Ryan's Sports Shop, a store he owns in Santa Clara, California. "They have a methodology and a system." Often, the details in any system are secondary to its mere existence.

Planning. "Proper planning can help sharpen a person's goals," says Atlanta's Mary Reed. A coach can help pick goals that are realistic and design training plans to achieve those goals, both long- and short-term.

Advice. Once a runner has been working with a coach for a long time, the training plan becomes obvious. One key role for coaches advising elite athletes is picking races, particularly knowing when to say no in this era of run for the money. But average runners need similar help to avoid overracing.

Injury prevention. A coach who carefully monitors an athlete's progress can recognize when the athlete begins to show signs of the fatigue from overtraining that often precede any injury. According to John Babington, "A coach's most important role may be preventing

which you can handle, both in total and in the number of good sessions a week. The training load you undertake must always be related to what you have been doing, not what you think you ought to do."

Don't get trapped. Historian Max Lerner once warned that we should learn from history but not be trapped by it. He was overtraining, which leads to injury, which puts you out of commission."

Plateau busting. Sooner or later, all runners reach the point at which they fail to improve. How to get off a plateau is a common problem. A good coach can suggest different types of training that may allow the plateaued runner to climb upward to a new level of performance.

Checklist. A good coach keeps a runner on course by making sure the athlete follows the system and plan. According to coach David Martin, Ph.D., "A coach remembers where the athlete is heading. He will have a checklist of what's important about different phases of the training plan. This frees the athlete to concentrate on the actual training itself."

Feedback. Most runners have a hard time evaluating their own training. Keeping a diary helps, but it's no substitute for a good coach. "A coach is an unbiased observer," says Lynn Jennings. "A coach can look at a workload and evaluate it more objectively than the athlete."

Cheerleader. Runners' muscles run on glycogen, but their minds often run on praise. They need encouragement. A coach can offer a shoulder to cry on after a bad race or a pat on the back after a good race. Exercise physiologist Dr. Jack Daniels, coach at State University of New York at Cortland, once said, "The primary reason to have a coach is to have somebody who can look at you and say, 'Man, you're lookin' good today.'"

Fun. A coach can make training fun by offering a variety of workouts and running routes. The coaching environment offers an opportunity to interact with other runners working with same coach. For those who run for enjoyment, this may be the best reason to hire a coach.

---

thinking of global issues such as war, but the advice is apropos for running, too. One of the dangers of having records for several decades of training on your shelves is believing that what worked once may work again. Some of my best training years were 1956, 1964, 1972, 1980, and 1991. I made breakthroughs or won championships in each of those years because of major shifts in my approach to training—sometimes more miles, sometimes more quality—but I could no more duplicate those workouts or workout patterns than I could fly to the moon. I approached my training differently in each of those bonanza years, and I will continue to do so in the future.

Our bodies change. Our situations change. Our motivations change. We age. Everything is different. A particular danger is for someone who starts running again after a slack period of a dozen or more years to think he can train like he did in high school. There are a lot of other things you did in high school that you wouldn't—or shouldn't—do again. Be wise.

> *There are a lot of other things you did in high school that you wouldn't— or shouldn't— do again.*

Make smart changes. Coach Babington suggested only one small adaptation to Jennings: Increase mileage. She added only 10 to 20 miles to her weekly total. Both coach and athlete realized that if she made too radical a shift in her training routine, they risked undoing all her previous gains.

At one point in my career, I tried to increase the number of quarters in my interval workouts (going from 10 to 20) and to decrease the times (going from 70 seconds to 60). Before I could reach my goal of 20 60-second 400s, I crashed. Years later, I reflected on this training mistake with Frank McBride, who was coaching me at the time. "We violated at least two of Gerschler's five training principles," he admitted. (See chapter 8 for more about German coach Waldermar Gerschler and his theories on interval training.)

That's the kind of mistake you make only once if you're an intelligent runner. If you're superintelligent, you'll avoid making it even once. In plotting your training progression, concentrate on improving one area at a time—and go about it gingerly.

Get out of the rut. Runners often get stuck on plateaus and fail to improve because they fail to change their training. Distance running will help you run faster; so will speedwork. But if you're stuck on one type of training to the complete exclusion of all others, you probably will fail to maximize your performance. One way to improve is to do something different, almost regardless of what that something is.

Be innovative. Change training sites. Join a different health club. Find a coach. Shift sports. If you're a track runner, you might benefit from doing some road running. Road racers probably should move to the track—or try cross-country. If your focus is marathons, try some 5-Ks; if your focus is 5-Ks, try a marathon.

At various times in my career, I've shifted more of my competitive focus to cross-country skiing or triathlons just to break the routine. There are many types of distance running, including orienteering (running with compass and map) and biathlons (shooting and skiing). In recent years, trail races have become quite popular, with many of the participants focused on competing in picturesque—but challenging—surroundings, instead of some time on a stopwatch. If you move from one discipline to another, it will provide new goals, if nothing else.

Program some rest. The hard/easy training pioneered by the late Bill Bowerman of the University of Oregon works well. By taking an easy day or two, runners can come back on their hard days and run that much harder. As I age, I find I need to pay much more attention to this approach. Former Ball State researcher Dr. David Costill claims that muscle changes occur on the rest day following a hard training session, rather than on the hard day. If you work hard day after day, you eventually tear down muscle.

During the summer of 1984, I had a conversation with British ace Sebastian Coe about a month before he won the 1500 meters and placed second in the 800 meters at the Olympic Games in Los Angeles. Coe was then 27; he had just torn through a workout of 20 × 200 meters, averaging 27 seconds, resting only 25 to 45 seconds between each. He ran his final one in 22.5, a time good enough to win at least most high school 200 races. It was a mind-boggling workout, but afterward, Coe commented that several years earlier, when he was 20 or 21, he could do quality sessions such as that 4 or 5 days in a row. "Now that I'm older, I need more rest," he said, straight-faced.

"Most athletes will find that two hard sessions and one race per week is as much as they can take, with the other days being easy running for recuperation," says Tulluh.

Respect your environment. If you wake up in the morning and find the street in front of your house covered with a sheet of ice from a freezing rain, that's probably not the day to head to the track for a workout of repeat quarters—unless that track is indoors. Obviously, everybody needs to take note of the weather for specific workouts. But the best way to prepare for weather is to do so well in advance, when you plan your schedule.

Living in the Midwest, I know that winter offers a good period for long aerobic runs, since I can run slowly while wearing several layers of clothes and picking my way across icy patches or puddles in the road. Spring is a good time for fast anaerobic runs, since the footing is good and the weather's still cool. Summer is a time for repetition running, since I can pause between fast bursts to cool down or even take a drink. But this scenario wouldn't necessarily hold true for a runner in Arizona or Alaska. And now that I've acquired a second home in Ponte Vedra Beach, Florida, near Jacksonville, I've started to rethink my training to take advantage of the warmer winter weather plus the availability of a smooth and flat beach for training sessions. In planning your training, you have to be aware of the environment in which you run.

Progress carefully toward your goal. To improve with each performance, you need to carefully and progressively adapt your training. This is the principle of overload, whose historic innovator, the ancient Greek wrestler Milo, got stronger each day by lifting onto his shoulders a calf that eventually became a bull.

When we increase our mileage on a daily or weekly basis, we essentially are doing the same thing.

But a lot of, well, bull is offered to runners about how they should progress. Some theories say to increase mileage by 10 percent a week or to run interval quarters a second faster each week. I don't believe in formulas. As you progress, make certain that you do so conservatively. But do progress.

Put it in writing. One way to motivate yourself is visually, with either a chart or a poster on your wall. If your goal is a specific race time, maybe you should pass those numbers every day when you go out to train.

I'm a big believer in visual aids. One year, I designed my schedule for the season by drawing a calendar with 8 months of dates. On it, I outlined in red my scheduled

In planning your training, you have to be aware of the environment in which you run.

mileage for each week and the race dates where I wanted to hit my peak. The calendar hung on the wall in my basement, where I do my stretching and weight training. I passed that chart every day when I left to run. I scribbled mileage and times on it, too, in addition to recording them in my diary. That let me know whether I was still on schedule with my planned training.

I don't do that every year, but sometimes, having a visual reminder of your goals and the training needed to attain them can help motivate you. Many runners use the training schedules for marathons and other distances on my Web site. A number of these runners have told me how they download the schedules and post them where they can see them regularly.

Review regularly. By reviewing my plans from time to time, I discover whether my original planning was overly optimistic. If it's April and my longest run over the past 3 months was 12 miles, but I plotted 18 miles for that date, I realize I may need to take a more realistic look at my plans and my goals. It may be time to return to the first tip: Plan ahead. ∎

DETRAINING AND RETRAINING

THE BEST WAY TO GET BACK IN SHAPE

Not everybody runs at the same level year after year after year. We move from peaks to valleys, gearing up for a road race and gearing down when other interests take precedence. Sometimes, we become injured. Sometimes, we become bored. Sometimes, we quit running (or run less) rather than fight the winds of winter or the dog days of summer. Sometimes, we switch sports, shifting into skiing or swimming or cycling, activities that keep us fit but do little to help us run fast. When we move back to the 5-K or marathon, we sometimes encounter troubles.

If it has been a while since you last ran (not to mention raced), or if you eased off your training to a maintenance level and you want to get back in shape, here is both how to do it and how not to do it.

GETTING BACK ON TRACK ■

Runners stay sharp mentally by reevaluating goals and accepting new challenges. We add miles to finish a marathon; we add speed to run a 5-K. That keeps us motivated. But even though you already possess a strong aerobic base, you can't make a major training shift without careful thought. When increasing intensity (or mileage), you first need to move very slowly.

What happens to the body when we move back to a level of fitness to compete in races and set PRs? The mind remembers those quarters run on the track that are so vital for peak performance, but maybe the body isn't ready for that level of stress. As mentioned in chapter 14, past training diaries can be traps as well as assets in planning your first steps to coming back to that level of performance.

When increasing intensity or mileage, you first need to move very slowly.

Complicating matters are the effects of aging: It is easier to resume fast training in your twenties or thirties than in your forties and fifties. And for those beyond 60, some scientists suggest that walking may be all the aerobic exercise we need. Of course, another factor is how long you have been away from running.

Also, use cross-training carefully. Carl Foster, Ph.D., director of cardiac rehabilitation and exercise training at Sinai-Samaritan Medical Center in Milwaukee, warns against overconfidence bred from this important training tool. "Staying active in other sports is a two-edged sword," he says. "Your cardiac output may be high if you bike or swim or ski, but your muscles and joints may not be ready for the different stresses in running. If you're in good general shape, it's too easy to overdo it. Then you're sore and creaky, and you can beat yourself up orthopedically."

The same is true after any change in goals.

Scientists now can describe the effects of detraining, or how quickly we go out of shape. At the University of Texas at Austin, Dr. Edward Coyle convinced a group of highly trained runners (who ran 80 miles a week) and cyclists (who rode 250 miles a week) to quit training.

Their measured oxygen uptake scores declined rapidly at first, then less so. The best trained, those who had worked hardest to get in shape, lost the most. Those less trained had less to lose. Dr. Coyle determined that athletes lost half of their aerobic fitness within 12 to 21 days, then half of their remaining fitness level within the next 12- to 21-day period, and so on. After 3 months, all were detrained.

Scientists find it more difficult to measure retraining, or how long it takes to get back in shape. "There's very little data," conceded the late Dr. Michael Pollock of the University of Florida. Nevertheless, scientists can make some educated guesses.

Dr. Coyle suggests that for every week lost, it takes 2 weeks to regain the original level of fitness. Former Ball State researcher Dr. David Costill estimates that you can regain aerobic fitness within 4 to 8 weeks. "Strength changes take longer," he claims.

Strength, of course, equals speed. It will take you longer to regain your ability to run fast than your ability to run far.

This is why layoffs trouble many runners. As a high school coach, I was asked by one of my students how much she lost by taking off the week between Christmas and the New Year. Citing Dr. Coyle, I told her that she would need 2 weeks to get back to where she was previously.

Most scientists believe that people with previous conditioning can regain their speed sooner than people starting from scratch. In other words, a born-again runner has an advantage over one who is just starting. "The muscles may have some memory," muses Dr. Costill, "or maybe we're smarter with our training the second time." Dr. Costill's colleague William Fink adds, "A lot depends on how far you've gotten out of shape. There comes a point where you've lost everything, when starting over means truly starting from scratch."

REGAINING PAST PEAKS ■

The very best athletes find it most difficult to regain past peaks. When you're at the elite level, improvements of a few seconds require Herculean efforts involving months, maybe years, of hard training. At that level, you can't afford time off; it's too difficult to reclimb the mountain. Alberto Salazar was America's top marathoner between the 1980 and 1984 Olympics, setting records at the Boston and New York City Marathons and running 10-K times well under 28 minutes. In 1990, Salazar attempted a comeback, which he abandoned when he was unable to break 29 minutes. Salazar remained in excellent physical shape; he simply lost his speed.

In Dr. Coyle's detraining studies, he identified one reason for the immediate fitness decline—loss of blood volume. During the first 12 to 21 days away from training, you lose as much as a half-quart (500 milliliters) of blood. "Previously, researchers thought detraining was because of deterioration of the heart. Actually, the heart had less blood to pump to the muscles," states Dr. Coyle.

When you retrain, you regain that lost blood volume. It's a natural form of blood-doping. Not only can you transport oxygen to the muscles more efficiently again, but you also have more fluid available for sweating, which helps cool your body. For this reason, you are better off resuming training during

When you're at the elite level, improvements of a few seconds require Herculean efforts involving months, maybe years, of hard training.

the cool days of spring rather than waiting for summer, when your body may not be acclimatized to the heat. Dr. Coyle says runners can regain plasma blood volume within a week, although reproduction of red blood cells takes longer.

Not all training benefits vanish during long layoffs. Fast-twitch muscles hold some of their endurance. Muscle capillaries, which increase by 40 to 50 percent during training, remain and retain their ability to eliminate the waste products of exercise such as lactic acid.

But not all systems of the body detrain or retrain equally. Your skeletal system, for instance, may not accept the strain of training at your previous level, particularly as you age. Remember, a runner who loses 6 years of training must also cope with 6 years of normal aging.

TRAIN SMARTER ■

Dr. Kenneth Sparks, director of clinical program development for St. Vincent Charity Hospital in Cleveland and member of a world-record 2-mile relay team in his twenties, resumed hard training as he approached age 40. He returned to a fast 4:16 mile and 2:39:00 marathon, but he also needed surgery after injuring an Achilles tendon. "If you've been a competitor in the past, you're used to training on the edge," says Dr. Sparks. "This may be all right when you're young, when you heal rapidly. As you age, you need to train smarter and be more in tune with your body. Every time you go out to run, it could be your last workout, because of an injury."

Runners who return inevitably experience sore muscles, but not because of lactic acid, which is often identified as a culprit. According to Frederick C. Hagerman of Ohio University's department of zoological and biomedical sciences, your body can rapidly remetabolize the lactic acid that pools in your muscles during hard exercise. More of a problem is caused by different motor patterns.

Dr. Costill agrees. "You're not used to coordinating the new activity," he explains. "After you've practiced it several times, your muscles discover the right motor patterns, and you won't get sore."

For this reason, a born-again runner should not face muscles as sore as when he first learned to run, assuming he is conservative in his retraining. According to James D. Richardson of Miami-Dade Community College's physical education department, "Most muscle soreness is temporary and apparently has no negative, long-term effect."

Retraining for the 5-K need not be that difficult. And it is certainly easier than starting to run for the first time. Remember the fun it once was to run fast? Remember the good feeling of wind in your hair? If you are returning to short-distance events after being away for whatever reason, the following tips may make your journey back more pleasant.

Have a goal in mind. A goal may be as simple as going out to do your first run. Ask yourself why you want to run again. To get in shape? To improve your previous times? To compete in a particular race? Plan your training well ahead so as to achieve that goal.

Consider how long you've been gone. Depending upon your time away from fast training, you will have an easy or hard time coming back. Expect to spend at least 2 days getting back in shape for every day lost.

Forget the past. Workouts done years ago bear no relevance to what you can do today—and can be a cause of injury if you try to duplicate them without your past level of fitness. Once you regain your base fitness, you can ask yourself whether you want

FOR MARATHONERS ONLY

For marathoners who are switching events—downsizing, so to speak—the rules are somewhat different. You're already in great shape. You simply have to refocus your training if you want to improve your speed and compete in races such as the 5-K. Here are some tips to help you in your search for speed.

Shorten your long runs. Typically, runners in marathon training do a weekly long, easy run, often on Sunday mornings. They usually run distances up to 20 miles and beyond, which can take several hours. Olympic marathoner Benji Durden, who now coaches runners of various abilities in Boulder, Colorado, suggests placing a cap of 2 hours on Sunday training, keeping the mileage down to 15 or less. "Along with that cap comes an increase in tempo," Durden advises. "People need to pick up the pace in their long runs."

Cut your weekly mileage. The more miles you run each week, the slower those miles must be. By cutting mileage, you permit yourself to train at a faster tempo. You can run fresh and run fast. There are two ways to cut mileage: One is to cut the distance of each daily run; the other is to plan more rest days.

Race at shorter distances. "Marathoners tend to run a lot of 5-K races," says Durden. "If your goal race is that distance, you need to compete at still shorter distances." Participating in 5-K races will help improve your speed. Also, consider a move to the track to run 1500- and

to (or can) resume old training patterns, including speedwork.

Decide if you can do it better this time. In your previous life as a runner, did you make mistakes that can be avoided this time? Reevaluate your entire approach to training. Don't get trapped in old training habits that maybe didn't produce the best results.

Consider your age. Runners in their twenties can head back to the track after layoffs as though they never took any time off. It becomes progressively more difficult to regain lost speed once into your thirties, forties, fifties, and beyond. But it's not impos-

800-meter races. Even if those distances are beneath your ability level, training for them can help improve your speed.

Move down in distance gingerly. If you suddenly switch to fast races on the track, you raise the risk of injury. Remember, your body is not accustomed to sudden bursts of speed. So be cautious in both your training and your racing at these new, relatively fast paces.

Shift the focus of your training. Instead of doing speed training 1 day a week and tempo training another, shift to 2 speed days. When marathoners do interval training, they often do long repeats, up to 1 mile. For shorter races, you need to run some shorter repeats, such as 200 and 400 meters.

Reintroduce yourself to the track. To get yourself into the mood for running fast, hang out where the sprinters train: on the track. You don't need to use starting blocks, but working out where you can accurately monitor your speed with a stopwatch over precisely measured distances can reintroduce you to the feel of running fast.

Set realistic goals. Don't believe computer charts that suggest if you ran your last marathon in under 4 hours, you can do a 24:30 5-K. Such charts don't account for the fact that you may have more slow-twitch than fast-twitch fibers. Set realistic short-term goals. Echoing Yogi Berra, Durden says, "If you get there, you get there."

sible. Use techniques such as stretching and creative rest that you might have ignored previously.

Approach speedwork cautiously. Some speedwork seems necessary to regain peak performance. But until you rebuild your aerobic base, workouts that are too intense may cause excessive fatigue and discourage you. Even with that base built, your tendons and ligaments may not support the power developed by your lungs and muscles.

Recognize that strength returns slowest. Just as strength is slowest to fade when you stop running, it takes longest to return. Strength also equals speed. You will find it toughest to regain the top end of your conditioning, even when you're back in reasonably good shape.

Don't race too soon. Competition can be a good way to measure your speed, but you risk injury by going too hard. It also takes time away from training. Go into early races with a relaxed mood, and don't worry about fast times.

Be cautious. If you've previously been injured, you should be particularly cautious. One important question to ask: "Have I determined the cause of the injury?" Rest is sometimes not enough. You may reinjure yourself if you train at your previous level.

Keep the faith. At times, it may seem the road back is too long to travel. But you can move back to road racing and perform at a high level. All it takes is discipline and patience. ■

READY TO RACE

TEST YOUR ABILITY TO RUN FAST

Many runners fail to recognize the value of a thorough warmup. While competing in the Fall Frolic Four, a 4-mile race in Hammond, Indiana, I noticed that only a few of the participants took the time to warm up; probably a minority of that minority warmed up well. Sure, a number of runners popped out of the gym 15 or 20 minutes before the start of that cold and windy day to briefly jog up and down the street, but I suspect that was the extent of the warmup for most.

Warming up is rarely discussed. And it's made complicated by the fact that runners fanning the fitness boom today never participated in track in high school, where they might have been coached in the values of the warmup. Everybody knows about stretching, but that's only part of a good warmup.

How important is a good warmup? It probably won't lower your race time by more than a few seconds—let's say 5 to 10 seconds. That seems inconsequential over the length of a 10-K race that lasts more than a half-hour—unless you are shoulder-to-shoulder with some running buddy you've wanted to beat for the last 4 years. But let's face facts: You wouldn't be reading this book if you didn't want to shave every possible second off your performance. At the elite level, hundredths of a second can make a difference of thousands of dollars.

A correct warmup routine is also valuable for preventing injuries. Cold muscles are more likely to pull than warm muscles. Then there's the matter of comfort. You can run more relaxed when warm than when cold. Minor irritations such as side stitches are less likely to occur if you warm up before going to the line. And since psychological considerations often overshadow physical talents when it comes to success, a good warmup can focus your mind as much as your body. By warming up thoroughly, you signal your body that this is a day for running fast.

Of course, warming up can seem like an inconvenience or a bother. You have to get to the start earlier than you might otherwise. At many races, getting an adequate warmup is difficult, if not impossible. At major races with several thousand entrants, you may be forced to go to the line early and wait to hold your spot on the starting grid. This can be quite a handicap, particularly for a short race. In a marathon, you often can start slow, planning to warm up gradually over the first few miles. But you can't afford to start too slowly in races of only a few miles. It's a simple fact of racing life: The shorter the race, the faster the pace, and the warmer your muscles need to be to reach full speed rapidly.

Certainly, the warmup is most important in race situations because you go from a standing start to full speed within seconds after hearing the starter's gun. But a full warmup with stretching should not be overlooked during training either, particularly on those hard days when you run fast repetitions on the track.

The warmup is particularly important for running in cold weather, when the temperature falls below 50°F and you don extra clothes to retain body heat. On the other hand, don't assume that you can skip the warmup during warm weather because you are hot and sweaty. Pay special attention to the warmup on those days when you feel you need it the least. Your muscles still need the extra performance boost that warmups deliver.

All told, the warmup is a subject to which every runner should give full consideration. So let's do just that, beginning with warming up before workouts and later considering prerace warmups.

THE WARMUP BEFORE THE WORKOUT ■

Few runners have time to spend an hour warming up before their daily workouts. Even for races, warming up seems a bother. Nevertheless, as I've already said, the faster you plan to run, the more you need to warm up. Here's how to do it right.

Make It a Habit

When I coach high school runners, I try to instill good warmup habits, which is not easy to do. One problem is that every runner needs to find a warmup routine to suit his rhythm. But team unity prohibits having two dozen runners warming up two dozen ways, particularly in cross-country, where the team usually tours the course as part of their warmup. In track, runners more often can warm up on their own, since they compete in different events.

At the beginning of the season, I set aside one workout where we practice warming up and nothing else. We go through it by the numbers. We even use the routine as a complete workout the day before a meet. We simply jog, stretch, stride, and jog, then go home.

Getting a proper warmup often can be a problem at midweek races and meets held away from our home track. Once we arrive after an hour-long bus ride, we have barely 30 minutes to get ready to run. So we do the best we can.

Most runners in open races don't have this problem, since they're not required to arrive or leave with a team. So they have no excuse for not warming up properly.

Can a proper warmup help you avoid injury? Can it make you a faster runner? I believe the answer to both questions is yes. A proper warmup and cooldown should limit the damage you can do to your body, particularly when used before and after the intense workouts that are the heart of any program designed to help you run fast.

There are three components to my workout warmup, which I also stress to my high school runners. These steps are simple, and they prepare my muscles for a productive workout. One, I jog for 10 to 20 minutes. Two, I go through my stretching routine, as I describe below. And three, my final step, I do a set of three or four easy sprints of 50 to 150 meters. These serve to wake up my muscles.

A Dozen Ways to Stretch for Success

Stretching is a subject that has launched a thousand magazine illustrations, but most runners probably can figure out how to stretch on their own or by watching other runners. If you want to learn from a book, I'd recommend Bob Anderson's *Stretching*.

You can also check out the American Running Association's (ARA) four-page pamphlet "The Top 8 Stretches for Runners." It illustrates stretches that implement the following ARA recommendations: Never stretch a cold muscle; use the static stretch; don't bounce or lunge; breathe relaxed and naturally; never stretch to the point of pain; ease into and out of the stretch slowly and rhythmically; and concentrate on how you feel in the stretch.

To order the pamphlet, contact ARA at 4405 East West Highway, Bethesda, MD 20814; (800) 776-2732; www.americanrunning.org.

I developed my own standard stretching routine over a period of time, without any particular scientific basis other than it feels good to me. I suggest you do the same. The purpose of stretching preworkout, prerace, or pre-anything is to make you feel good as well as to get loose. Don't do some exercise just because you saw it in Anderson's book or because every other runner you know stretches that way. If it doesn't work for you, don't do it. Anderson would tell you the same.

Having said that, let me tell you that most of my stretches flow from one to another. That wastes less time, which is important if you have a limited period for a stretching routine. Here's the Higdon list of stretches.

Overhead reach. Stand with your feet slightly spread and reach overhead. Focus on your posture and reach for the sky. Personally, I enjoy another version of this stretch. When I run to the nearby golf course, there's a favorite evergreen tree with a branch just in my reach. I hang from it and enjoy the aromatic smell of the tree. But you can stand anywhere that you find a cubic meter of ground and do this stretch. It's my opener.

Hang 10. Stand with your feet slightly spread, bend forward from the waist, and let your fingers dangle toward the ground. The farther your legs are spread, the easier it is to touch the ground. But there is no shame in this. If some other runner tells me my knees are slightly bent, I ask them how fast they ran their last 10-K. Unless it was 5 minutes faster than I've run, I don't listen to their advice. Again, do what works best for you.

Twist and turn. Still standing, put your hands on your hips, bend at the waist, and rotate slowly—forward, sideways, and back. Do a few rotations in the clockwise direction, then in the counterclockwise direction. Wait a minute, you say, isn't stretching supposed to be static? I'll check my rule book and leave a message on your telephone answering machine.

Heel hold. Support yourself with one hand on a wall or tree and grasp your ankle with the other hand, pulling it toward your buttocks. There are two ways to do heel holds. One way is to grasp your left ankle with your right hand, then your right ankle with your left hand. The other way is to grasp your left ankle with your left hand, then your right ankle with your right hand. Various experts have written why one heel hold is superior to the other. I sometimes do one, sometimes the other, sometimes both, sometimes neither. I don't want to offend the experts by playing favorites.

Wall lean. Every runner knows this one. It's a safe, effective way to stretch your calf muscles. Find a wall or a stationary object such as a tree, and stand about 2 feet away from it. Keep your heels planted firmly on the ground and place your hands on the wall, shoulder-width apart. Keeping your back straight, bend your elbows and gently lean forward. It feels good, plus it's an excellent stretch before fast races, where the calf muscles come into play.

There are a couple of variations on the wall lean. One is to lean with both feet together; another is to lean with one foot forward (knee bent) and one foot back, then switch. Take your pick.

A massage therapist I visited in Duluth, Minnesota, following Grandma's Marathon taught me an interesting variation of the split-leg wall lean. After stretching in one position, you move the front foot left and right, which stretches slightly different muscle combinations.

To stretch your calf muscles without the wall, stand tiptoe on stairs, allowing your heels to hang over the edge. Do the same going up escalators, too. Never miss an opportunity for a good stretch.

The great behind. Hit the deck now—literally. Squat to get low enough to touch the floor with your hands near your behind. Then simply roll over backward, gently, with your toes pointing upward, your knees tucked against your forehead, and your arms spread wide at a 45-degree angle for balance. This is the Higdon equivalent of contemplating your navel while everybody else at the race contemplates something else. But don't be self-conscious; your object is to get loose.

Hurdle. Sit on the floor with your legs in front of you. Bend your left leg to the side and keep your right leg straight in front of you. Support yourself with your left hand and reach for your toes with your right. Reach only as far as comfortably possible, without any pain. Don't force this stretch. After you've stretched your right leg, switch your position to stretch your left leg.

To do this stretch effectively, try to picture what two-time Olympic champ Edwin Moses looks like going over the 400-meter hurdles. I have a signed poster from him on my basement wall on which his front leg is bent. If Edwin Moses can run a world record 47.02 with a bent leg, I see no reason why lesser runners should force their legs flat against the floor in this stretch.

Butterfly. While you're sitting on the floor, put your legs straight out in front of you. Bend your knees so that they are pointing out to the sides and your feet are touching sole to sole. In this position, wrap your hands around your feet and press outward with your arms against the inside of your thighs, extending the stretch.

Knee pull. Lie flat on your back, and with your knee bent, bring one leg toward your chest, assisting it by pulling with both hands just below the knee. Do the same with your other leg. I've been doing this stretch for years for no other reason than it feels good, but I saw the stretch pictured in a *Runner's World* article titled "An Ounce of Prevention." I must be on the right track.

Horizontal reach. This stretch is just like the overhead reach, the first stretch in this list, except you lie on your back. Point your toes and reach above your head with your fingertips. Hold the stretch for as long as it feels comfortable, then roll over and do the horizontal reach again, this time facedown. I pretend I'm 7 feet tall and playing in the National Basketball Association. This is a comfortable stretch that I feel I could hold forever, but I seldom maintain a stretch as long as the de rigueur 30 seconds recommended by other experts.

Belt-down pushup. I use this pushup variation not to strengthen my arms but to loosen my back. The position is the same as for regular pushups, except that your lower body remains "nailed" to the ground and you push up only the upper body. I usually do about five of these.

Starter's crouch. Few distance runners will find themselves in this position in a race situation, but I find it an effective stretching exercise. Pretending you're Carl Lewis at the start of the 100 meters, rise into a set position, but with the back leg fully extended. This gives you another variation on the wall lean. (But don't attempt to press your heel flat on the ground.) Switch legs, hold the stretch, then switch legs back and forth rapidly—a dynamic stretch. Remember, I don't limit myself to static stretches.

This ends the floor portion of my stretching routine. I rise and repeat one or two of the standing stretches with which I began my routine, most often the overhead reach or the twist and turn. If time is short, I may skip some stretches.

Can I complete a dozen stretches, some of them involving several variations, in 5 to 10 minutes? Sure. Each stretch flows from one to the other, and I hold each only as long as I feel comfortable. This way, I don't waste time. I'm not out to set an endurance record for stretching; I'm out to stretch to get ready for a comfortable, productive run. I follow my workout with an easy jog to cool down. It helps prevent injuries and keeps me in top form for racing.

A WARMUP FOR THE FINAL HOUR ■

Let me tell you about my personal warmup routine before each race. I like to arrive 60 to 90 minutes before race time. Sometimes, I'll cut it closer for a race I'm treating mostly as a hard workout (a summer fun run, for example), but an hour is almost minimal for any race in which I hope to perform well. Arriving early allows me time to pick up my number and visit the rest rooms before I start my warmup countdown. One plus in getting there early: You won't have to waste as much time standing in lines.

On some occasions, I'll do a pre-warmup at home before climbing into the car to go to the race. This pre-warmup may be less than a mile, just enough to loosen my bowels so I can visit the toilet before leaving for the race. I may stop for gas en route if I need another pit stop. And in the last few minutes of my drive, I'm still scouting for hidden toilets without people standing in line. You can waste a good warmup by being forced to stand in line for 10 to 15 minutes because the race organizers failed to provide adequate rest room facilities.

One advantage that road races have over track meets is that you can predict with some certainty the time the race will begin. If the entry blank announces an 8:00 A.M. start, a well-organized race will begin precisely at that time. At track meets, the mere number of scheduled races often causes delays, or races start earlier than stated, which is sometimes worse. Track runners often need to be more adaptable about their warmups than road runners.

60 MINUTES AND COUNTING ■

Sixty minutes before race time, I usually start my countdown. I try to use the same routine before each race, certainly before the important ones, because it is a routine that works for me. Here's how it goes.

Jog (10 to 20 minutes). How far I go in my prerace jog depends on how loose I feel arriving at the start. A drive of more than an hour to the race, or hard training the week before from which I haven't fully recovered, may require me to spend more time and warm up more slowly. Generally, I like to go a couple of miles in my warmup.

If I'm familiar with the area, I may jog to a location where I do the remainder of my warmup alone. It depends partly on how much the race means to me. Before important races, I may not want to waste my concentration chatting with other runners.

Relax (5 to 10 minutes). If I have not yet picked up my number, now is the time I do it. This may be time for another visit to the toilet, although everybody else has the same idea at this time.

Stretch (5 to 10 minutes). I try to find some quiet area (not always easy at large races) where I have enough room to stretch without being disturbed by too many people. If it's warm, I prefer to stretch outdoors on the grass, under the shade of a tree. As with my workout warmup, I begin with standing stretches, move to floor stretches, and finish by repeating some of the standing stretches.

T MINUS 30 ■

With 30 minutes left, I usually have finished stretching. At this point, I move into the next phase of my warmup.

Flexible play (5 to 10 minutes). This is a dynamic extension of my stretching routine that includes bounding and strides, with jogging and walking in between. I don't utilize my full set of bounding exercises (described in chapter 6) but do two or three at the most. High knees and high heels are handy because they are simple and less stressful. (See "High Knees" on page 151 and "High Heels" on page 153.) You might find them helpful, too. But try them out in your workout first. Don't include bounding in your race warmup unless you bound regularly as part of your training.

More essential are the strides. Run three or four easy sprints of 50 to 150 meters at a pace not much faster than your race pace to remind your legs about the task at hand. I like to accelerate very gradually, hit a good pace in the middle, then gradually decelerate. I walk and jog between strides. Before a road race, I pick out a straight section of street for this routine. If possible, I choose a stretch that slants slightly downhill, doing my fast strides that way because it makes me feel faster. For the same reason, I always run my strides downwind.

In teaching warmup routines to his team at Southwestern Michigan College in Dowagiac, coach Ron Gunn has them do a 200-meter run at race pace exactly 20 minutes before race time. I've followed this approach on occasion and feel it works particularly well on those days when nothing you do seems to loosen you up. Just pushing that extra distance at a fast pace seems to help. Yes, you'll use energy that you may otherwise have conserved for the race, but in 5-K and 10-K races, energy conservation is not usually a problem. You should have ample energy for the job at hand; if a long stride during the prerace warmup aids your ability to get loose, go for it.

Another variation on this routine is to run three strides of increasing length: 20, 30, and 40 seconds, or 100, 150, and 200 meters.

Final preparations (10 to 15 minutes). I've finished my warmup. What remains is to get ready to race. Usually, I wait until now to don my racing top, preferring to go to the line with a dry shirt rather than one that's wet with sweat. On a cool day, I want to avoid getting even slightly chilled and losing the benefits of the warmup. Also, I warm up in training shoes, then change to my lighter racing flats.

I carefully knot my shoelaces to prevent them from coming untied midway through a race. This happened to me only once, while racing in the Vulcan Run, a 10-K in Birmingham, Alabama. It was maybe 2 miles into the race, and I didn't want to run the rest of the way with shoelaces dangling, so I stopped to tie them. I

RACE ETIQUETTE

You may feel out of place the first time you appear at a 5-K race. This is natural. It happens whenever we do something new and don't understand the rules.

Rest assured that every other runner there has had a "first race" experience. They didn't know what to expect the first time they walked into a gym full of runners, but they learned fast. Here are a few tips.

Obtain an entry blank. Contact the race organizers to get a copy, or find one online. Send a stamped self-addressed return envelope. Read the entry form carefully. It will contain important details about the time of the race, where registration is held, and (hopefully) directions on how to get there. The more you know, the more comfortable you'll feel at your first race.

Enter early. This is partly for motivational reasons. By filing your entry, you make a commitment to run that race. That's very important if you're a beginner. Your entering early simplifies registration both for you and race organizers, plus the entry fee often is less. Some races will acknowledge your entry; others will not.

Plan what to take. Most runners like to plan what outfit to wear, including shoes. Lay your gear out the night before, so you don't forget anything, especially not your race number. Plan for all kinds of weather. Most runners come dressed to run, but you might want to take some extra clothes for postrace activities.

Pin your number on the front. In track meets, athletes often wear numbers on their backs; in road races, they wear numbers on the figure it cost me at least 30 seconds. To avoid a recurrence, I tie my shoes once, then jog to the line. By the time I reach the line, the laces have loosened somewhat, so I pull them snugger and tie them again with a double knot. Finally, I tie a square knot over that. Removing my shoes takes time after the race, but I accept that.

In the last few minutes, I jog easily and maybe take one or two more very short strides or stretch some more. Waiting for the

front. Bring a couple of extra safety pins to make sure you can secure your number at all four corners.

Arrive early. Since this is your first race, you might as well enjoy the total experience and not feel rushed. Arrive at least 30 to 60 minutes before the scheduled race start. Allow time to pick up your number, warm up, and visit the toilet. (The earlier you arrive, the shorter the lines you'll encounter.) Watch what other runners do, and do the same. When everybody starts moving toward the starting line, that's your cue too.

Start in back. Don't make the mistake of starting near the front, otherwise you'll spend the first mile watching everybody run past you. Start toward the back. People are cheerier in the middle of the pack, since their goal is usually only to finish the race, not run any world records. You may lose some time crossing the starting line, particularly in big races, but time isn't important to you in your first race—or shouldn't be.

Pace yourself. One reason for starting in back is to avoid running the first mile too fast, either because of enthusiasm or because faster runners pull you along. Once you cross the starting line, settle into your normal training pace—or run even slower. You'll enjoy your first race more if you run comfortably and see what's happening. Save personal records (known as PR's, by the way) for later races.

Savor the moment. Every beginner's first race is a special moment. There will be other running highs as you continue in the sport, but do your best to enjoy your first 5-K as much as you can.

gun, I let my arms hang and shake my wrists in a last-minute battle with my nerves.

At high school races in Indiana, the starter often tells the runners to "shag out," meaning they sprint off the line for 50 to 75 meters, then gather in a circle to give a team cheer before jogging back to the start. The physiological reason for the shag is to elevate the pulse rate to a point where the heart can pump blood with immediate efficiency. In my case (and this probably is also true of most well-trained runners), my pulse rate returns to normal so rapidly that I would need to make such a sprint within the final minute to guarantee a high pulse rate at the start. But the dynamics of most road races rarely permit shag-outs by large numbers of runners. So I suggest you simply wait patiently, with the knowledge that, having followed the warmup routine in this chapter, you are as hot to trot as anyone else in the field. The gun sounds. And you're off.

WHEN ALL IS SAID AND DONE ■

Almost as fast as it starts, the race is over. You've crossed the finish line, and hopefully, you've sliced a few seconds off what is now your old PR. You're ready to go home now, right? Wrong. There's one more thing left to do—your cooldown.

A cooldown obviously won't aid you in running the race you just completed any faster, but it will help you recuperate more rapidly. It also helps you return to regular training more quickly, resulting in a stronger performance the next time you race.

Within 5 minutes after crossing the finish line, I begin my cooldown at the same pace as, but for half the distance of, my warmup jog. On cool days, I wear sweats. On warm days, I won't wait to change. As long as it doesn't interfere with the other runners, I like to turn around and jog back over the course, since it gives me an opportunity to see my friends finish. Sometimes I turn around and meet them at the line so we can cool down together. This is the beginning of the social hour.

Scientists may tell you that you should cool down to help process the removal of lactic acid and other waste products that may have pooled in your muscles during your final anaerobic sprint. This, they say, will prevent muscle soreness. That's only partially true. Lactic acid largely disappears from your system within a half-hour, whether or not you do a cooldown. The soreness and stiffness experienced after a race is more from minute muscle fiber tears—micro tears, the experts call them—than from lactic acid.

A cooldown is also a fun way to cap the experience. It gives you time to think about your race alone, and time to share it with others, if you like.

And the better shape you are in, the more you will enjoy this social time. In fact, that's one benefit of running short races. I've never been able to do much immediately after a marathon, other than stare at the cup of yogurt in my hand and wonder how I'm going to summon enough energy to walk back to my hotel clad in a silly aluminum blanket. But 5 minutes after most shorter races, I'm ready to run again. ■

EPILOGUE

Halfway through the "Star-Spangled Banner," singer John Toenbroek's voice cracked, and he missed the high note. The broad span between the highest and lowest notes in our national anthem causes a lot of singers to struggle. More than 6,000 of us standing on the starting line at the Gate River Run laughed. We had been humming along sotto voce until that point, but suddenly everybody took up the melody with gusto and helped Toenbroek, a Jacksonville Track Club officer, finish what he had begun.

It was one of those magic moments that you can't orchestrate if you're a race director. I was moved. Tears moistened my eyes as I sang along with my fellow runners—and I wasn't even taking the race seriously! After 2 days of talks and appearances connected with the Jacksonville, Florida, race, I was tired and not primed to run fast. Until that point, I had planned only to jump into the middle of the pack somewhere and let the crowd carry me along. Then the cannon sounded, signaling the start, and I was off and running, perhaps faster than I had planned.

Race day is when it all comes together. It's why we do tempo runs, fartlek, strides, sprints, and all of the other performance-enhancing exercises described in this book. While improved fitness clearly is on everybody's agenda—or should be—there comes a time to run fast, to feel the wind in your hair, even to race. Jumping into a 5-K, 10-K, or even a 15-K like the Gate River Run can be very motivational and can give meaning to all our training.

The Gate River Run is northeastern Florida's biggest and best race. Locals refer to it simply as the Gate. Fifteen kilometers (9.3 miles) long, the Gate is the USATAF National Championships at that distance. It has a scenic loop course that starts at Alltel Stadium (home of the Jacksonville Jaguars) and crosses two bridges over the St. Johns River. It is *the* race of choice for runners in northeastern Florida, including me, since my wife, Rose, and I recently acquired a second home in Ponte Vedra Beach.

As part of my introduction to our second city, I joined the Jacksonville Track Club and posted an 8-week training program leading to the Gate River Run on my Web site. Eight weeks is almost minimal if you plan to finish a 15-K comfortably, but after talking with a number of participants, I suspected that many did not train even that hard.

For many, the Gate was the only race they would run during the year—maybe the only race they would run in a lifetime. While 57 runners have run every one of the 23 River Runs held between 1978 and 2000, race director and founder Doug Alred still shakes his head in wonder when he notes that half of the entrants each year are running it for the first time.

ACCEPTING CHALLENGES ■

Life provides numerous rites of passage. We accept challenges, we succeed or fail, and we move on. The sponsoring Gate Petroleum Company owns three local clubs, including The Lodge & Club, which is near our condo in Ponte Vedra Beach. While teaching classes for those clubs, I ran with one woman who had trained for many years and who frequently ran workouts 6 to 8 miles long—yet this was going to be her first Gate!

After a workout during which I had a hard time matching her pace, she said, "I'm worried about finishing." She had no concept of how easy it might be to bridge the gap between training and racing. Yet she had accepted running the Gate as a challenge, and it motivated her for at least the 8 weeks she followed my schedule to train for it.

The race itself had highs and lows, just like the singing of the "Star-Spangled Banner." Two highs were those bridges over the St. Johns River: the Main Street Bridge in the first mile, the Hart Bridge in the second mile. Temperatures rising into the mid-70s posed a threat to the undertrained or to those seeking fast times, but coming from the North, I knew I'd never complain about March weather that allows me to wear shorts and a singlet comfortably. Despite the presence of 10,000 runners competing in the 15-K, a companion 5-K, and a kid's mile that attracted 2,000, traffic was light. The lines before the portable toilets were short. Finding a position on the starting line was easy, despite the numbers.

Going into the Gate, I knew I was undertrained. I was working on this book, and that absorbed some of the energy that should have gone into my training. As a result, I set a conservative time goal, hoping only to break 1:30. Positioning myself where I thought I was well back from the front-runners, I was surprised when it took me only 19 seconds to cross the line after the starting cannon fired.

The crowd around me was tight, but I was able to run at my planned pace almost immediately. Running defensively so as not to trip, I failed to notice the clock showing the first mile split, but I would see all the rest. Aid stations roughly every mile provided all the water I wanted to drink. The first challenge just past the mile mark was the Main Street Bridge. Not only the climb was challenging but also the grating underfoot. Running the bridge in the race, however, seemed easier than the several times I had run it during Wednesday-night workouts with the Jacksonville Track Club (JTC). The hill repeats done with the JTC runners definitely helped me on the up- and downhill. We quickly moved into the trendy San Marco district along the river, where people lined the sidewalks, cheering us on. There were not as many spectators as at marathons in Chicago and Boston, but there was lots of warm support.

Near mile 3, I caught Bob Carr, who directs the JTC's Wednesday-night track workouts at The Bolles School. Intervals on the track with Carr and the Bolles gang had become one of my Wednesday-night pleasures since shifting my winter training base to Florida. Having run each of the previous Gates, Carr sported a low number that permitted him to start near the front.

For most of the next 4 miles, Carr and I kept passing and repassing each other. Carr chided me by saying that by cutting the tangents more tightly on turns, he was able to regain ground I gained on the straightaways in between. In contrast, my strategy was to run wide to avoid having runners cut me off and trip me. One clueless woman wearing earphones who suddenly darted diagonally almost did that in the early miles.

Our *mano a mano* ended with about 2 miles to go at the foot of the Hart Bridge, when I walked at an aid station to take extra water. I figured I needed an extra push to get over the bridge, whose span rises several hundred feet over the St. Johns River in returning us to where we started. But as I gulped down two cups of water, Carr put me away for good. Obviously, he had taken those hill repeats more seriously than I had.

The bridge ascent and descent went well, meaning I had too little time to appreciate the view of downtown Jacksonville upriver. I finally caught Carr after we both had cleared the finishing chute. He won his 70-74 age division. I placed only fourth in my younger division. Nevertheless, I was happy because I ran 10 minutes faster than my admittedly modest time goal. Putting my arm around Carr, I told him, "You're going to have to coach me next year so I can beat you."

Our race was over. We had run the Gate. Somewhere in those miles between bridges, I had found the motivation to keep moving. I finished knowing that I would train harder next winter with the Gate as my goal. With the right training, I would be running fast again. ∎

INDEX

Underscored page references indicate boxed text.

A

Acceleration sprints, 59
Aerobic activity, 127
Aerobic fitness
    building base of, 21–24
        training schedule for, 23
    losing and regaining, 212
Aerobic intervals, 142
Aging
    retraining and, 211, 214,
        216–17
    strength and, 188
    weight training and, 183–84,
        188
Altitude, training and, 171
Anaerobic activity, 127
Anaerobic threshold, 21, 77–79,
    126–30. See also Lactate
    threshold
    determining, 128–30
Anaerobic threshold training. See
    Tempo training
Andersson, Arne, 118
Arm carriage, form and, 66
A.T. running. See Tempo training

B

Babington, John, 199–200
Ballistic stretching. See Dynamic
    flexibility drills
Barefoot running, for awareness, 71
Base training, 14–16

Beatty, Jim, 63–64, 110
Beginning runner(s), 2–12
    fartlek training for, 120–21
    getting started as, 3–7
    motivation for, 5–7, 5
    training for first races by, 7–8,
        9–12, 12
Bell, Sam, 86
Belt-down pushups, 226
Benham, Ed, 13–14, 15–16
Benson, Roy, 149–52, 154–56, 157,
    160
Bent-over row, 193–94
Blood volume, fitness levels and,
    213–14
Boston Marathon, hill training for,
    181
Bounding, 71, 159, 163
Bowerman, Bill, 101, 102–3, 160–62,
    165
Butterfly stretch, 225
Butt kicker. See High-heels drill

C

Calisthenics, for strength, 195
Caloric expenditure, 18
    from junk miles, 33
Carr, Bob, 89, 237
Carriage, form and, 65, 69
Cerutty, Percy, 167
Classes, for beginners, 4–6
    locating, 7
Clean and press, 193

Coaches. *See also* Self-coaching
  benefits of having, <u>204</u>–5
  training with, 199–201
Coe, Sebastian, 111, 207–8
Competition phase of 3/1 training,
  36–37, <u>37</u>
Conconi, Francesco, 125
Conconis. *See* Tempo training
Cooldowns, 232–33
Coordination drills, <u>59</u>. *See also*
  Dynamic flexibility drills
Courtney, Tom, 83–84
Cross-country fartlek training,
  122–23
Cross-training,
  cautions about, 197–98, 211
  on rest days, 47
Cruise intervals, 111, 125
Cumulative caloric through-put, 18
Cunningham, Glenn, 83
Curl, 196

D

Date pace, 101, 102
Deflection point, 125–26
Detraining, 212
Diaries, running, 203
Distance runners vs. sprinters,
  184–85, 186–87
Distance running
  for endurance, 16–21
  for speed, 25–30
  types of, 207
Distances, in interval training, 94,
  111
Double leg hop, <u>159</u>, 163
Downhill running. *See also* Hill
    training
  speed and, 70, <u>180</u>
  techniques for, 178–81, <u>180</u>
Drills. *See* Dynamic flexibility drills
Drum-major drill, 152–53
Duration, 42–43

Durden, Benji, 134
Dynamic flexibility drills, 149–164,
    <u>158</u>–<u>59</u>
  bounding, 71, <u>159</u>, 163
  double leg hop, <u>159</u>, 163
  drum major, 152–53
  fast feet, <u>158</u>, 160–62
  high heels, 153–54, <u>158</u>–<u>59</u>,
    228–29
  high knees, <u>59</u>, 151–52, <u>158</u>,
    228–29
  injury risk from, 163, 164
  in prerace warmup, 228–29
  skipping, <u>59</u>, 154–57, <u>159</u>
  toe walk, 157, 160

E

Economy. *See also* Efficiency
  form and, 60–63, <u>69</u>,
    71–72
  interval training and, <u>106</u>
  junk miles and, <u>33</u>
  repeats and, 88
Ectomorphs, weight training by,
    187–88
Edelen, Buddy, <u>68</u>
Efficiency. *See also* Economy
  form and, 57–58, 64–66, 67
  speed endurance and, 39
Elliott, Herb, 167
Endurance training, 16–21. *See also*
    Speed endurance
Exercise machines, 196–97
  vs. free weights, <u>194</u>

F

Fanny flicker. *See* High-heels drill
Fartlek training, 117–23
  for beginning runners, 120–21
  cross-country, 122–23
  formula for, 121
  vs. interval training, 118–19

stopwatch, 142
tempo changes in, 119
Fast continuous runs (FCRs). *See*
　　Tempo training
Fast-feet drill, 158, 160–62
Fast-twitch muscles
　　detraining and, 214
　　glycogen depletion and, 27, 29,
　　　31
　　race pace training and, 44
　　vs. slow-twitch muscles, 27,
　　　79–80
FCRs. *See* Tempo training
5-K races, first
　　tips for, 230–31
　　training for, 7–8, 9–12
　　　schedule for, 12
Flexibility, form and, 62
Flexibility drills. *See* Dynamic
　　flexibility drills
Footstrike, 151
　　barefoot running and, 71
　　for distance vs. speed, 150
　　efficiency and, 67
　　form and, 65, 68–69
Form, 55–72
　　elements of, 65–66
　　flexibility and, 62
　　for hill running
　　　downhill, 179–80, 180
　　　uphill, 172, 177
　　smoothness and, 62–63
　　speed and, 161
　　teaching, 59
　　techniques to improve, 69–72
　　tips on, 68–69
　　videotaping, 71
Free weights, 194
Frequency, 42, 43

G

Gate River Run, 234–37
Gerschler, Waldermar, 90, 93–94

Glycogen depletion, 18, 26–28, 27,
　　29, 30–31, 126–27
Goal pace, 101
Goals
　　charting, 209
　　for retraining, 215
　　setting, 203, 204
　　　for beginning runners, 5
Great-behind stretch, 224–25
Green, Norm, 191
Grelle, Jim, 110
Groups, running in, 5–6, 99
Gunn, Ron, 174, 175–76

H

Hägg, Gundar, 118
Halberg, Murray, 25–26, 28
Half squat, 185–86
Hand carriage, 69
Hang 10, 223
Harbig, Rudolf, 90
Hard/easy training, 49
Haydon, Ted, 108–9
Hayward, Bill, 161–62
Head position, form and, 66, 69
Heartbreak Hill, 170–71
Heel hold, 154, 224
Heel raises, 186
High-heels drill, 153–54, 158–59,
　　228–29
High-knees drill, 59, 151–52, 158,
　　228–29
Hill training, 165–81
　　benefits of, 70–71, 169
　　for Boston Marathon, 181
　　injury risk from, 175, 176
　　research on, 168–69, 176
　　techniques for
　　　downhill, 178–81, 180
　　　uphill, 172, 177
Hip extensions, 186
Hip flexors, strengthening, 152
Holmer, Gosta, 117, 120

Horizontal reach, 225–26
Hurdle, 225
Hypertrophy, 189

I

Igloi, Mihaly, 110
Impact shock, of hill running, 176
Injuries
    coaches' role in preventing,
        204–5
    plantar fasciitis, 175
    retraining and previous, 218
    risk of, from
        dynamic flexibility drills, 163,
            164
        hill training, 175, 176
        interval training, 106, 110, 116
    speedwork and, 141
Intensity, 138. See also Pace
    aerobic gain and, 41–42, 43
    increasing, 20
    levels of, 43–44, 46–47
Interval training, 89–116
    benefits of, 70, 98–99, 114
    cautions for use of, 106
    charting, 96, 109
    distances for, 111
    vs. fartlek, 118–19
    frequency of, 114–15
    for improved form, 70
    length of rest in, 94, 111–12
    locations for, 115–16
    origins of, 93–94
    overtraining with, 110
        avoiding, 116
    pace for, 99–103, 112–13
    progressive programs of, 104–5
    repetitions in
        number of, 112
        pace for, 112–13
    research on, 91–92
    vs. sprints, 139
    times for, 115

types of rest in, 113–14
variables in, 94–97
    manipulating, 104–5, 109

J

Jennings, Lynn, 199–201
Jogging, in prerace warmup, 228
Johnson, Michael, 137
Junk miles, 32–33

K

Kennedy, Bob, 55–56, 59, 119
Knee pull, 153, 225

L

Lactate threshold, 39, 44. See also
        Anaerobic threshold
    tempo training and, 125–26
    training to increase, 46, 78
Lactate threshold training. See
        Tempo training
Larrieu Smith, Francie, 21–22
Leg curl, 196
"Legging up," 13–14, 15–16
Lewis, Carl, 137
Lindsay, Herb, 171
Liquori, Marty, 171–73, 176
Long runs, for endurance, 16–21.
        See also Distance running
Lupfert, Stefan, 107
Lydiard, Arthur, 165, 167–68

M

Marathoners, former, retraining
        tips for, 216–17
Marathon training
    for Boston Marathon, 181
    tapering programs for, 145–46

Maximum heart rate (MHR), <u>40</u>
    aerobic base and, <u>21</u>
    aerobic vs. anaerobic activity
        and, 128
    deflection point and, 125
    endurance training and, 42, 43
    intensity and, 44–46
    lactic acid accumulation and,
        79
    max VO$_2$ and, <u>40</u>
    measuring, <u>45</u>
    pace and, 132
Max VO$_2$, 38, <u>40</u>. *See also* Oxygen
        uptake
    endurance training and, 42
    exercise intensity and, 41–42
    lactic acid accumulation and, 39,
        44
    maximum heart rate and, <u>40</u>
    modifying, 43
McBride, Frank, 107
Measurements, of performance,
        130–31
MHR. *See* Maximum heart rate
Mileage,
    cutting, <u>216</u>
    increasing, 208–9, 19, 20
        with junk miles, <u>33</u>
Military press, 196
Moore, Kenny, 178–79
Motivation. *See also* Goals
    for beginning runners, 5–7, <u>5</u>
    from coaches, <u>204</u>
Muscle imbalances, strength
        training for, <u>192</u>
Muscles. *See also* Fast-twitch
        muscles; Slow-twitch
        muscles; Strength training
    adaptation of, for endurance,
        40–41
    glycogen depletion in, 18, 26–28,
        <u>27</u>, 29, 30–31, 126–27
    lactic acid accumulation in,
        77–78, 129, 142, 214–15, 233

sore, <u>11</u>
    causes of, <u>11</u>, 233
    from retraining, 214–15
    strengthening, with hill training,
        173–74

N

Nautilus machines, 196–97

O

O'Connor, W. H. "Skip," 121
Older runners. *See* Aging
Overhead reach, 223
Overload interval training programs,
        104–5
Overstriding, 63, 65
Overtraining
    coaches' role in preventing, <u>204–5</u>
    with interval training, 110, 116
    symptoms of, 16
Owairaka, New Zealand, training
        course, 25, 29–30
Oxygen uptake, 38. *See also* Max
        VO$_2$
    aerobic fitness and, 21, 212
    aerobic vs. anaerobic activity and,
        127

P

Pace. *See also* Date pace; Goal pace;
        Intensity; Race pace
    for fartlek training, <u>119</u>
    high intensity, 43–44
    for interval training, 99–103,
        112–13
    low intensity, 46–47
    maintaining even, 22
    medium intensity, 44, 46
    for repeats, 85–86
    speedwork and, 81
    for tempo training, <u>124</u>, 132–33
    for 3/1 training, 31

Peaks
    interval training to achieve, 104–5
    regaining, 213
Personal Records (PRs), 8–9
Pick-ups, 142
Plantar fasciitis, 175
Plyometrics. See Dynamic flexibility
    drills
Pre-warmups, 227
PRs, 8–9
Pulse monitors, 45, 130–31
Pushups, 226

Rest intervals
    in interval training, 94, 108–9,
        111–12, 113–14
    between repeats, 86–87, 88
Retraining, 210–18
    age and, 211, 216–17
    by former marathoners, 216–17
    time required for, 212
    tips for, 215–18
Rodgers, Bill, 67, 166, 170
Running clubs, locating, 7
Running diaries, 203

R

Racehorses, comparison of to
        runners, 15–16
Race pace, 44. See also Pace
    determining, 81
    in interval training, 100, 112–13
Races. See also specific types
    first
        tips for, 230–31
        training for, 7–8, 9–12, 12,
            23–24, 23
        warmups for, 219–20, 227–32
Reaction time, speed and, 161–62
Recovery. See also Rest days
    junk miles for, 32–33
    strides for, 143–44
    after workouts, 50, 51
Reed, Mary, 120–21
Relaxation sprints, 59
Repeats, 82–88
    distances for, 85–86
    improving economy with, 88
    pace for, 43–44, 85–86
    rest intervals between, 86–87,
        88
    vs. sprints, 139
Resistance training. See Strength
        training; Weight training
Rest days, 10, 47, 207–8. See also
        Recovery
    scheduling, 49

S

Salazar, Alberto, 58, 213
Samuelson, Joan Benoit, 66–67,
        170–71
Sandoval, Tony, 67
Schlau, Bob, 190–91
Schul, Bob, 110
Scott, Steve, 88
Self-coaching, 201–9
Shag-outs, 232
Shoes, tying, 230–31
Shorter, Frank, 67, 81, 103, 196
Skeletal system, retraining and,
        214
Skipping, 153–57
    for distance, 59, 156–57, 159
    for height, 156, 159
Slow running, 20–21
    to improve speed, 25–30
    junk miles as, 32–33
Slow-twitch muscles
    vs. fast-twitch muscles, 79–80
    glycogen depletion and, 26–27,
        29, 30–31
Smoothness, form and, 62–63
Snell, Peter, 25–26, 28
Speed drills. See Dynamic flexibility
        drills
Speed endurance, 38–47
    physiological factors of, 38–39
    training for, 39–44, 46–47

Speedwork, 76–77, 78. *See also*
    specific types
    attitudes toward, 73–76
    pace for, 81
    physiological benefits of, 77–80
    slow running vs., 28–29
    types of, 81–82
Sprinters vs. distance runners,
        184–85, 186–87
Sprints, 137
    acceleration, 59
    benefits of, 142–43
    vs. interval training, 139
    length of, 141
    in prerace warmup, 229
    relaxation, 59
    vs. repeats, 139
    short, 142
    surfaces for running, 140
    variation in, 143
Stadium running, 172
Starter's crouch, 226
Steady state running. *See* Tempo
        training
Stone, Curt, 62–63
Stopwatch fartlek, 142
Straightaways, 140
Strength
    hill training for, 173–75
    junk miles for, 33
    regaining, 212, 217–18
    speedwork for, 185
Strength training, 182–98. *See also*
        Weight training
    debate on benefits of, 183–84,
        189–90
    exercise machines for, 196–97
    for muscle imbalances, 192
    for upper-body strength, 190
Stretching
    dynamic, 149–51
    exercises
        belt-down pushups, 226
        butterfly, 225
        great behind, 224–25

hang 10, 223
heel hold, 154, 224
horizontal reach, 225–26
hurdle, 225
knee pull, 153, 225
overhead reach, 223
starter's crouch, 226
twist and turn, 223–24
wall lean, 224
    junk miles and, 33
    in prerace warmup, 228
    publications on, 222–23
Stress load, 19–20
Stride length,
    form and, 63–64, 65, 69
    of sprinters vs. distance runners,
        184–85
Strides, 138, 143
    for recovery, 143–44
    in warmups, 144–46, 229
Surges, 138, 146–48

T

Tapering programs, 145
Tempo. *See* Pace
Tempo training, 123–134
    benefits of, 131
    length of, 132, 133–34
    pace of, 124, 132–33
    structure of, 133
    tips for, 124
10-K races, training for first,
        23–24
    schedule for, 23
3/1 training, 30–31, 34–37
    competition phase of, 36–37, 37
    endurance-building phase of,
        34–35, 36
    pace for, 31
Toe walk, 157, 160
Track meets, warming up for, 227
Tracks
    interval training on, 115
    running sprints on, 140

Training. *See also specific types*
  changing, 204–7
  charting, 209
  for 5-K races, 7–8, 9–12, 12
  for marathons, 145–46
    Boston, 181
  planning, 48–52, 202–9, 204
  setting goals for, 203, 204
  simplifying, 17
  for speed endurance, 52–54
  for 10-K races, 23, 23–24
  for 3/1 competition, 37
  for 3/1 endurance building, 36
  variety in, 53
  weather and, 208
Triathletes, 197–98
Twist and turn, 223–24

U

Uphill running. *See also* Hill
    training
  benefits of, 70–71
  techniques for, 172, 177
Upright row, 194–95
Up-tempo aerobic running. *See*
    Tempo training

V

Videotaping, for form awareness, 71
VO$_2$. *See* Max VO$_2$

W

Walking, as training, 10–11
Walk/run combination, 10
Wall lean, 224
Warmups, 219–232
  before races, 144–46, 219–20
    routine for, 227–32

reasons for, 219–20
  strides as part of, 144–46, 229
  before workouts, 221–22
Weather, training and, 208
Weight training. *See also* Strength
    training
  exercises
    bent-over row, 193–94
    clean and press, 193
    curl, 196
    half squat, 185–86
    heel raises, 186
    hip extensions, 186
    military press, 196
    upright row, 194–95
  for muscle imbalances, 192
  by older runners, 184, 190–91
  for sprinters vs. distance runners,
    186–87
  tips for, 194–95
Welch, Priscilla, 3
Williams, Gar, 108–9
Wilt, Fred, 68
Women, strength training by, 188
Workouts. *See also* Training
    programs
  fartlek formula for, 121
  recording, 202–3
  recovery from, 144
  stress load of, 19–20

Y

Yakimov, A., 86–87
  fartlek formula of, 121–22
  rest intervals of, 87, 88

Z

Zatopek, Emil, 58, 74, 93